UNTIL THE SEA
SHALL FREE THEM

UNTIL THE SEA
SHALL FREE THEM

*Life, Death, and Survival in
the Merchant Marine*

ROBERT FRUMP

BLUEJACKET BOOKS

NAVAL INSTITUTE PRESS
Annapolis, Maryland

Naval Institute Press
291 Wood Road
Annapolis, MD 21402

First Bluejacket Books edition, 2007
ISBN-10: 1-59114-284-9
ISBN-13: 978-1-59114-284-3

Library of Congress Cataloging-in-Publication Data
Frump, Robert.
  Until the sea shall free them : life, death, and survival in the Merchant Marine /
Robert Frump.—1st Bluejacket books ed.
      p. cm.—(Bluejacket books)
  Originally published: New York : Doubleday, 2002.
  Includes bibliographical references.
  ISBN-13: 978-1-59114-284-3 (alk. paper)
  1. Marine Electric (Ship) 2. Shipwrecks—North Atlantic Ocean. 3. Marine accidents—
Investigation—United States. I. Title.
G530.M3135F78 2007
363.12'309163—dc22

2006027581

Printed in the United States of America on acid-free paper ∞

14 13 12 11 10 09 08 07   9 8 7 6 5 4 3 2
First printing

for SUZANNE

CONTENTS

Part Three: TOWARD HOME

UNTIL THE SEA
SHALL FREE THEM

Part One

AT SEA

And Jesus was a sailor
When he walked upon the water
And he spent a long time watching
From his lonely wooden tower.
And when he knew for certain
Only drowning men could see him
He said, "All men shall be sailors then
Until the sea shall free them. . . ."

LEONARD COHEN

Chapter One

CASTING OFF

*Whenever I find myself growing grim about the mouth; whenever it is
a damp, drizzly November in my soul; whenever I find myself
involuntarily pausing before coffin warehouses, and bringing up the rear
of every funeral I meet; and especially whenever . . . it requires a
strong moral principle to prevent me from deliberately stepping into the
street and methodically knocking people's hats off—then, I account it
high time to get to sea as soon as I can.*

HERMAN MELVILLE

10:00 P.M. / THURSDAY, FEB. 10, 1983 / COAL TERMINAL
NORFOLK, VIRGINIA

At the loading pier near Norfolk, Bob Cusick, the veteran chief
mate, spread steam coal into the holds of the *Marine Electric* like a
pastry chef layering a cake. No chunk was larger than a Ping-Pong
ball, and some of the coal was just black powder. In bulk, the coal
formed a huge mass, heavier than 10,000 automobiles, and it had to
be loaded carefully so that the ship remained balanced.

Huge chutes passed over the ship and dumped black coal evenly
at Cusick's command. Normally, it took three passes to load a ship
this size, but Bob Cusick had done this more than a few times. He
almost never needed the third, "finishing" pass. That was an advantage of time on the water, of time on the piers. There was a lot he
knew, a lot he'd seen that the younger kids aboard ship might
never see.

Still, Cusick always felt the excitement of leaving, of casting off,
of starting the voyage. All of them, all thirty-four seamen and officers, felt it, even if this would be just a milk run up the coast,

Virginia to Massachusetts and back, shuttling coal to the power plants of New England.

There were a number of green kids on the ship who felt the excitement more than Cusick, and he wondered what they must think he was doing now. For anyone with just a few months at sea would think Bob Cusick was cheating. Clearly, the chief mate of the *Marine Electric* was overloading his ship—she had sunk below the legal load line. You could see it, if you knew just enough about the business not to know what you didn't know. Cusick had filled the hatches with 23,000 tons of coal on top of the 1,800 tons already there. And now the ship was five inches below its legal load line.

Or so it seemed. The truth was that Marine Transport Lines, the owner, never asked Cusick to overload a ship. That was one thing he liked about this job.

Another truth was that Cusick had checked the salinity of the harbor water carefully. It measured 1.013 on his hydrometer. That meant the harbor water was far less salty than ocean water. So when the *Marine Electric* sailed into the ocean, she would rise magically, like some huge high school science fair display, leaving her load line comfortably above the waterline.

Only there was nothing magic about it. It was professional procedure. And it was how Cusick got and kept a job that paid him well at a time when American maritime work was scarce.

He liked this job, and he liked the men he worked with. Most all of them, with their different ranks and duties, had drifted back to the ship as he was loading it.

They were members of diverse tribes with diverse skills, and on some ships, the tribes never got along. There were the officers, of course. Deck officers, like the third mate, navigated and steered the ship. Engineers, like the first assistant engineer, kept the turbines humming and the power up. Ordinary seamen fell near the bottom of the organizational chart, just learning the business. Able-bodied seamen, or ABs, were veteran, skilled seamen. Oilers and wipers worked the engine room down below, assisting the engineers. At the bottom of the officer social order were the cadets—the men and women still in a maritime academy who shipped out for the first time on an American merchant vessel.

Fissures would form along these differences in rank and mission on many ships. The deck officers and engineers grumbled at each other and did not fraternize. Deck crews and the engine room workers followed the lead of the officers. They blamed each other for problems and held grudges.

But Cusick, the chief mate and second in command of the *Marine Electric,* mingled with all the men and set the tone for the ship. They had their differences, as men do, but they all pretty much got along.

Certainly all classes and ranks on the *Marine Electric* joined together to poke gentle fun at George Wickboldt, the cadet. The cadet was in love, they said. It seemed a real romance. Cusick's friend Mike Price, the first assistant engineer, had taken the cadet under his wing and treated him like family, even took him home to Massachusetts. There Wickboldt met a pretty young girl named Cathy. They had hit it off, became an item, and the whole ship kidded George about his love life. Price even speculated that the two kids might get married some day.

But the crew, all of them, made certain the ribbing never turned nasty. This was so because all of them knew the Wickboldt story, and there was an unspoken agreement among them to watch out for the kid.

The cadet's family lived on Long Island near the Sound, and the four sons of the Wickboldt family had been called to sea. The family dream was to restore a large wooded property they owned on a lake in New Hampshire. There, no matter how far the seafaring sons roamed, they could have places near their parents. A year earlier, they'd begun planning to renovate the old house there.

And while George Wickboldt was quiet about the story, the crew all knew what happened to that dream. All of them heard what had happened only a year before to George's older brother Steven. And all of them knew it could as easily happen to them.

Take the wrong turn. Stop for a moment. Do some inconsequential thing you would not even think about. Go left instead of right. On board a ship you could be dead or maimed in an instant.

* * *

Twenty-four-year-old Steven Wickboldt sailed on the *Golden Dolphin,* a modern oil tanker. He was a conscientious man who took pride in his work. It was a Wickboldt family tradition.

But his ship had two routine maintenance problems in March 1982 as she sailed from Louisiana to Dubai on the Persian Gulf. The first problem was common to all tankers. Sludge had accumulated in the cargo tanks. It had to be removed. The only way to do it was the old-fashioned way: sending men down in the tanks with shovels to muck it out manually.

The other problem was more technical and required skilled labor. The steam lines that ran into the cargo tanks were so corroded that they did not work. These lines were important because oil sometimes had to be warmed to make it portable and pumpable. And the sludge now lining the cargo tanks of the *Golden Dolphin* would be much easier to remove if the steam lines and heating coils in the tank were activated. The heat turned the oil from a hard, unpliable solid to a more liquid, movable muck.

On the *Golden Dolphin,* the steam lines connecting the engine room to the cargo holds snaked along the deck and had succumbed to the corrosive powers of saltwater. The crew had tried to seal the leaks with fiberglass and epoxy patches, but to no avail. Steam leaked so badly that the pipes no longer did their job. It was clear the steam lines on deck had to be replaced, and the only way to do that was to break out the welding equipment and put in new lines.

Steve Wickboldt was safe in the engine room when the welding started on deck. At the same time, about 3:20 P.M. on March 6, Seamen Roy Leonard, Martin Wright, and Manuel Rodriguez ended a coffee break and entered the number-four cargo hatch to begin mucking out the sludge. Seaman Zemlock went to the mucking winch—a hoist that would carry the sludge up and out of the tanks below. Norman Beavers, who as bosun supervised the deck crew, popped down below to join the men.

At 3:45, the welding crew continued to fit new steam pipes. This was "hot work" on a tanker, not to be taken lightly. But the crew was some distance from the number-four hatch, fifty feet or more away from any combustible fumes coming from the oil.

Paul Rippee, the chief engineer, was supervising the welding.

He asked the chief mate to tell the third assistant engineer, a man named Fitzpatrick, to pick up a 1⅛th inch impact wrench and bring it to the worksite. The chief mate, heading for his stint at the wheel, saw Fitzpatrick and relayed the message. Fitzpatrick fetched the wrench and was walking forward to the welding site. Just ten seconds more and he'd be there.

In the engine room, men were changing shifts. First Assistant Engineer Cronin showed up early, at 3:45, to stand his watch. Steve Wickboldt could now take a break. It wasn't common to see hot work on board a tanker, and Steve wanted to see how it was done. He jogged forward to lend a hand.

Then, as always in such times, events happened both quickly and slowly, as if caught by a slow-motion camera. Fitzpatrick, walking with the wrench, could see the welding team. Wickboldt was about to join them; the kid had slowed to a walk. The chief engineer, wearing his blue jumpsuit, was looking off the port side of the ship. Fitzpatrick raised the wrench as if to say, *"Hey, Chief, I've got what you wanted."* But he did not catch the chief's eye. Fitzpatrick saw a metal strip on the deck and looked down, afraid he might trip. He heard a long whooshing sound, then a noise like a firecracker inside a barrel. A wall of fire rose straight up. Pieces of metal started flying and landing around him.

One piece looked like the steam pipe. Fitzpatrick did not stop to examine it. He ran aft for his life, to the rear of the ship. A thirty-eight-knot wind was blowing over the *Golden Dolphin,* whipping the flames like a blowtorch. He found shelter from the falling debris behind the deckhouse, then peeked around a corner to survey the starboard side of the ship. The cargo tanks from below had been blown out and up, so that now their bottoms were above the deckline, pointing jagged steel toward the sky. The whole huge midsection of the ship was aflame.

The general alarm was sounding. Smoke and fire engulfed the deck. There was no sign of the small group of men who had been huddling over the hot work. Friends and colleagues—Paul Rippee, Wickboldt, all of them—were simply gone.

Zemlock, operating the winch when it happened, by all rights should have been killed instantly. As he was hauling out buckets of sludge and dumping them into fifty-five-gallon drums, he felt and heard a vibration directly beneath him. He was looking down into the tank, but instead of being burned, he was hurled away from the opening. He heard one explosion. He was in the air, floating, when the second one came. Fate had it that he was blown aft forty feet, away from the inferno forward. He did not remember landing, only that when he did, he was sitting.

He looked forward. The force of one explosion had blown up part of the cargo hold bulkhead straight in front of the spot where he landed. The shattered bulkhead had shielded him from the flames. Yet another explosion had blown the deck out directly behind him. He sat, stunned, protected by jagged metal armor on both sides. He waited a moment, then picked his way toward the stern.

Steven Wickboldt, the men on the welding crew, and the men in the tanks, all nine of them, died instantly. What had happened was dreadfully simple. The heat from the welding torch had entered the steam line that still ran into the cargo holds. Although the tank in which the men were working was gas-free, the other holds were in that most perilous of tanker conditions—empty of oil, but not empty of vapors. The steam coils lining these tanks were connected to the steam line the men were welding. The cargo coils were corroded. Thus, vapor from the tanks wafted up through the steam line, venting to the deck where the men were welding. A spark or flame or heat from the acetylene torch in effect lit a fuse running from one part of the ship dozens of yards to the explosive vapors of the empty oil tanks forward.

Which explains the "whoosh" sound many of the survivors heard. It was the gaseous fuse linking torch to tank.

On the bridge, the captain ordered hard left rudder. This turned the ship sharply and cut down the fierceness of the wind blowing the fire forward to aft. Then he hit the abandon ship button. The remaining men found lifeboats. They were rescued a few hours later by a passing merchant vessel and sat there on the deck and watched as the hull of their tanker burned and glowed cherry red.

*   *   *

Nearly a year later, the men of the *Marine Electric* knew the lesson. Even good men, even smart men, even men who thought they had things under control, could die in a thousand different ways. The flames did not care. The steel did not care. Most particularly, the ocean did not care.

But the men of the *Marine Electric* cared. They watched out for Cadet George Wickboldt. Like all cadets, he needed to prove himself. And he took some hazing about his love life. But in many ways, they figured, he had already paid his dues. Anyone whose brother could die like that, and who then went to sea, anyway, well . . . the men did not talk about it much. Such things did not need to be said.

Philip Corl, the master of the *Marine Electric,* Cusick's boss, could look down from the bridge on all of this and figure he was a lucky man. Captains in the American Merchant Marine could make annual incomes equal to those of many doctors and lawyers but usually paid a price. They spent months at sea.

The *Marine Electric* run was an easy one. She ferried coal from Virginia to an electric utility at Brayton Point, Massachusetts, near Boston. It was about thirty-two hours each way, and the earlier trip down just a few days before had been glass-smooth, unusual for the North Atlantic in winter.

Corl, like Cusick, was an old hand, in his late fifties. He had signed on two days earlier as the relief master—the captain who took over when the regular captain was on vacation—and did so quite eagerly. Hour for hour, captains made a nice living, but only when they worked. More and more, there were fewer and fewer jobs in the American Merchant Marine. For years, Corl had stayed clear of such unemployment. He'd put behind him the memories of service in World War II and the sparse jobs of peacetime and moved west to deal cards at a friend's casino. That work in the desert had dried up, though, and Corl, himself a cardplayer, knew he had beaten the odds when he signed on with Marine Transport Lines a few months back. Corl had a plum. Hundreds of officers were without work. He was lucky, and he was grateful.

They were all lucky. There was none of the discomfort of long trips to Somalia or Egypt, carrying government grain. The *Marine Electric* carried coal in the coastal trade. Miners pulled it from the ground in Virginia and West Virginia and Kentucky and Illinois. It came east to Norfolk by train, but it was cheaper from there to ship north by water. And so the coal was dumped into the holds of the *Marine Electric,* which carried it up the coast to the Boston area.

There, they burned it to heat the water that created the steam that turned the turbines that generated the electricity to light and heat homes and workplaces and to power toasters, televisions, stereos, vacuum cleaners, ovens, coffeepots, and hair dryers. The *Marine Electric* and the coal she carried helped make New England twinkle. At night, as the men out at sea stared at the land, they could watch the lights and understand that the cities were glowing because of them and the coal they carried. It gave them meaning. A connection.

For his part, Cusick did not need to philosophize. He had always been connected to the sea. Had always loved the life at sea. And he loved the job he had on the *Marine Electric.* He had been at sea since age eighteen and with the *Marine Electric* for five years. He was second in command, a year older than Corl, and he knew his ship inside out.

With Corl looking on from above, Cusick computed the load factors again. There were nuances. Important ones. There always were in large ships, particularly the old ones like the *Marine Electric.* The ship had been built during World War II as a T-2 type tanker—state of the art at the time—and then modified and extended in 1961 for dry cargo bulk duty with a new midsection.

There was nothing new about her now, though. The bow and stern were almost forty years old, and the "new" midsection was officially "overage" by insurance standards. If you were in charge of loading cargo, as Cusick was, you had to be careful how you distributed the weight in any ship and, particularly in an old girl like this.

Earlier, the hatches for the five cargo holds had been rolled back like huge horizontal garage doors. The rail cars had dumped their coal onto conveyor belts. The belts then carried the coal to chutes. The chutes hosed the coal down the hatches and into the holds. This could not be done sloppily. Dump the coal too densely into the middle hatches, leave the fore and aft light, and the ship sagged. Dump it too heavily into the fore and aft, with the center light, and it "hogged"—rose up like a hog's back. Either way was dangerous. The *Marine Electric* was a small ship by the standards of the new supertankers, but immense by human scale. Stretch two football fields end to end, and you had her. Hogging or sagging meant a ship of that size could fracture and founder at sea, if she hit the waves wrong.

These things Cusick knew automatically and did automatically. Up to Somerset, Massachusetts. Down to Norfolk. Load the coal. Two passes and he was done, really. Same old same old, and fine by him. Just to make sure on this trip, he put in a few more dollops of coal on that third trimming pass. In hatch number five, he added 400 more tons. In hatch number one, he placed 700 more tons. These light touches were the equivalent of a pastry chef's signature touches. A few hundred tons here, a few there. Then, no more. It was finished.

He then went over his loading log and measurements with William H. Long, a good friend and old salt, retired from his days at sea as an officer with the *Marine Electric* but still working dockside. Bill Long copied Cusick's loading measurements as the chief mate read them off. The copy was just that, a sort of working checklist. Long always threw his paper away, and Cusick carried the formal record on board the ship.

Cusick could think of all the good things about the crew and ship and be grateful. But there were also certain things Cusick tried not to think about. Because these kinds of thoughts worked against all the good things, all the right things about the *Marine Electric*. These thoughts conflicted with the what-a-great-deal-we-got-here version of the ship.

Cusick knew better than anyone that the ship was falling apart. The owners were good owners, as these things went. Marine Transport Lines, Inc. was a big, modern corporation that was now in the middle of some big deal on Wall Street. The company was a joint owner in a new project, building a new ship, the *Energy Independence,* one of the few new ones built in U.S. yards. In that, the company was among the best of shipping lines.

But every trip, Cusick would sketch on his clipboard one more crack in the hatch covers. There were more than ninety now. He had the crew slop Red Hand over the cracks—marine-strength epoxy patching. They welded "doublers" over them—big sheets of quarter-inch steel. The company sometimes put the ship in for repairs, but she never came out right. Some mariners called ships like the *Marine Electric* "tired iron." They were like used cars. Even if you treated them like classics, you never knew what would break next.

Cusick worried enough that when the *Marine Electric* was taken off the coal route a few months before to carry grain to Haifa, Israel, he had opted out. He knew the shape of the *Marine Electric* better than anyone. Would he ride her up and down the coast of the North Atlantic? You bet. The U.S. Coast Guard could always come out and get them. They were only thirty miles from shore.

But cross the North Atlantic and go through the Mediterranean all the way to Israel? Cusick had always taken risks. Not this one, though. He passed. He remembered that just two years earlier, another old ship, the SS *Poet,* had gone down in the Atlantic carrying government grain. No one was found. No one survived.

Cusick was not alone in his concern. The *Marine Electric*'s first mate, Clayton Babineau, also passed on the transatlantic voyage. He took the summer off and worked on the roof of his house while the *Marine Electric* delivered grain to Israel. *"When are they going to cut that tub into razor blades?"* friends would ask Babineau. Babineau would grin back and say, *"You can't cut rust into razor blades."*

But Babineau was unamused by much of what he saw on the old ship. He was a methodical, serious man, whose absorption in detail drove his wife to distraction. Mary Babineau loved him dearly but hated his endless lists. He even had a packet marked for her if he was ever lost at sea, detailing what she should do—lists of assets, lists of lawyers, who to call, bills to be paid, union officers to contact.

"Don't worry," he would tell Mary. "It's never going to happen. The thought of you as a rich widow is enough to keep me safe."

Very funny, she would say, and Mary, a devout Catholic, would pray harder, hope that Clayt would loosen up on the lists, and pray she never would have to reach for the packet she knew was in that desk drawer.

But Babineau found he could not loosen up on the condition of the ship. Clayt liked the job, but hated the ship. He liked the job because the home front had been tumultuous recently. He was needed there, and the coastal run let him spend a lot of time at home. He had two teenagers and a daughter in her twenties, now out of the nest. Teenagers always are a challenge, but it was the older girl's actions that bothered him and Mary. She wanted to marry a guy who was not in any way, shape, or form included on his lists. Mary agreed.

The parents weren't winning this debate, but they weren't giving up on it, either. Their older daughter was nearly estranged. Home time was important until this thing was seen through one way or the other.

Clayt also liked his position in the company. He'd just gotten word that he would be the new relief chief mate, filling in when Cusick took vacations. And that would mean, in a few months, he would be the relief mate on a brand-new ship—the *Energy Independence*. When she came in service, he would have a scarce position on one of the safest ships imaginable.

If Babineau could hold on a little longer, keep his nose clean with the company, and keep the *Marine Electric* on the water instead of under it, he'd be set.

So it had been no small thing several weeks back when he had called the Coast Guard about the *Marine Electric*. Mary was in Clayt's study when he phoned. The ship was in a Rhode Island repair yard in the winter of 1982 when he dialed up the local Coast Guard inspectors.

"Listen," he said, "here's what's wrong with the ship. Go on board and just take a look. You'll see the cracks in the deck. You can't miss them. Check the hatches."

"Will do," said the Coast Guard guy.

But the *Marine Electric* sailed a short time later, and the complaint made in Rhode Island was not forwarded to other ports where she put in. Babineau never got any response, never saw any results of his call, and watched in fact as inspectors of the American Bureau of Shipping and the Coast Guard stepped over obvious safety violations. The crew had circled cracks in the deck with chalk, then spraypainted circles around them. The inspectors were careful both not to trip over the deficiencies and to ignore them in their inspection reports. Clayt's list of what was wrong with the ship grew longer as the condition of the ship became uglier.

Still, the men took pride in their work and in the *Marine Electric*. They kept her painted, and the rust didn't show from a distance. Cusick kept the deck crew busy on that, though when they scraped the rust off the hatch covers, sometimes daylight would show through.

Eugene F. Kelly, Jr., had caught that spirit of pride, even though he was only the relief third mate—a part-timer. He liked the ship and liked the crew and hoped the *Marine Electric* would become a permanent hitch.

He had a wife and seven-month-old daughter at home, and this was, as the third mate often said, a "milquetoast run." He thought every once in a while it would be nice to work on the new big tankers, use his head a little more, run the modern inert gas systems that kept the supertankers from exploding. Or maybe work on one of the military sealift ships, oversee refueling in mid-ocean. That would be a challenge. He was only thirty-one and needed challenges, he thought. A little more danger could be good for him.

But life on the *Marine Electric* was perfect in so many ways. He was a sportsman, and the winter waterfowl season was open. When he was landlocked, he could hunt and be with his family.

The old salts could have the transatlantic runs, two weeks each way, with just the ocean to stare at. Most of the men on the *Marine Electric* parked their cars at the power plant in Massachusetts. When Kelly and the crew came in, they zipped home. "Like we were shore workers," an officer once remarked.

Besides, the *Energy Independence* would be finished soon. Six months, Kelly figured, and all of them would have the same cushy job on a brand-new ship.

There is a saying among the families of seamen, among wives, lovers, mothers.

Some men go to sea to get away. Some men go to sea to get home.

The *Marine Electric* had its share of the former, men who knew no other life and were most comfortable at sea. Like the men of the old clipper ships or the fictional whaler Ishmael, they needed the sea to get away from land and all its social complexities.

But most of the *Marine Electric* crewmen were "home ported"— with a regular departure port close to their homes. They went to sea so they could get home to land. The sea provided for their land life, and they were grateful. They didn't want to worry about the age of the ship. They thought themselves blessed.

Besides, new ship, old ship, always there was risk. A state-of-the art West German ship, the *Munchen,* had gone down in the mid-Atlantic a few years earlier. A brand-new British ship, the *Derbyshire,* sank in the Pacific in 1980. All hands perished, including some women on the *Derby.*

It was a global story, a global worry, that stretched back to the first man who floated atop a log in saltwater. Those who went to sea faced peril, period. Worrying too much was a waste.

Perhaps it was the knowledge that he captained a rust bucket that made Corl do what he did. Or perhaps a premonition. Cusick couldn't figure it out. Not on the face of it, at least. Was the old man superstitious? They were both old-timers and seasoned professionals. So Cusick was surprised at Corl's decision about his wife, Alice. It was more and more common these days for officers' wives to accompany their husbands on trips, particularly milk runs like this one. So the plan had been for Alice Corl to board in Massachusetts, take the trip to Norfolk, see a bit of Virginia while the ship loaded, and scoot back up the coast with her husband.

But Corl hemmed and hawed about her coming. Finally, he declared that the quarters weren't large enough. "Alice," he said, "skip this trip. Stay in a hotel in Boston, Alice. I'll see you on the flip-flop, on the return trip. Have fun in the city."

His decision made no sense to Cusick. Or to anyone. The quarters weren't huge, but they were big enough for a couple. People ate in shifts anyway. Of course, men in the maritime trades often talked around things. It was rare that a softness of heart would surface.

Premonitions were not part of the science of navigation and engine room maintenance.

What else could Corl have said? That the trip didn't feel right? That the ship was unsafe? The men would have muttered all thirty-two hours south and thirty-two hours north about that one. About how the old man felt that the ship was jinxed.

And in that sense, it made perfect sense to Cusick and everyone else on the crew. They just didn't want to talk about it.

They didn't have to talk about it. If the officers felt concern about the ship, they could go to the bridge and watch the radar. Etched in green flows on the scope was their salvation. Off there on the left going up. Down there on the right coming down. The continental shelf. Land. The Coast Guard was only thirty miles away. Jobs were scarce. They didn't get any better than this. Who wanted to complain? Who wanted to lose this good thing?

The crew had all signed on over the last few days as the ship loaded, and there were the usual manning mix-ups, misunderstandings, and last-minute quirks.

Jose O. Quinones had just made chief cook, and there was no way he would miss his first voyage with that title. He was making certain his galley was well-stocked with comfort food. He wanted to keep the *Marine Electric*'s reputation as a "good feeder."

Others were more casual about the trip.

Walter Parkhurst was a relief able-bodied seaman, an "AB," and had sailed down from Massachusetts. Edward W. Matthews, a Baltimore man, had been on leave. But there was a misunderstanding, and now both men showed up on the pier in Norfolk. Men on the ship took sides. Some, mostly friends of Matthews, told Matthews he should demand his berth, that it was his by rights. Matthews wanted the ride.

Cusick knew his union rules, though, and took Parkhurst aside.

"Parkie, you have a right to sail now," Cusick told him. "I'll back you with the union. The rules are the rules, and you can sail if you want. You're cleared to get on the ship. Just give me the word."

Parkie gave it some thought and a few minutes later found the chief mate.

"Oh, what the hell, Mate," he told Cusick. "I'll get off here." Matthews got his berth.

Davy Wright, a steady AB, was coming back to the ship, too, but was careful to follow the rules. He had been on vacation. The union had strict rules about time off and time on and rigorously enforced vacations. Because jobs were scarce, the union spread the jobs out by demanding mandatory times on the beach. Now Wright had been on the beach long enough to go back to sea. He stopped by the union hall to make sure all was in order.

He was out the door with his ticket punched when the union man ran out after him. "Hey, sorry, Davy. There's a mistake here. You're one day short. You need one day more on land. You're going to have to catch the ship up north."

So Davy joined Parkie on the beach.

And then there was the Gashounder. He was a good guy when you could catch him sober, but Kelly remembered giving him a ride one night and how the liquor fumes from the guy filled the cab of his truck. The Gashounder would go to sleep and snore, slip a little on the seat, then slide over and slump against Kelly, drooling on him. It got to the point where Kelly had to shove the guy hard over to the door. There he drooled against the window, emitting fumes of vomit and booze.

"Thank Christ!" Kelly said, when he learned that Cusick had fired the Gashounder. It was something the chief mate had hated to do. Drinking was a problem on board ships, and not just among the seamen. Cusick had a good friend, an officer, who was a bad drinker, so bad that the story of the guy was a legend in the fleet.

In Da Nang, South Vietnam, in the old days, the friend once took the ship's small motor launch to a bar across the bay. When the Viet Cong mortared the area after a few hours, the launch came hurtling full speed back to the ship. The Marine guard on the ship watched as a man stood in the bow of the launch, stripped off all his clothes, and dove into the water.

The launch swerved out to sea, and the naked man swam madly

to the ship. He ran up the ladder yelling that people were shooting at him, waved his arms wildly, then disappeared down below. The young Marine ran to the officer on the bridge and said, "We just had a crazy guy run stark naked onto the ship. We better tell the captain."

"Good luck," the officer on watch said laconically. "That *was* the captain."

In the rough culture of the Merchant Marine, stories like that were numerous and—too often, perhaps—accepted as part of life at sea.

But no one accepted the Gashounder. Just a few days earlier, in Massachusetts, as they were getting ready to leave for Norfolk, he was drunk again in his cabin, and this time he would not get up. He told Charlie Johnson, the bosun, that he just wanted to sleep. When he was told of the problem, Cusick sighed and went down to the man's berth.

"Come on, fella, time to go to work," Cusick said.

"I ain'ta gonna," the Gashounder said.

"You gotta," Cusick said twice. The man lay still, in a stupor.

Then Cusick said, "Listen, you're a good man when you're sober, but this can't go on like this. Get your O.T. sheet and your gear and get off."

A few minutes later, the Gashounder was back, a supplicant. He wasn't a mean drunk. "Look, Mate, you've been fair with me all along and I've been an asshole. I know that. Can I ask you one favor, though? Can I keep my gear on the ship and pick it up in Brayton?"

"Sure," Cusick said. And then the Gashounder left for the bars, and a young seaman named Paul Dewey signed on.

For Cusick's part, there were no ominous premonitions on this trip. Just common sense. And precision.

This night, he took additional precautions. There was a very bad storm bearing down on the East Coast, and the Virginians, not used to driving in ice and snow, would soon be skidding into one another left and right. Already it was cold and rainy. Gale warnings were out. They could expect winds of twenty-five to thirty-five knots.

The *Marine Electric* and Cusick had seen dozens of storms like this one. It would be a bad one, but nothing to write home about. Not "the perfect storm." It had formed over the Gulf of Mexico and was headed north. The *Marine Electric* would plow through as she had for nearly forty years. The bow would plunge. The waves would pump high. There would be a whoosh and bang of water hitting steel and a ka-thump as if someone had whacked a very big washtub with a board. Sometimes green water would bury the frontmost part of the ship, actually submerge the bow and much of the deck beneath a big wave. Then the buoyancy of the bow would assert itself, and she would clear the wave to meet the next one.

Cusick instructed the crew members to pay special attention to the huge hatches. The covers were very heavy affairs and normally needed only a few fasteners—or dogs, as they were called—to secure the hatches, one dog at each corner, one or two per side. With heavy weather coming, Cusick ordered them all dogged down to the maximum. The hatch covers weighed tons. The water in the waves could weigh tons more. If water crashed through the hatches? Many a ship had sunk precisely because that had happened. So in the cold and the rain, the crew put down every dog they could. Not all of the fasteners worked. Many of the hatches had holes in them and gaskets that did not fit well.

Still, it seemed good enough. She had seen worse, the old girl. She was good enough. In as good a shape as ever she was these past several years.

There were 745 tons of fuel, food, and fresh water on board, about 24,800 tons of coal, and thirty-four men. The bow drew thirty-four feet of water on the button. The stern, thirty-four feet, eight inches. The center, thirty-four feet, four inches. No hogging or sagging here. Over the course of two full football fields, only an eight-inch difference, stern to bow. Cusick was a pro.

They had only one small problem as they left. Steve Browning was not there.

Corl and Kelly thought it odd that Browning was a no-show. The guy was a responsible assistant engineer and serious about his work. The storm must have delayed him.

Well, they could make it without him. They had enough engineers. This was just a little coastal run.

And then she was set to go. Shortly before midnight, in the last hour of February 10, a Thursday, the propeller of the ship surged. Tugs pushed and pulled the old collier away from the dock. The thick mooring lines were heaved on board and stored. And she was off, the crew and officers feeling the little thrill that accompanies any voyage. They were casting off. They were en route.

The tickle of excitement soon settled into cozy routine.

It would be many hours before the ship's officers heard the radio crackle news about a fishing boat in trouble.

Theodora was her name, and she would change everything.

Chapter Two

THE RESCUE
OF THE THEODORA

Does anyone know
Where the love of God goes,
When the waves
Turn the minutes
To hours?

GORDON LIGHTFOOT
The Wreck of
the Edmund Fitzgerald

2:00 A.M. / FRIDAY, FEB. 11, 1983 / ON BOARD THE *MARINE ELECTRIC*
MOUTH OF THE CHESAPEAKE BAY

As the ship cut across the Chesapeake Bay toward open sea, Bob Cusick roamed the deck, more than a little worried. He paid special attention to securing the bow area. There was no doubt it would be pounded by waves. He even ordered the anchors secured earlier than usual in anticipation of the storm to come. Normally, they kept the anchors ready until they got past the long Chesapeake Bay Bridge Tunnel that spanned the mouth of the bay. But not this time. Cusick wanted the work done before they hit open sea. The waves were already rough.

In fact, the water was rough enough that the harbor pilot was considering staying on board the big ship. Pilots supervise navigation in shallow local waters, then hop off onto small pilot boats once the local hazards are cleared. It would be a tough hop for the pilot on this night. He would have to climb down a ladder and then, as the ship and the boat both pitched, jump to the pilot boat.

On this day, he was scheduled to transfer at two in the morning. Cusick made sure the ladder was secured for the pilot. Ladders, anchors, hatches. They could come loose in a big blow. He made sure they all were dogged, tied down and secured. All the anchor systems were in place. The anchor windlass was secure. The stopper—a chisel-like piece of steel—was secure in a link of the big anchor chain. And the devil's claw, a device that snagged the chain if it started to fall, was snugged in nice and tight, held by its own smaller chain and a turnbuckle-type tightener.

On the bridge, Kelly had been listening to the harbor pilot debate with himself. The seas were high. The pilot pickup boat was small. Would it be easier to ride the *Marine Electric* to Massachusetts in this storm? Or should he risk going down the fragile pilot's ladder to the wave-tossed harbor craft?

The pilot boat was alongside the *Marine Electric,* and now it was time for a decision. Ride the ship? Take the boat?

"I'm getting off," the pilot said, and a few moments later, he descended the ladder, sprayed by the waves. He timed his jump correctly and soon was safe on the deck of the boat below.

Almost instantly, another figure mounted the ladder, and this one made his way *up,* hand over hand.

Steve Browning's head popped above the rail of the *Marine Electric,* and he smiled sheepishly as Kelly ribbed him. He had been late at the dock, but he ran to the pilot boat and hitched a ride out. They could kid him all they wanted. The weather was bad. The ship was bad. Losing a good job was worse.

And now they were under way in the open sea, cutting handily through four-foot waves, which blew with the wind north northeast on a course of 38 1/2 degrees true from Chesapeake Light to Narragansett Bay up north, a distance of 322 nautical miles.

One officer, two able-bodied seamen, and an ordinary seaman manned the ship in shifts of four hours each. It is a quiet and warm routine on the bridge, much like being secure in a comfortable cabin. They were making eight knots. The head wind caused the ship to pitch and roll some. And soon, as Cusick thought she would, the *Marine Electric* was shipping water over her main deck and hatches. Each time this happened, the ship responded well.

During the night, the waves reached ten to fifteen feet, with Force 8 conditions with winds at thirty to forty knots—about thirty-five to forty-five miles per hour.

By dawn, the blow was a Force 10 storm from the northeast, with winds of sixty miles per hour and seas between twenty and forty feet—nothing to laugh about.

Still, there was no need to panic. The *Marine Electric* took it well, shipping seas and bouncing back with no sign of sluggishness. By afternoon, green seas were boarding the ship's bow area, hammering the hatches and pouring across the forward area.

Par for the course. The *Marine Electric* took it all with the serenity of a forty-year-old veteran of the sea.

Secure, the officers and engineers settled into their social shipboard routines. There was a howling gale outside, but inside, the ship served up a constant buffet of food and warm drink. Most ships had reputations as good feeders. Few ships had bad cooks, because they did not last. The word got out. No one wanted to put up with a bad cook, because food was central to the rhythms and morale of a vessel. Quinones's skill in the kitchen was one reason many of the men were, if not portly, *ample.* Food was not just sustenance. In a routine that infrequently varied, on a sea that looked the same, often, one day to the next, food was the one changing item. In a closed, self-sealed environment, food was recreation.

The rest was routine, and often the routine was boring. Officers and men served two four-hour shifts a day. Even if they slept eight hours, they had six hours to knock about the ship. Some watched videos. Some read. Some studied. Some talked.

Cusick listened to music, and his tastes ranged from Mozart to a recent discovery, Stan Rogers, a Canadian folk singer. He and his wife, Bea, had wandered down to a café near their home in Scituate, Massachusetts, one evening and heard an amateur group sing Rogers's sea tales and ballads. Cusick liked the singer so much, he bought a cassette player for his cabin.

There was always time for talk.

Bill Scott, one of the men in the engine room, passed the time in part by shooting the breeze about motorcycles. He had a big BMW, a road bike. Others in the crew, Cusick among them, were partial to Harleys. As the gales howled outside, hours could pass as they debated the merits of the horizontally opposed cylinders of the German bike versus the big-bore Harleys.

Cusick spent a lot of time talking to Mike Price, the thirty-five-year-old engineer who had played cupid with Cadet George Wickboldt. Normally, engineers and deck officers kept to their own kind. But Price and Cusick had grown to be close friends. Price had shared his dreams with Cusick. At sea, Price was down below in the bowels of the ship, nursing the engine, tweaking it, keeping it going. It was a good job, but his wife, Marsha, had cried when he had left two weeks before, and he missed Heather, his eight-year-old daughter.

Like Cusick, Price was married with one daughter. It was a custom, a routine, for the men to talk about those dreams of Price's when the ship was under way. How it was going to be. What Cusick had done in his youth. What Price was doing in his. The older man listened to the younger man. Encouraged him. It was almost as if they were father and son.

"The thing is," Price would say, "I can make it on land . . . if George Dolak listens to me and we both sign on the *Marine Electric* for a while, one man on, one man off."

Price and Dolak envisioned their own foreign-car repair service. Jags, BMWs, Mercedes, and other high-ticket automobiles. Some marine engine repair work, too.

One man would go to sea for a few months while the other ran the shop. Then they would rotate. If they did that for a year, they could get the business going. Then both men could stay on land. He knew Dolak could get a berth on the ship, but Price had to talk him into it. Dolak was the night engineer on the dock at Brayton Point, tending to the ship's needs but never sailing her. It wouldn't be hard for him to get on the *Marine Electric* full time.

Clayt Babineau had lists. Price had plans. In his youth, Price's family had moved from urban New Jersey to a small town in Massachusetts, and he instantly cracked the code of the small-town ethic. In high school, he was not the largest man on the football team, but he was the best defensive lineman Coach James Stehlin had ever seen. Never, in his entire career, had he seen anyone like Price. Amiable, good-natured off the field and in the locker room, Price was fierce, focused, driven, not to be denied on the field.

In 1966, Price had a big plan. Win the state championship. They were in mid-season when one of the more popular kids on the team, a good player, was caught drinking.

The team council handled such things. Thumbs up or thumbs down. On the team or off.

"Cut the guy a break," one of the players said. "It was one time. Give him another chance."

"Hear, hear," someone else said, and the guy was all but back, cleared by his peers.

"Yeah, let's give him one more chance," Price said. "And then when I start drinking and break training, give me one more chance. Give the next guy a chance, and the next.

"But that's not what we said we were going to do," Price continued. "We said we were going all the way, no compromises this year. If that's what we're going to do, this guy doesn't get another chance."

The guy was off the team. Price, as co-captain, Number 62 on the defensive line, led the school to the Eastern Massachusetts Class B Championship that year.

Nothing, his coach said, kept Mike Price from his goals. Nothing.

Still, his plans did not keep him from worrying about the ship. He told his wife, Marsha, what was wrong with the *Marine Electric,* and now she worried too. Price looked at the old tub. He looked at Heather, his beautiful daughter. He looked hard at his plans. He looked at Marsha's tears each time he left. He figured the odds.

Nothing was without risk. No pain, no gain. He stuck to his plans and kept pitching Dolak. The guy would come around, would see the vision.

No one turned Price away from a goal, but Marsha Price had come the closest. In high school, she was the pretty girl from one high school over. She had heard about Price the football star from friends, came to see him play, and met him a few days later in the parking lot of the A&P near the field. Price asked her out, and that was it.

Even the weeks at sea were easy for the couple at first. He would send flowers, write, and call whenever he was in port. Sometimes, he was away sixty or 120 days at a time, but it worked. When Marsha and Mike decided to have a child, though, Marsha had a request. Stay on land while I'm pregnant, and he did. He worked a land job for nine months, then shipped out the tenth month.

"I'm just not built for a land job," he said. "My place is with the ocean—I'm not the type to sit behind a desk."

When he was home, Heather and Mike were inseparable, and they shared the same spirit. When Mike would take his daughter to the highest point in a ski resort or the deepest water in a swimming pool, Marsha would bite her nails and shout warnings. But Heather? She loved it. Wanted to be at the highest point, loved swimming to the deepest water.

But even Price's sense of adventure had its limits, and he was not certain the limits included the *Marine Electric*. He had signed on in November 1982 and told Marsha it would be great, that he would see them every two or three days. He had just gotten his first engineer's license, and one day he hoped to make chief engineer.

His stories about the ship began to weigh on Marsha deeply. Two weeks before the February trip, they fought over his job.

"Isn't it enough?" she said after he described a fault in the ship. "Listen to what you're saying. Isn't that enough to get off the ship?"

"It's going to be dry-docked in February," he told her. "And if anything happens to us, the Coast Guard will come out and get us."

But then the dry-docking was postponed, and the ship continued sailing. When he was down in Virginia, on the day the ship sailed, Marsha renewed her argument, played back to him all the bad things he himself had said about the ship, told him on the phone as he prepared to board the ship in Virginia that he needed to leave that old rust bucket.

Price stopped arguing, and there was a smile in his voice, it seemed.

"Do you really want me to get off this ship?" he asked.

"Yes," Marsha said. "Right now."

Price sighed. Hey, he could modify the dream. Not give it up, but change it a little.

"Okay," he said. "One more trip. I'll take the ship up to Massachusetts, and that will be it."

"That sounds good to me," Marsha said.

"We'll go out to dinner with George Dolak Saturday night, and that will be the end of the *Marine Electric*," Mike said.

Later, right before the ship sailed, he called again, just checking in. Marsha Price had been watching the weather reports and saw there was a bad storm brewing.

"Mike, there's a big storm," she said. "Get off that ship now."

Mike laughed it off.

"We're better off at sea than tied up at the dock," he said. "We'll just ride it out."

"Have you seen the weather reports?" Marsha said. "Do you *know* how serious this storm is?"

"There's no one to replace me," Price said. "I have to stay. Don't worry. I'll be home tomorrow, and we'll go to dinner."

Marsha Price knew when her husband had made up his mind. She put Heather on the phone, and they talked about what they would do on the weekend. Her father told her he loved her very much, and they said good-bye.

Price would talk to Marsha about the ship, but the crew and officers said little about it to each other, other than the passing joke. Bob Cusick would talk to Price for hours about dreams and kids and land jobs, but neither of them talked much about the ship's condition. They talked around the subject or ignored it. Such rationalization among seamen in the coastal trades was nothing new. It dated back decades, more than a century. It was tradition.

"The class of shipping which is engaged in the coal trade, as a general rule, is a very inferior class . . ." said James Hall, an early maritime British reformer, in 1870. "I have been for many years engaged in loading ships in the coasting trade, and many are the faces of those captains, whose vessels I have loaded, who have gone to sea never to return again to port.

"Strange as it may appear, men who are accustomed to trade be-tween two ports will, for the advantage of being frequently at their homes, incur the risks of navigating such ships," Hall said.

Cusick did not know the history of this tendency. He simply liked the security of working for one firm on regular routes close to home. He was a company man. Tradition, service, and home were important to him. Growing up in the Roxbury section of Boston, Cusick had seen his father do well, serving first as a butler, then working for years in upscale service positions at the Boston Plaza Hotel. The man provided nicely for his family, and they lived in a thirteen-room house. Cusick, in his own way, was following the same tradition.

Bob Cusick had his master's license, in fact, and could have cap-tained the ship. It just wasn't his style. He was a number-two guy, not a number one. He could have had Corl's job as relief master, and some of the union guys had encouraged him to take it. But he passed. He would have to take the ship on its grain runs across the Atlantic every once in a while as a captain. If he were a number one, he would have to run those old hatches, that old bow, through the rough seas.

Moreover, if he were master, he'd be away from the men. If you were a master, you had to keep your distance. No talks with Price. No shooting the breeze about Harleys. He wasn't the kind of chief mate who gave orders and then retired to the officer's mess. He was out on the deck, sometimes handling lines, moving with the men, working hand in glove with the bosun, Charlie Johnson.

The men, the officers, all saw him as the ship's older uncle. Very experienced. A good guy. Asked that the job be done and done right, showed you how if you had questions, wouldn't put up with nonsense from the Gashounder.

Those who knew him well knew Cusick was both funny and somehow, at odd moments, sad. Most of the time, he had a light in his eyes, a twinkle, as if he had seen God's Green Pastures and un-derstood and loved God's Great Cosmic Joke.

The sad look would come in unguarded moments when he stared out to sea. All seamen have a variety of that look when they have been at sea for long periods. Their faces go slack. They focus on nothing, except perhaps the far line of the horizon. Cusick's stare seemed even farther, a 5,000-yard stare, as if he were looking into the Abyss, had just lost his five best friends. Which in fact was not far from the truth, if you went back far enough with Bob Cusick.

Few saw that look, though, and knew instead the man's slightly subversive sense of humor and wit. Often it struck from the blue and from the most innocent of faces. Once, some friends and Cusick were listening to a woman who had traveled worldwide and was decrying the American prudishness about topless beaches. Toplessness was common everywhere else, except America. Only in America, she said, had she ever been given a ticket for baring her breasts.

Cusick looked concerned, perplexed. "Was the ticket for public nudity," he asked, deadpan, "or under the legal size limit?"

Sometimes the skewered never knew they were done in. The Cusicks once had a house guest, a hopeless yuppie who drank the right wines and drove the right cars. They rolled out the red carpet for him, and Bea served her famous special waffles, laced with freshly picked wild blueberries. Accompanying the waffles was the house brand of syrup, a common bottle of Log Cabin.

The yuppie took one bite and exclaimed, "These waffles are awful."

Bea was hurt and showed it, and there might have been sharp words in another household. Bob Cusick simply looked concerned and said, "Bea, shame on us, we didn't give our friend the special syrup."

Bea started to say there was no special syrup when Bob surreptitiously shushed her and added aloud, "I think there's a bottle in the basement."

He bootlegged the Log Cabin syrup on his hip so the man could not see it, then padded down the basement stairs. There, he had an old, empty maple syrup bottle of a brand equivalent to fine single-barrel bourbon. He quickly filled it with Log Cabin and went back up the stairs. Bea had made a fresh batch of waffles, and Cusick ceremoniously drizzled the "new" syrup over them.

"Try this," he said.

"Ahhh, now these are waffles," the poseur announced.

And it was that sort of quiet humor that percolated up from Bob Cusick. When they patched holes in the ship with cement, he began calling the *Marine Electric* the *Marine Sidewalk* because there was more concrete in her than in all the sidewalks in Scituate. People would see him coming with a mischievous look in his eyes and they knew a joke was afoot.

It was that sort of good-natured feeling for the men that led to long talks with Price and a few others. They were a good crew and had been together a long time. They were like brothers, Cusick thought, as he talked to Price and Charlie Johnson. Like family.

All of the pleasant shipboard routine, the ropes they all knew by rote, was broken the next day when they saw the fishing boat.

Cusick had ducked out of the comfortable warmth of the cabins and was out on deck in the blizzard. About three o'clock in the afternoon on Friday, February 11, he was wrestling with the mooring lines, working with a seaman to make them more secure, when they first saw the *Theodora,* like a ghost ship through the storm.

She did not look like much, and they wondered what she was doing out in weather like this. At sixty-five feet, the *Theodora* was a tenth the size of the *Marine Electric.* She could easily sit on the bigger ship's deck.

Some of the rogue waves—monsters formed by combined wave peaks—were nearly as high as the fishing boat was long. The *Marine Electric* pounded through the waves; the *Theodora* sailed up and down them. Up the steep pitch of one wave to the crest, then down the slope toward the trough.

Still, she seemed to be doing well enough. Fishermen were crazy sometimes, but they knew the risks, too. Or so it seemed. There were no calls for help. Nothing on the radio. No flares. No distress flags. So the *Marine Electric* sailed right past her.

But a little later, the *Theodora* was in big trouble. Her crew and captain soon were frantically calling the Coast Guard. They were taking on water. The pumps were lagging behind, and they did not know exactly where they were—a big problem when you were asking to be rescued. Big ships like the *Marine Electric* had radar and

Loran-C's—instruments that gave fairly precise readouts of latitude and longitude and location. The *Theodora,* which had left Cape May, New Jersey, the previous day, knew only that she was off Chincoteague, Virginia, by maybe thirty miles.

The distress signal from the *Theodora* scrambled a helicopter out of Elizabeth City, North Carolina, just south of Norfolk. The call came about 3:20 in the afternoon, and by 4:00 P.M. a chopper, one of the big H-3s, was scouring the scene. Up above, a C-130 fixed-wing Coast Guard plane was searching as well.

And they came up with . . . nothing. The boat was so small, the sea so large, the snow and rain blowing so hard that the Coast Guard could not find the *Theodora.* The helicopter swept the seas, burning precious fuel, to no avail. The fishing boat was a small cork in a vast ocean.

It was about this time that the Coast Guard put out a call for help, asking for a fix on the *Theodora* and for assistance in finding and rescuing the ship. It is a time-honored tradition, as well as a legal responsibility, to come to the aid of vessels in distress, so the *Marine Electric* responded.

We passed the fishing boat a while back, the *Marine Electric* officers said, and then gave the latitude and longitude of the rough position.

Would it be possible, the Coast Guard requested, for the *Marine Electric* to turn to and stand by the *Theodora?* It was no small request. Reversing course in a Force 10 gale meant that the ship, two football fields in length, had to turn sideways to the oncoming winds and waves. On shore, the Coast Guard was often a nuisance, inspecting ships and holding up loadings and departures. At sea, the Coast Guard was a revered presence, the rescuer of lost seamen. When they called, seamen responded. The *Marine Electric* would return.

Captain Corl immediately began the dangerous maneuver and made a neat trick of it. To turn, the big ship needed to come about in the face of twenty- to forty-foot waves. This exposed the sides and the rear of the ship to walls of water the size of a three-story house. The crew and officers remarked later that the old man had done well. The *Marine Electric* was only "in the trough"—turned sideways to the waves—for perhaps one or two wave cycles.

Now the *Marine Electric* was taking the seas on its stern. The ship rolled more, but there were fewer waves over the deck. Soon, they could see the *Theodora* clearly on radar and then visually, two miles away. The *Marine Electric* bridge kept sending out the location, and a little before 5:00 P.M., they heard, cutting through the howl of the gale, the whirl of the helicopter overhead.

Cusick's Theorem had proved right. *The Coast Guard will come out and get you.* He watched as the helicopter hovered like a descending angel. And what a sight it was! From nowhere, in the blizzard and rain, this celestial presence appeared. A floodlight on the 'copter heightened the angel-like quality of the errand of mercy. Motes of snow and rain gave the beam of light texture and depth. A golden cone poured down on the *Theodora.* At that moment, there wasn't a man on the big ship who didn't have a warm spot in his heart for the Coast Guard. And maybe a lump in his throat. Knowing they were out there was a comfort. Seeing them at work was a balm. Cusick's Theorem had proved correct.

Would they take the men off now? Would the basket drop and men be pulled up from the angry ocean? No. The captain and crew were game—they would try to save their boat. Extra pumps were lowered to the pitching deck of the *Theodora.* The crew would pump water out of their boat and see if she could make it.

By 5:30, the chopper was heading back to North Carolina, its mission over. Using the extra pumps, the *Theodora*'s crew could guide her to safety. The Coast Guard cutter *Highland* was on its way from Chincoteague and would be there before midnight.

But just in case, the Coast Guard asked, would the *Marine Electric* play big brother until the cutter got there?

The *Marine Electric* stayed. But the weather was worsening, and when the *Theodora* turned toward Chincoteague, on a course of 270 degrees, the seas began battering the *Marine Electric.* The fishing boat rode them like a cork. The big ship confronted them like a dike. The tops of waves were clipped off by the *Marine Electric*'s starboard side, and green seas boarded the ship, sweeping over the deck and the hatch covers. It was as if the ship lay at the end of a beach directly in heavy surf. As the snow turned into a bad rain squall, Corl raised the Coast Guard and told them of his troubles.

Stick it out if you can, the Coast Guard said.

About 6:30 P.M., Corl keyed the mike and raised the Coast Guard again. "I'm taking an awful beating out here. I'm going to be in trouble myself pretty soon. I don't know how I can hold—heave to on this course. I'm rolling, taking water, green water over—over my starboard side, all the way across my deck."

The battered master of the *Theodora* keyed his mike then and said he was okay, he'd make it. The pumps had turned the trick. He was making headway. The *Highland* would be there by midnight. So, for his part, the *Marine Electric* could leave. The Coast Guard agreed.

"I thank you very much, old dog, and I really appreciate what you did. . . . Thank you very much, and good luck to you," Jennings Hayward, the captain of the *Theodora,* radioed.

No problem, the *Marine Electric* radioed back, all in a day's work. Corl turned the ship neatly again through the trough of the wave and back into the heavy seas, thinking, Thank God that's over. The men were back on their coastal routine.

Chapter Three

INTO THE WATER

Our problem is: We don't know exactly what our situation is.

Captain Corl's radio transmission
to the Coast Guard

6:25 P.M. / FEB. 11, 1983 / ON BOARD THE *MARINE ELECTRIC*
NORTH ATLANTIC SEA-LANES

The *Marine Electric* turned in the cold of the storm and set a course for the utility dock at Brayton Point, far away in Somerset, Massachusetts, and her crew and officers turned back to their warm routine.

There is a feeling on a bridge at night almost like that in a hunters' lodge or gentlemen's club. There are no harsh or loud words. Conversation percolates quietly, like an old-fashioned coffee maker. Quiet jokes are passed among the three or four men on watch. Hot liquids are sipped. All stare forward toward an invisible point they themselves are unsure of. The future. What's out there through the window? Where will it come from?

Eugene Kelly was the eight-to-twelve shift third mate, and the bridge was his. There was nothing particularly tricky about the voyage now, and he did not expect to see anything bad out front. The weather was awful, but not the worst he had seen. The ship turned into the seas and took them well. The trick, really, was just to hold one's own. If Kelly made two miles on his shift in this weather, he would do well.

Outside, waves crashed into the ship, but the bow forced its way through them like a fullback shaking off tacklers. There would be a mighty heave, and the top of the wave would come rushing across the deck and hatches. The whole front of the ship would be buried. Then, explosively, the bow rose, as if shrugging its shoulders of this nuisance, rising above the water, ready to take on the next wave.

It was routine. When one first goes to sea on a modern ship, the wonder is of man's accomplishments. In quiet water, modern ships are so huge it is as if they are an island, with the water passing by like some swift river. Hit the open sea, though, and one is amazed at the magnificence of the ocean. The ship begins swaying gently, rocking in gentle rollers. Then, as the sea roughens, the ship shudders and shakes and pitches, and a vast ship seems a small cork. How, one wonders, did man ever come to brave such elements, face them, and return again?

Only veterans could stand on the bridge as Kelly did and know that the seeming turbulence was well under control, that the ship was built to specifications that allowed it to do exactly this and more. Strong steel, watertight compartments, the displacement of water, the force of gravity—all these meant the bow would burst back up into the cold air.

So it was with a sense of security that the officers not on watch took their rest. Cusick in his cabin, Corl sleeping behind the bridge on a settee in the chart room.

And when Kelly's relief came, he too turned in without a worry. They had been up for hours. Same old same old, was Kelly's message to Richard Roberts, the relief mate. And when Dewey, the new man, came up to relieve the able seaman on his twelve-to-four watch, he asked, "Okay?" and the man replied simply, "Nothing out there."

Over the next two hours, they would slowly lose this sense of certainty. Roberts and Dewey would stare through the window and, for the first time, not be sure about the future. It was not what they saw, really. It was what they felt. Or felt they felt. They thought they noticed a small shift about 1:00 A.M. on Saturday, February 12. It was hard to say. It was as if they were driving a car and thought they might have a flat, but couldn't really tell. Was the bow sluggish? They thought so. It did not seem to be rising from the water as it should. But again, it was hard to tell, because the sea and spray were everywhere. It was the dead of night and hard to see. It was not so disturbing that they woke the captain. Dewey left on a break between 1:00 and 1:50 and was unconcerned enough to be reading a novel when one of the engineers passed by and asked if the ship was down by the head—too low in front. Guess so, Dewey said. Some. But it was no big deal. Nothing to worry much about.

Shortly before 2 A.M., when Dewey went back to the bridge to take the helm, Captain Corl was awake. Still nothing urgent. The temperature had reached twenty-eight degrees Fahrenheit, and when that happened, the officers routinely turned on steam to warm the anchor, hatch, and mooring winches to keep them from freezing. The phone to the engine room wasn't working, so Corl sent a seaman to tell the engineers.

But out front it was growing worse. Dewey could see green water board the ship and wash back as far as the number-two hatch— covering the front third of the ship. Less and less would the bow hunch its shoulders and throw back the waves. More and more, it simply plowed through them. Dewey thought it was getting worse.

By 2:30 A.M., Corl was worried. The bow was very sluggish. Was that normal? Corl had only been on the *Marine Electric* a short time. Cusick was the veteran on the ship. Corl crept down to Cusick's quarters and gently roused him. "Mate, I believe we are in trouble," he said. "I think she's going—settling by the head." Then he shrugged and added sheepishly, "This may be my imagination with the way the seas are running. I can't really tell, but I think she's settling by the head."

"Settling by the head" meant that the ship was slowly sinking, front part first. But was she? Was the tire flat or not? Was the bow sluggish or not? The more you listened for it, the more it seemed flat. Then, when you listened again, you weren't so sure. Was the ship sinking slowly in the bow? Corl had been watching and listening too long to be sure.

Cusick went first to get Richard Powers, the chief engineer. The two friends, both *Marine Electric* veterans, mounted the stairs to the bridge and looked out to the bow. They knew how she rode seas.

They were horrified. It was apparent they were in trouble. The bow was not lifting properly. The seas were roaring down the deck. The old girl never rode the seas like this.

They had to act fast. Otherwise, all might be lost. Immediately, they let Corl know they were in trouble. Probably big trouble.

Corl did three things. He called the Coast Guard. Then he set the engineers to pumping and redistributing ballast. He ordered all crew and officers awakened, and then he told them to prepare the lifeboats.

Now he faced a difficult decision. Captains could not abandon ship too soon. Always, they would be safer riding out the storm in a 605-foot, 24,000-ton coal carrier than in a twenty-five-foot lifeboat. Even with her deck awash, the *Marine Electric* was a safer haven than out there.

He had only to look at the case of the SS *Marine Merchant,* a Liberty ship from the war, loaded with sulphur, when she ran into trouble off New Hampshire in April 1961. The ship split in two, but the main deck held the two halves together—like a broken index finger held together only by the skin. Her captain made ready to abandon ship, but weighed that option against staying on board the old vessel. There were Force 10 storm conditions in the chilly North Atlantic—about what the *Marine Electric* faced now. He stood pat. Morning came. The weather lightened. All men made it.

That case and others bore down on Corl. There was no indication that the ship was actually sinking, only that they were having trouble. They could all walk away from this dry. Could wait out the weather and step daintily onto a rescue cutter from the Coast Guard. Even get a tow in, ship and cargo undamaged.

And that, too, was a concern. The master had a responsibility to his men, yes, but weighed always against his responsibility to the owner and shipper. If he abandoned ship too soon, he could be held liable and lose his license. If he left the ship to the elements before it was clear the ship was sinking, he would violate civil law and modern laws of a master's conduct. Settling at the head was not sinking. He had an obligation to the owners to preserve the ship unless it was clear that the ship was sinking.

If he needed a reminder of that, there was the case of the *Smith*

Voyager, another World War II leftover, which developed a severe twenty-degree list in the South Atlantic in 1964, on its way to India with a cargo of grain. Water had breached the hatches and was spraying into the engine room. The crew took to the lifeboats, and most of them were rescued. But a formal Marine Board of Investigation found the master in error for letting his men go. The ship eventually sank, and that might not have happened had the captain kept his men on board, the board said. The master was brought up on charges, and his license and livelihood threatened.

Even more powerful than the threat of formal action were the traditions and customs of the sea. The old saying about the master going down with his ship was not an ancient myth. It happened in contemporary times. Kurt Carlsen, master of the *Flying Enterprise*, stayed with his ship in 1952 and was celebrated for his heroism by a ticker-tape parade in New York City. The tendency, the tradition, was to fight to save the ship. And these extremes were taken for granted, whether or not you got the ticker tape.

No one, for example, made a big fuss over what the captain and crew did in the late 1960s aboard the *Badger State*—one of the most heroic and least-known voyages in contemporary history.

The *Badger State* crew refused to leave a leaking, listing ammunition ship with bombs rolling around in its holds, when told to do so by their captain. Not just the captain, but the entire crew, was prepared to go down.

And many of them did.

She was bound for Da Nang during the Vietnam War, an old Liberty ship built in 1944, about five years past the twenty-year age limit when most ships are retired or officially called "overage." In her holds were more than 5,000 tons of bombs. Steel bands held the bombs to each other and to their metal pallet frames. So large were the 2,000-pound bombs that their noses protruded from the pallets by twenty-nine inches. One hundred pallets of the one-ton finned cylinders, unfused but still deadly, created a whole layer in the cargo hold. Wood planking helped hold it in place. Wood sheathing guarded the hull and the pallets from contact. Any voids or spaces were jammed with wood to keep the pallets from shifting.

Another scheduled load of munitions did not arrive, and the captain, Charles T. Wilson, considered the vessel light, not trimmed optimally. He asked for more cargo, but it was not forthcoming. Then the loading officials and the master decided the weight of the bombs alone would hold them in place. With a few minor shifts in cargo, Wilson was ready to go. As insurance, he asked for spare wood bracing, or dunnage, in case the cargoes needed further bracing. It was a prescient request.

On December 14, 1969, the *Badger State* sailed from Bangor, Washington. No one foresaw the heavy weather ahead. As they hit high winds and waves, the master reported the ship was uncomfortable, with "stiff" riding characteristics and a "snap roll" in the waves.

Conditions grew worse. By December 16, the ship was encountering "following" winds and waves—coming from behind it—and "confused swells," waves that were not predictable. Captain Wilson had twenty-foot swells coming from one direction, ten-foot swells from another. This meant he was constantly calling for hard rudder turns, attempting to keep the bow into the seas. But where were the seas coming from?

The ship was now rolling to forty degrees—then to forty-five degrees. A forty-five-degree tilt is about the angle you place your head when you are attempting to dislodge water from your ear after a swim. But the *Badger State* could not afford to dislodge anything—particularly its cargo.

Without power and steering for a time, the old ship took the seas roughly and kept snap-rolling to and fro. By the time steering was restored, there was the worst sort of news: The 500-pound bombs had shifted and come loose. The wood holding them secure had splintered and cracked from the pressure brought by the rolling. One bomb now pressed against the hull.

The crew responded valiantly, entering the holds, wrestling the bombs back into place and resecuring them while the ship continued to roll. The spare dunnage came in handy—all seemed stabilized for now. The *Badger State* slowed, and a cement patch was placed over a ten-inch hole in the hull in the shaft area. It seemed the ship had stumbled but had not fallen.

Yet, the cargo continued to shift. Constantly, the crew was using wood to brace the bombs. Worse, heavy rolling to thirty-five degrees continued. Even when the rolling slackened, the bombs had built up enough kinetic momentum from their caterwauling below to continue the calamitous shifting. Some of the bombs packed nose to nose had burst their wood restraints and had overshot one another. When this happened, the steel strapping came loose. The bands were breaking. Now some of the individual bombs were loose. The shoring material available—the dunnage carried on board—was rapidly disappearing.

But the weather forecast was for improved conditions, and the *Badger State* was directed to hold its course.

Then, in number-three hold, where there was no access, the men heard heavy banging noises, as if an angry intruder were pounding on the door. The bombs were loose down there. The men knew they could not reshore those missiles. They could not reach them. The captain requested diversion to a safe port, and the Military Command directed the *Badger State* to Pearl Harbor.

The men continued to reshore the bombs they could reach. Whenever the ship rolled past twenty degrees, however, the bombs came loose, cracking and splintering the wood. This went on for a week, but it looked as if they would make it to Pearl. They were holding their own.

Then, on Christmas Day, a severe and unpredicted storm hit hard. Hurricane-force winds struck the *Badger State*. The seas seemed to come from all directions. Winds were at forty to fifty knots. Waves swept over them, thirty to forty feet high. There was no way to control the rolls or the cargo now. Fixtures that had not moved in decades—galley refrigerators, engine room equipment—were sliding about wildly. At one time, the ship rolled fifty degrees to starboard—close to capsizing. The bombs were loose in all holds now.

Told to divert to Midway, the captain could not turn because of the rolls and the unstable cargo. The crew struggled below and, incredibly, rescued many of the bombs. The storm slackened. The *Badger State* had cheated death and destruction again.

On December 26, a second, even worse storm struck. One mountainous wave rolled the ship fifty degrees to starboard. Like a besotted top, the ship righted briefly and then rolled fifty-two degrees to port. The port lifeboat was destroyed. The metal bands on the pallets of the 2,000-pound bombs burst like a ribbon on a Christmas present. The bombs began to roll and slide, striking each other and the steel hull. Five-inch holes were punched in the ship's side by the heavy battering of the bombs. Other bombs toppled through open hatches to lower cargo holds.

The crew rallied again. All hands were mustered. No one could go down into the holds. So the men clustered above, frantic, as the vessel rolled in the storm, throwing into the holds anything they could find in an attempt to stop the big bombs from rolling.

First, they took the hatch covers partly off. Then they threw all their mattresses down into the melee of sliding, rolling bombs. Then they threw rags, mooring lines, anything. And when that did not work, they took their frozen meats from the kitchen freezer. In desperation, they threw steaks, turkeys, pork rolls, mutton, chickens, and frozen vegetables and desserts into the skittering cargo.

Finally, after they had even thrown in spare life jackets, they lowered one end of a hatch cover pontoon on top of some of the bombs.

Some of the bombs were checked. But others frolicked about as if in a rave. Sparks flew. Heat formed. The hull was battered. Kinetic energy gave the bombs a life of their own.

The Greek merchant ship *Khian Star 40,* miles away, received a distress message. Navy search and rescue heard it as well.

And now the last hours were playing out. An exhausted crew had not slept in days because of the emergency and the severe rolling. Captain Wilson had been on the bridge without rest for four straight days.

The men could see the *Khian Star* on the horizon. Hope was in sight. These were severe conditions, and the heavy waves would make an evacuation difficult, but it could be done. Captain Wilson considered launching the lifeboats and letting the men strike out for the *Star.* He would man the *Badger State* with a volunteer skeleton crew.

He proposed the idea. He polled the crew to see if they approved. But the men stood fast. The would not leave the ship. They would not leave their captain. They all volunteered to stay. The captain stopped polling.

Then the men heard a muffled explosion. The cargo hold covers were blown into the air. The cargo booms were bent and twisted by the force of the blast. Out came the life preservers, aflame. Food and other debris scattered high in the air and fell back onto the deck. On the right side of the hull, above the waterline but far below the deck, a jagged hole twelve by eight feet had appeared. One of the 2,000-pound bombs had detonated. Miraculously, none of the others had.

Wilson had had enough—he sounded the abandon ship signal. The engine room was evacuated. Thirty-five crew members boarded the starboard lifeboat and were lowered away. So high were the waves that the lifeboat, upon hitting the water, was carried back up to the deck and banged about.

Despite the heavy seas and winds, the boat was soon launched successfully. The odds for getting away seemed good.

But the men discovered that the lifeboat's sea painter—a device that dragged in the water and held the boat steady against the wind and waves—had disappeared, probably broken off when the boat had banged into the deck. The men began operating the hand propelling gears in an attempt to get steerage in the bad seas. But nothing happened, and they could not hold their own against the swells. The rudder on the lifeboat could not be shipped or installed, so the men had no way to direct the vessel.

The boat was thrown back against the ship. It drifted helplessly toward the open wound in the ship, the large hole where the bomb had exploded. It moved directly under the gaping hold.

And, as if in slow motion, a 2,000-pound bomb rolled out of the hold through the hole and fell onto the men and the lifeboat below.

It did not detonate. It did not have to. A ton-heavy bomb striking a small lifeboat needed no explosives. The boat capsized and sunk. The men, those not killed by the weight of the bomb, were spilled into the cold water.

Above them, on the flying bridge, the captain and the four crew members still on board were trying to launch life rafts. The rafts were deployed, but the fierce winds quickly swept them away. The captain told the men to put life rings over their life preservers, and they prepared to jump into the forty-eight-degree sea. Life in such temperatures is measured in minutes, not hours.

They looked down at the water and saw their fellow crewmen scattered about. Burnette, the third mate, threw life rings to them. Second Mate Ziehm and Seaman Hottendorf went over first, jumping together. Then Burnette jumped. Then Captain Wilson. Only Fireman-watertender Kaneo remained. He hesitated. The water was cold and rough. Smoke still poured from the cargo hatch. The men below him were swimming desperately away from the ship, knowing she would blow any moment. Kaneo was caught between two negatives. He looked at the smoking cargo holds. He looked at the cold water. Kaneo jumped.

To the rescue came the *Khian Star.* Her crew had seen the explosion thirty minutes before coming upon the scene. All around the *Badger State* now there were dead and dying men in the water. Some were still clinging to the wrecked lifeboat. Others were swimming away from the ship—expecting an explosion any second.

Still others made for the *Khian Star*—but were quickly carried off by the twenty-foot swells and lost.

Then, as if in a horror film, the huge albatrosses that had been following the ship began to attack the men, diving at them and pecking them. It was as if the furies of hell themselves were dogging the men of the *Badger State.*

From above now, a U.S. Air Force plane swept low and dropped rafts. They inflated, then flipped end over end, useless save one. Third Cook Donald Byrd, near the overturned lifeboat, grabbed the line of a raft. He held fast. Seaman Henderson swam to the raft. He helped Third Mate Sam Bondy on board, then jumped in himself. They pulled Seaman Richard C. Murray in. Then Bosun Richard Hughes and Seaman James McLure and Wiper Forencio Serafino. Electrician Konstantinos Mpountalis hung alongside, but the men in the boat were now so weak they could not bring him in. Byrd, who had held the raft, was nowhere to be seen. Lost.

One of the men, Murray, was so weak and sleepy he could not hold up his head. Hypothermia was claiming him. Henderson held him and slapped him roughly, reviving him.

In heavy seas, maneuvering carefully around a damaged munitions ship, the Greeks made a pass at the lifeboat and the rafts with Jacob's ladders, net slings, and lines at the ready. So high were the waves that Henderson's raft almost washed on board by itself. But it did not. So the *Khian Star* crew threw lines. They tied lines around McLure and Serafino. And they were saved.

Then Henderson grabbed a Jacob's ladder from the ship. And he was saved. The others were so weak they could not hold well to the ropes. The crew members above were swept by waves, up to their waists at times in the swells. Several of the *Badger State* men were taken by the sea in this manner, washed away within inches of rescue, grasping for the *Khian Star* crewmen's hands. Others were brought up in any manner possible. Tangled in lines. Feet first. It did not matter.

She picked up six men, but soon the *Khian Star* saw only dead men floating, headdown, in the water. A huge albatross swept in to peck at the dead. Even then, the Greeks did not quit. One Greek crew member—Ioannis Kantziakis—tied a line around himself and dove from the deck to rescue an unlucky American, but the man was already dead. The *Khian* kept at it, seeking out each individual seaman but finding mostly dead bodies. There were exceptions: The last survivor she picked up was five miles from the wreck.

All told, the *Khian* rescued fourteen men, including the master and two men who had jumped into the sea with him. Captain Wilson joined the *Khian*'s Captain Niros on the bridge. The crewmen were given blankets and hot food.

In the end, twenty-six died.

And that was how masters and crews could fight to save their ships. That was the high-water mark of bravery. And if not every master and crew could be expected to go to those lengths, they were expected not to embarrass the standard. They demanded that of themselves.

• • •

Compared to the *Badger State,* the *Marine Electric* was in positively excellent shape. On the *Marine Electric,* Corl really had no choice but to risk staying on the ship. He could not launch boats into those waves, only to have the ship survive. He would be the laughingstock of the Merchant Marine and lose his license. He might be able to stand that, but he also might lose men in the process—send them needlessly into mounting seas.

It was a lot easier to chopper men off a floating, foundering ship than to put men into lifeboats in twenty-foot waves. So, let's see where it leads, he told his fellow officers. Let's cut the risks, but stay on the ship and ride this out—at least until the helicopters come. The men could leave then. And if it was clearly hopeless, the officers would follow.

So he attempted to eliminate the risks as best he could. Corl, the casino dealer, on the bridge, figuring the odds. Take a card? Stand pat? Fold? House odds were a statistical gift if you dealt for the house. But now Corl was a player. The sea was the house, and the cards it dealt rolled into the ship with great crashes of spray and green water over the hatches.

Shortly before three o'clock in the morning, Corl took a half-step. At 2:51, he keyed the mike on the VHF-FM radio, channel 16, and raised the Coast Guard. It was the first official acknowledgment that the ship just might not make it.

"I'm approximately thirty miles from Delaware Bay entrance, and I'm going down by the head. I seem to be taking water forward.

"I am a coal carrier. Five-hatch coal carrier. I am loaded with twenty-three thousand tons of coal.

"I am positively in bad shape. We need someone to come out and give us some assistance if possible.

"Our problem is: We don't know exactly what our situation is."

Three minutes later, the captain gave the word to Bob Cusick. Tell the officers to assemble at the bridge. With life jackets. Have the crew go to the lifeboats and stand by. You handle the lifeboats.

To the Coast Guard: *"I am steering zero thirty. My position is as follows: 37 degrees 51.8 minutes north; west 74 degrees 45.5 minutes west."*

And three minutes later:

"I'm altering my course to due north to try to head for Delaware Bay entrance."

"Are you in any danger of sinking at this time?" the Coast Guard radio dispatcher asked.

"It's hard to say," Corl replied. *"My bow seems to be going down. We seem to be awash forward. We can't get . . . up there. We don't have any lights to shine up to see what's going on. I'm not listing. I seem to be going down by the head fast."*

Could they send a helicopter with a searchlight and shine it on the bow? That would help.

One should be there in about twenty minutes, the Coast Guard said. This would mean the helicopter would arrive at about 3:20 in the morning.

Kelly was shaken awake gently at three o'clock by a seaman. The captain wanted to see all the officers on the bridge now, with their life jackets. Not a drill.

Kelly calmly washed his face with soap and warm water. He brushed his teeth. Then he crept up to the darkened bridge and stared out toward the front of the *Marine Electric*.

Kelly could see nothing at first as his eyes adjusted, "night blind" as if he had just walked into a darkened movie theater. He stayed to the rear of the bridge, away from the window, while he gained his night vision. He could hear a burble of concern from the tight knot of officers on the bridge. As Kelly stepped to the large window looking forward, the picture came into terrible focus. Ahead of him, waves broke over the bow of the *Marine Electric* some 400 feet forward. Some washed the full length of the ship to break against the deckhouse. Green water swirled over the front hatches, burying them under tons of weight.

Kelly could see six to seven feet of water washing on the deck. The ship was five to eight degrees down by the head. He had felt that list when his feet hit the deck in his cabin; felt that the ship was out of plumb and tilted head down.

Paul Dewey, who had replaced the Gashounder, was on the bridge, too. He could see Powers, the chief engineer, out on the starboard wing—the outside area just to the right of the bridge— directing the man on watch to shine a powerful tankerman's light forward. They were all peering through the mist, the rain, the spray of the waves, trying to give the horror a face and a form. The tankerman's light was a powerful battery-operated torch that pierced through the foam and blow. "The number-one hatch is cracked," Powers said. It was open. Busted. That could mean tons of water were reaching the holds, weighing the ship down and out of trim.

From the engine room area, Price's voice crackled over the hand-held radio. He, Wickboldt, Scott, and the others were far below, frantically manning the pumps and making sure the power plant held up. The turbines hummed there, with the same comforting bass drone that filled all ship engine rooms. That, at least, was reassuring. All they needed was for the mighty engines to fail. Pumps, steering, headway—all would be lost. They would fall into the trough of the huge waves, and God help them then.

"I'm getting good pressure on the pumps," Price said. On the starboard side. Which meant there was water flooding the holds there, and the pumps were disgorging it.

"Do you want to gravitate from the starboard tanks to the port tanks?" Price called out over the radio. Did the captain want to shift the water to even the vessel's trim from an increasingly heavy right side to a lighter left side?

"Keep pumping!" Corl replied.

"I'm getting a lot of water out of number-one port," Scott replied over the radio.

Frantically, they pumped and prayed. Neither seemed to help. Slowly, the ship developed an ominous list to starboard. At 3:50 A.M., the list was five degrees. This meant the ship rolled to fourteen degrees with the waves. By 4:03, there was an eight-degree list.

There was no choice now. They had to counterbalance the list to starboard.

"Flood the port tanks," Corl ordered the engine room. Price and Scott and Browning and Wickboldt, far down below, fought their battle, flipping switches, pulling levers as the powerful turbine engines hummed steadily and faithfully.

Cusick was on the bridge and saw the list. He left immediately to join the crew on the boat deck. The ship was listing so far over they could not man the port lifeboat. It was dangling high above the sea with no clear line to the water. The port lifeboat was useless, he thought. On the starboard side, the ship was rolling so that the lifeboat, dangling free, was only five feet above the water at times.

Still, few of them believed they would actually go into the water. The lifeboat covers had been folded carefully and stored nearby, ready to be placed back on the boat. They all had seen the angel of mercy, the helicopter, descend with a holy shaft of light on the *Theodora*. Now they were looking for the same angel. Many of them were watching the heavens. They were casual, almost, and their discussions were conversational in tone, not panicked.

Near the lifeboats, Cusick paced among his crew, comforting them, keeping them upbeat. The blizzard whipped around them, and spray from the rolling monster waves pelted their faces like bb's.

Babineau drew close and muttered in a low voice, "Mate, are we going to make it okay do you think?"

"Absolutely," Cusick said. "The Coast Guard is going to come out and get us."

But the doubt was there somewhere inside Cusick, too, so he went to his right-hand man, the bosun Charlie Johnson. Upbeat, looking for confirmation, Cusick asked Johnson, conversationally, almost as if wondering whether a slight rain might clear up soon:

"What do you think, Charlie? Are we going to make it?"

Johnson turned to him. Normally, he was can-do, no-problem, cheerful. Now his face was long, not fearful but knowing, and ever so sad. He paused for a long moment and then said with certainty:

"No, Mate. We're not going to make it. We're not going to make it at all."

Johnson's mournful face hung in his line of sight. Then Cusick was all business. He turned to the lifeboats.

Kelly was moving between the bridges and the boats. Norman Sevigny, an older seaman at fifty-three with close-cropped gray hair, climbed into the lifeboat on the starboard side to insert a plug in the drain hole. The plug was loose in the bottom, to allow rainwater and spray to drain out, and was inserted only when the boat was to be used. Norman scrambled back with the plug in his hand.

"Sir, she's too rusty. I can't get the plug in," Sevigny said.

Kelly did not pause. "Use channel locks," Kelly said. "Use your Visegrip pliers."

"I don't have any," Sevigny said.

"Then go below and get some now," Kelly said.

Norman did not hesitate. He disappeared deep into the listing ship. These old guys, Kelly thought. Pros. Real seamen.

Would he have the courage to run down below on this ship right now? Kelly did not know. This ship? This sea? This moment? No way, he thought to himself. No way he would go. Kelly thought Sevigny's scramble the bravest deed he had ever seen.

Long minutes later, Norman Sevigny emerged triumphant with the pliers held high in one hand, the plug in the other. He scrambled back into the boat.

"All set," he said a minute later. "Plug's in."

Still, the little act of heroism did not make Kelly more optimistic. On deck, Kelly approached Babineau and gave him his candid but quiet assessment of the situation.

"Clayt," Kelly muttered under his breath so the crew didn't hear. "This old fucking tub isn't going to make it."

"Nah, you're wrong," Babineau said. "She's going to come through. We're going to be okay."

A short time later, as the men waited at the boat station, it was not a reasoned action that Kelly took, nothing he had thought out. Nothing that was in any textbook. But he returned to the upper deck and tossed the life rings, one by one, out into the darkness. He had seen the lifeboat, just five feet off the water. He had seen the bow settling. Seen the list. Perhaps someone could use those life rings if they abandoned ship. Who knew? God, give us every chance. Let us take every chance.

Some of the rings bounced off overhead protrusions and fell back on board the ship. But others sailed clear. Like big Frisbees, they arced and soared gracefully into the night wind. Kelly watched them until they were lost in the froth and spray.

On the bridge, Albion Lane, nicknamed Sparks, rushed to the bridge. Two ships were in the area, he told the officers. He had raised two ships via Morse code.

There was an air of expectancy.

One was an hour away, the other a little more, Lane said.

There was a spontaneous sigh of disbelief and despair. They all knew now they would not last that long.

Then the ship took another list. This time to ten degrees. It was almost a lurch.

The captain called down to the engine room, to Price and Wickboldt and the others.

"Secure the engine!" he said. "Stop the engine! Evacuate the engine room. Get out of there! Now!"

He turned to Dewey. "Leave the helm," he said. "There is no sense steering her. She isn't answering the helm." The seaman cranked the wheel hard to port and went toward the outside ladder leading from the bridge to the boat deck.

"No!" Kelly yelled. "Don't try the outside ladder. It's no good that way." Kelly had seen the dangerous list and the tilt of the deck. "Use the inside stairs." It was safer. Dewey might fall off the outside ladder, it was so tilted.

At 4:14 A.M., Corl keyed the mike to the Coast Guard again.

"We are abandoning ship. We are abandoning ship right now."

"Sparks" Lane had returned to the radio room, tapping out the ship's position in Morse code on the 500 khz emergency frequency. Now it was time to go. In the small world of radio and telegraph operators, succinctly phrased last messages can be an art form. The telegraph operator of a doomed Japanese fishing vessel once tapped out in dots and dashes this final good-bye: "Danger like dagger now."

Lane seemed less poetic in the final moments of the *Marine Electric*. Those who have heard the tapes, say he tapped out simply, "30 30 AR." But poetry is in the ear of the beholder, and the professionals listening on the 500 frequency interpreted the nuance of the sparse series of numbers and letters, the dots and dashes and were haunted by them. What they heard was something like: *"This is the last broadcast from this station. Forever. Out."*

The operators on the 500 khz frequency were dead silent. As was the tradition, they maintained quiet for 60 seconds to honor a lost operator.

But Lane was not lost yet, and he had no time to be honored. He ran from the radio room and headed for the lifeboat station.

Captain Corl reached for a life jacket, the last man to put one on. He had been talking to the Coast Guard. "What color are your lifeboats?" the radio crackled. "State the color of your lifeboats."

Kelly had a silly, angry thought.

You shitheads! You're the Coast Guard. You MAKE us paint them orange. What a question!

But he reacted fluidly, professionally.

Corl's arm was hung up in the life jacket, so Kelly reached around him for the mike. *"Orange. International orange!"* Kelly yelled back to the Coast Guard.

Kelly pulled the ship's whistle repeatedly. Blast after blast. Corl went through the door to the outside deck of the bridge—the same passage Kelly had warned Dewey not to take. Little choices. Little choices had big consequences now.

Now Kelly would make his own desperate run down the inside passage. Earlier, he had changed into heavier clothing. Leg warmers, a hooded jacket, a heavy knit cap. Then he had carefully packed a knapsack. His two cameras. A knife. His electric calculator. Binoculars. A small transistor radio. They all went into the bag. He had placed his billfold deep in a pocket. Put his glasses into his shirt pocket and then buttoned it. Then he had grabbed his car keys, as if he were leaving for the weekend, shoved them deep in his pocket.

But he had left that knapsack on his bunk. Now he would try to get it. As he rushed down the inside passageway, the list seemed to increase. He came to his cabin. He rushed past it. No way he was going to take the extra five seconds to pick it up. He needed desperately to get to the boats, to get outside.

Kelly carried a walkie-talkie, and over it now Michael Price's voice crackled.

"Do the officers want the engine room pumps tied down?" Price asked.

Kelly could not believe it. He and Wickboldt and the others were still below.

"Mike!" Kelly yelled into his radio. *"Get the hell out of there! We are going down!"*

Then Kelly jumped from the stairs, the walkie-talkie coming loose from his hand and tumbling before him. The radio crashed and splintered. Kelly landed hard. Lying prone on the steel floor of the ship, he thought: *I've got to get up and get out of here.*

Below Kelly, at the lifeboats, Cusick still had hope. Now, as he attempted to keep up morale, he stomped as he paced in the cold. He noticed, even in this wind, that his coat kept him warm.

Well, Bea was right about the coat, he thought. He looked at it now, all smeared with coal dust, just as he had told her it would be. Oh, he had given her hell over that coat.

Hardly ever would Bob Cusick argue with his wife, Bea. He'd met her at a friend's home after the war and asked her out. They went to a Gilbert and Sullivan operetta and then to a restaurant, Steubens, which had an orchestra that played waltzes. Cusick knew the German words to "Vienna, the City of My Dreams," and he sang them to Bea as they waltzed. *"Vien, Vien nur du allein . . ."* Bea said that's nice, but sing it in English now. He looked at her there on the dance floor as they swayed through the waltz and sang instead what was on his mind: *"Bea, Bea it's only you . . ."*

There was a second date shortly thereafter. They went to a nice restaurant, and Bob walked her home. He would write in his journal that the evening had been enchanting. He said good night to her at the gate to the house and then watched her walk away from him on a path framed by snow-laden branches. He thought about how it would be many long hours until he saw her again.

He called out to her, and she stopped. A light snow was beginning to fall. He walked up to her and could see a light shining in her eyes. He unbuttoned her bulky fur coat so he could draw her close to him and enclose her in his arms.

"Before you turn in for the night," Bob Cusick said then, "I want you to know that I love you and that we should be together for the rest of our lives. I'll always try to make you happy and keep a smile on your face."

That was how they fell in love. Staying in love took work, but their relationship was a smooth and easy one for the most part. The two recent exceptions had come over little things, both of them over what Bob wore. The first was hardly even a spat. Bea was a knitter and wanted to make Bob a sea cap from raw wool. "Leave the lanolin in the wool," Bob said. "I read it helps insulate and sheds water."

"Oh, it will look crude that way, and you can't add color," Bea said, upset. "I can't wash the wool if I keep the lanolin in, and there're all these twigs and dirt in the raw wool. I want you to look nice."

"Leave the lanolin in," Bob said. "Please."

She did. He won. Whatever detritus clung to the raw wool, he picked loose. He had the cap on now, tucked down around his ears, and the lanolin shed water and wind, just as he had thought it would.

But the coat was another matter. One day, shortly after this past Christmas, Bea passed by one of those boutiquey outdoor-equipment stores in Plymouth. There she saw a rugged, beautiful blue coat. The tag said it was made of Thinsulate, one of those new fibers that insulated against the cold even when wet. She paid $85 for it and gave it to Bob.

He was stunned! $85! He shopped at Sears and wore basics. He could pay $35 and get a perfectly good, warm coat that he wouldn't have to worry about.

"You don't buy an $85 coat for a dirty old coal boat," he scolded her.

But Bea got mad right back. "Don't you give me hell for this!" she said. "I'm not taking it back, and you're going to wear it. You're cheap! You're never cheap with us, only with yourself. We're keeping it. You're wearing it. You're going to look nice. I don't want to hear anything more about it."

Bob Cusick followed the first three orders. He kept the coat. He wore it. He looked nice in it.

But he would not let the argument rest. Gradually, coal dust splotched the pretty blue color. "See what a dirty old coal boat does to a nice coat," he would tell Bea. He couldn't help himself. He could not let this little thing go.

Cusick was wearing the silly thing now. He had to admit that it was nice and warm as the blizzard began to blow. Tight around the waist and the wrists, with a hood he could bring up and secure tightly, too. At the lifeboat, he thought, *You were right, Bea. You were right about the coat.*

He looked up. In the sea-lanes off the American coast, he figured, the Coast Guard would just come out and get them if they had these sorts of problems. Cusick's Theorem. The practical applications of. Please let it be true. It would be true.

His mind raced like this as he ran the crew through the well-practiced lifeboat drill. Take the covers off the boats. (But we'll just have to put them back on once the Coast Guard gets here, so fold them neatly, boys.) Swing the boats out on their davits. (But we won't have to use them once the Coast Guard gets here.)

The lifeboat drill that was not a drill went smoothly. The lifeboat lines were paying out, paying out. Dewey, down by the boat now, was reaching out, reaching out for a line.

Above them, Kelly recovered from his fall, stood up, and rushed outside on a mid-level deck. He could look down and see the boat swinging out. Above him, he could see Captain Corl literally climbing over the rail of the bridge, preparing to get free of the ship. He was still struggling with the life jacket. Did not seem to have it quite fastened. Seemed to be fumbling with it and with the rail as well. Far below him, he hoped, Price and the others in the engine room were slamming steel doors and pounding up steel ladders and stairs. Their footsteps would form a tympani of ascending rhythms on the steel. The regular rhythms of a ship. The regular sounds. But now at a frantic, panicked beat. Double time. Triple time. Price, the defensive lineman. They said he was fast. All of you down there, Kelly thought. Run. Run fast.

No time. No time. There was no time. The ship jerked, and Dewey, reaching out for the line, already off balance, tumbled into the ocean. The first to go.

Cusick could hear the groan and screech and crash of heavy equipment sliding and falling far below in the engine room. Then there came a sucking sound, like that of water draining in a tub— only a billion times louder. The *Marine Electric* capsized to starboard.

All of them were in the soup now. As the men by the lifeboat went into the water, the tall deckhouse rolled over on top of them. On top of Dewey and Cusick and the other men. The waves were twenty feet high. The water temperature was thirty-nine degrees. The air was twenty-nine degrees, but with a shrieking gale that dropped the windchill to fifteen degrees below zero. Men had little chance in such conditions. Some could die in as little as fifteen minutes.

Officers and seamen, cooks and engineers. All alike. No rank now. All paddling about in severely cold water. The ship they had sailed on was rolling over on them as they swam. They were being pushed down into the depths of the cold North Atlantic.

Chapter Four

THE SURVIVOR

*And they died. From torpedoes, aerial bombs, collisions, shell bursts,
and machine-gun bullets, frigid seas, flames, exploding cargoes. From
drowning trapped below decks or from freezing or starving adrift in
oarless lifeboats. Their casualty rate in World War II was exceeded only
by that of the U.S. Marine Corps.*

AUTHOR BRUCE L. FELKNOR
The U.S. Merchant Marine at War, 1775–1945

4:15 A.M. / SATURDAY, FEB. 12, 1983
IN THE WATER, NEAR THE *MARINE ELECTRIC*

On the *Marine Electric,* one minute Bob Cusick was shouting orders
into the gale, directing the lifeboat evacuation. Then there was that
awful sound, the draining, sucking sound as the ship capsized, and he
was in the water.

The ship rolled, and then the tall deckhouse, above where the
lifeboats were to be launched, came down on top of the men, pressing them down, carrying them down as they tried to swim up.

Cusick had been a snorkeler in his youth. He knew how to
swim underwater and hold his breath. Now, as the deckhouse
pushed him down, Cusick swam up, past the lighted porthole of the
chief engineer's cabin. He looked in. Everything looked normal inside. Comforting. Inviting. As if in a dream. Cusick clawed against
the steel of the deckhouse and swam some more. He was trying to
swim up, but he only felt the deckhouse pushing him down.

Dewey could feel the steel of the deckhouse pushing him down,
too. He was young. He swam energetically. But the harder he swam,
it seemed, the deeper he was pushed. He was moving up. His life

preserver assured that. But he was moving up *against* the capsizing ship and deckhouse. The physics of the equation was devastating.

Kelly had been standing on the ship mid-deck. He looked below him and saw the seas carry the lifeboat up in a great surge and push it against the smokestack of the ship above him. For the last hour, Kelly had been functioning automatically, making the right decisions automatically. Little things. Going down inside the ship, not outside. Stacking the life rings. Then lobbing them out into the abyss.

Now the ship was in its final seconds of life, and Kelly did things that were instinctive but of no use at all. He thought: *My grandfather died on this day exactly ten years ago.* Then he saw the sea coming for him as the ship made its final roll, the sea moving up the side of the ship, like a slowly rising tide.

He tried to move higher. Up the low rail on the deck in front of him. He put a foot on the first rail, and in slow motion, it seemed, as if in one of those dreams where you run but do not move, he climbed up the three-foot rail. Tried to get higher, as the ship was going lower, meeting the water. He looked up above him, higher, and saw Corl out on the bridge, climbing the rail, still struggling, it seemed, to fasten his loose life jacket.

And then, when Kelly could go no higher, as he tried to climb another rail that wasn't there, climb toward the sky away from it all, the sea was upon him. He bellowed into the storm with all his might. Where the cry came from, he did not know. It was just there. Deep from within and then out his mouth. A plaintive, savage, primordial cry, a desperate hollering for help, the sort of sound a zebra might make as the lions bring it down.

And then the sea had him. Just came up to meet him there on the rail. Grabbed him almost gently at first, then washed him clear of the ship.

Instantly, he was in a metal vise. That was exactly how it felt. Some strong steel vise was squeezing him, crushing his body and collapsing his chest. He could not breathe, could not move his lungs against the force. He gasped shallowly, desperately, hyperventilating in short gasps. Little puffs, little clouds of breath were whipped away by the gale.

Then he inhaled thick black oil. Bunkers spilled from the ship.

An awful, gagging sensation made it even harder to find the air, bring it into his lungs.

For ten minutes, he struggled to breathe. Then his body adjusted to the cold, and he coughed up the thick oil and drew a deep lungful of air.

And it struck him there in the water. It was not a figure of speech. The wind moaned through the waves. Not *like* a moan. It *was* a moan. A sad, singing, howling moan. It had pitch, timber, and tremolo that were almost human.

Kelly looked up. He was clear of the dangerous deckhouse because he had been higher up when the ship turned over.

But something was still higher than him. The ship's stack. He looked up at it and was frozen. He bobbed in the water. It was coming straight for him. He stared, transfixed, unable to move. The stack was coming for him, coming for him. He would be pushed down, like the men below him.

Cusick was down a long time, then felt a deck railing and knew he could reach the surface. He turned his body around the railing, and the trapped air in his synthetic quilted long underwear shot him to the surface.

But when he bobbed to the surface, his mind was immediately on another fear. The ship's propeller. Had the engines been turned off? Or was the prop still turning? He could be sucked into it. Or into the vacuum caused by the sinking hull. He struck out in the water. He swam hard away from the ship. Time vanished. He would turn on his back to rest, then swim some more.

He did not know how long he had been swimming when he came upon a large oar floating in the water. It was enough to help him stay afloat. The twenty-foot swells would raise him above the water and then plunge him into a valley. It was a repetitive ride, along the cycles of waves as high as a two-story house. Up to the top. Down to the bottom.

His mind wandered. Where were they, all his friends who had died? He had said they would be with him always. These were the very sea-lanes, the very same, where he had lost them, oh, so many years ago.

Floating in the water, he could think back and remember it all. The war had not yet started. His father had worked as a butler, and then at the elegant Plaza in Boston, but Bob Cusick would not serve on land, knew that at a young age.

He was fifteen when he became a Sea Scout—a waterborne Boy Scout. In 1938, when Germany invaded Poland, he and his friend Paul Keaveney saved their lunch money for gas for an old rum-runner confiscated by the Coast Guard. They sailed the SSS *Porpoise* from Boston up to Gloucester or down to Plymouth. They learned every knot—and then devoured officers' manuals and ship operation guides. Their scout leaders were former Navy and Merchant Marine officers who drilled them constantly. So by 1941, at age eighteen, Cusick was ready to ship out in the Merchant Marine with knowledge far beyond his years.

The war was something far away then—and the romance of fighting inescapable for a young man. Cusick was turned down by the Navy because his vision was not perfect. Keaveney was accepted. One Cusick dream was dead, but merchant mariners suddenly were in demand, and Cusick shipped on a large oil tanker, the *Axtell J. Byles,* which ran between Texas and Bayonne, New Jersey. The chief mate, Matthew Hannon, was pleasantly surprised at this young pup's advanced knowledge and took him under his wing. Cusick could work out a meridianal altitude and had his arms around longitude as well. Hannon mentored him and even let him take the wheel. The officers and crew treated Cusick as a bright and treasured mascot, and he learned quickly in the warm and nurturing atmosphere.

"I was happy," Cusick would write in a journal. "I was at sea. And the *Byles* was one of the largest tankers afloat."

Then one Sunday, when the *Byles* was loading oil in Port Arthur, Texas, Cusick went to a matinee movie. Midway through, the projector ground to a halt. The lights went on. The movie manager rushed into the theater and yelled that all servicemen and merchant mariners must return to their posts. The Japanese had just bombed Pearl Harbor.

Cusick returned to the *Byles* to find the crew frantically painting the orange and black markings of the ship flat gray to make it less of a target. By the time the tanker had rounded the Florida Keys, the job was done. The men and the ship turned north, not knowing what to expect in the sea-lanes ahead.

They could not have imagined. For at about the same time, six *Unterseebooten*—German U-boats—began heading west from the Bay of Biscay in France to prowl the Atlantic coastal sea-lanes of the United States. These six boats would soon create one of the worst maritime maelstroms ever known.

Cusick's youthful idyll had ended. The good times of the German U-boat commanders were just about to begin. The official title of the German operation was Operation *Paukenschlag*—or Drumbeat. But the commanders informally called the period *Die Gluckliche Zeit*—the Happy Time. The U-boats took about a month to reach the American shipping lanes. Just a handful of them—only six at first—were enough to hobble the American war effort.

One U-boat alone sank seven merchant ships in mid-January 1942. From Cape Cod in the north to Jacksonville, Florida, in the south, the Atlantic was aglow with the fires and explosions of hundreds of burning vessels. More than 300 went down in the first six months of submarine attacks—a rate that would have destroyed more than 40 percent of American shipping by year's end.

It was an abattoir.

At times, Americans still thinking the war distant could watch the deaths from shore. In February 1942, the *R. P. Resor* was torpedoed off Barnegat Light, New Jersey. The vessel exploded grandly. The crowds on shore were horror-struck.

Cusick and the crew of the *Byles* sailed into the heart of this killing field. All around them, vessels were torpedoed and sunk. Men were burned, blasted, drowned, frozen to death.

Yet nothing was done. The simplest precautions—established by years of wartime naval experience—were ignored.

There were no convoys. There was no air cover. There were no guns on the merchant ships. And the very people who gathered on shore, horror-struck, did not seem to realize a simple and clear fact: By keeping their coastal and resort lights ablaze, the cities were placing the merchant mariners directly in the periscope sights of the U-boats.

There was no blackout.

Ignoring the experience of World War I, the U.S. Navy declined to provide convoy support for tankers in the coastal trades. The escorts were in short supply and were needed elsewhere. Great Navy victories were underway in the Pacific. Steamship owners preferred individual schedules over convoys. Guns were eventually deployed on the merchant vessels, but resort towns and coastal cities declined to turn off their lights. It was bad for business.

The U-boat commanders could not believe their good luck. They silhouetted tankers against the lights, torpedoed them, and then surfaced to shell them with deck guns, saving their torpedoes.

The Germans sailed boldly into heavily fortified areas and suffered little consequence. Off Jacksonville in April 1942, the brand-new tanker *Gulfamerica* crossed paths with the U-123, framed in the periscope by the blazing and brilliant lights of the resort, which was then the largest city in Florida and in full "Spring Fling" mode. The U-123 torpedoed the ship, setting it ablaze.

A blinding red-and-yellow explosion lit the night sky, illuminating the beach and tourists as if by klieg lights. Then the U-123 surfaced and activated its deck gun. So close was the submarine to shore that the U-boat captain could clearly see crowds of soldiers and tourists on the Jacksonville beach. He feared he might overshoot the *Gulfamerica* and land a shell in the crowd. So he maneuvered to the land side of the *Gulfamerica* so he could shoot aiming out to sea.

The maneuver simultaneously showed the decency of the U-boat captain, the slowness of the American military response, and the U-boat commanders' feeling of safety and invulnerability. For by moving to the land side of the burning ship, the U-123 was moving to shallower water where it could not easily dive.

Moreover, the submarine was silhouetting itself against the flaming wreckage of the *Gulfamerica*. Now the tourists could clearly see the sub. And presumably, any land batteries along the fortified

Florida coast could as well—and easily pick off the U-123. Or planes could be scrambled to bomb and strafe the invader.

No response came in time to help the *Gulfamerica,* but a depth charge nearly caught the U-boat in shallow water. She lay on the bottom and then limped away to deep water. Through his periscope, the commander could see the vacationers rushing from their hotels to watch the still-burning ship.

"A rare show for the tourists, who probably were having supper now," the sub commander wrote in his log. "All the vacationers had seen an impressive special performance at Roosevelt's expense. A burning tanker, artillery fire, the silhouette of a U-boat—how often had all of that been seen in America?"

Even in his youth, Cusick could not believe the lack of support. No convoys. No guns. No air cover. No blackouts. The tankermen aboard such vessels had only a slight chance for survival. Quick-release life rafts were seen as the only chance. Other ships had them. The men on the *Byles* told the owners they would not sail without the rafts. The owners did not provide them. And so, many of them, including Cusick, declined to sign back on the ship in February 1942.

Now nineteen, Cusick puzzled what to do after leaving the *Byles.* A friend of his, Herman Mathisen, offered Cusick a slot on the *Lake Osweya.* A few days later, however, Mathisen sheepishly called to tell Bob the slot had been filled by the mate's nephew. Cusick then sought to sign on with the *Esso Boston* out of Bayonne, New Jersey. The union hall had sent him, and he struggled up the icy, vertical gangplank with his seabag. It was more like an ascent up a slippery cliff. Then he was turned back. The union hall had made a mistake. The *Esso Boston* was fully manned. He crept carefully down the gangplank, like a descending mountain climber, hand over hand, and started searching for a ship again.

Finally, he signed on with the *Edward Shea* and was back at sea amid the turmoil of Germany's Operation Drumbeat. In the countless hours waiting for the torpedoes to strike, droning up and down the shooting gallery, Cusick and a friend decided they would enlist in the Army. At least there they would have a fighting chance. At least there they would have guns.

So they did. They enlisted in the Army. The Army looked at

their experience and saw that they had been to sea and assigned them to an Army-owned cargo ship, the *Merrimack*. Cusick and his friend pleaded to be combat infantrymen. The Army said their country needed them at sea. Reluctantly, Cusick and his friend went back to face the German U-boats.

When the *Merrimack* went in for repairs, Cusick was transferred briefly to troopship duty. The war was brought home to Cusick when he took a brief shore leave in New Orleans and stopped by the family of his friend, Herman Mathisen. He was met by a grief-stricken family. Both Mathisen and his father had been torpedoed. The *Lake Osweya*, which Cusick had nearly signed on with, had been sunk en route from New York to Halifax. All thirty men had perished. The family had just learned it had lost both men at a single stroke. Cusick reeled from that meeting.

Then he learned that the *Merrimack*, the Army ship he had just served on, had been torpedoed as well, near the Panama Canal. Only nine men had survived.

Later, he learned that the *Byles*, his first ship, had been torpedoed.

Then he learned that the *Esso Boston*—the vessel he had been turned back from—had been torpedoed.

Then he learned that his old Sea Scout friend, Paul Keaveney—whom he had tried to enlist with—had died while on escort duty in the Navy, where Cusick probably would have been.

Bob Cusick understood then that he was just one step ahead of fate. He was traversing World War II as one might cross a swamp, stepping on a succession of snapping crocodiles.

At long last, the escorted convoys were formed, evening the chances. By the end of the war, Cusick was an officer. And a charmed survivor. As a young man, he had wandered into the bloodiest part of the war. So deadly was the action that, by the end of the war, the fatality rate of American merchant mariners was exceeded only by America's shock troops, the U.S. Marines.

Was all of that, then reduced to *this*, thirty-six years later? Death at the hands of a World War II rust bucket? Was he to escape the worst World War II had to offer, beat odds as steep as those of a D-Day infantryman? Go through all that and now die on a . . . a *milk run*? A cold and wet old man, beaten and exhausted?

In the cold, cold water off Virginia, Cusick thought of his past and wondered if he had a future. He was the oldest man there. He had the longest odds. He pulled the hood of Bea's silly coat over his head, over the wool watch cap. The coat was tight at the sleeves, tight around his waist, too. He was very cold, but the coat seemed to hold warm water around his body, like a makeshift wet suit.

At the top of the waves, he could see back toward the ship. He could see the strobe lights twinkling in the cold North Atlantic. He could hear cries for help. He could hear groans. He could see the ship in the distance, rolled over, slowly sinking, and hear the waves slapping against her hull.

God, the hull. Floating upside down like that. The engine room guys. His friend Price and the cadet, Wickboldt. Scott, the guy with the BMW motorcycles. They must still be in there, Cusick thought. If the ship rolled on him, then she must have rolled before they made it out. Cusick thought about that and felt sick. He hoped he was wrong. Tons of equipment had shifted. He had heard the noise. The boiler had probably tipped and then spilled its superheated steam. He hoped they had made it. And if not, he hoped it had been quick.

But he could not think about it for long. The cold and the waves were ruthless. They demanded attention. They demanded full focus. There was no time to worry about his friends. He could not help them. All he could do now was fight to survive.

The waves began to break over him. They would crest—and then crescendo down on him as if he were at the surf line. He held his breath. Long moments passed as the waves broke on top of him. It was exhausting. Each time a wave passed, Bob Cusick would strike out again and swim, swim. He was staying active in the cold, swimming where he did not know, but swimming.

Then Cusick had the sensation of a line wrapping around his right leg, just above the ankle. It had the feel of a nine-thread, a rope used for heaving lines and attaching life rings. The line drew tension. It began pulling him, pulling him sideways through the water. He kept hold of his oar and, with one arm, reached down to disentangle himself. He could not. He then held the oar with both hands, because the tension and the pull were strong enough that if he let go of the oar, or loosened his grip too much, he would be pulled off the oar. Was the line attached to the ship? A trick played by cold limbs and a desperate mind? Cusick did not know. It was pulling him somewhere, and he had no choice but to go.

It was cold. There was no moon. No stars. Only the glow of the spindrift on the water's surface. But it was enough for Bob Cusick to discern a slight variation in the darkness ahead of him. The tension on the line slackened. He thought it was gone. Free to move about on his own, Cusick paddled his oar toward the shape in the distance. For half an hour he paddled and swam, rested, caught his breath, paddled again.

He could see the shape now. It was one of the ship's lifeboats. Not the starboard one he had tried to launch. That one had been thrown against the stack. It was the lifeboat from the other side of the ship. The one they had not been able to launch because it was so high out of the water.

As he got closer, his heart sank again. The boat had been torn badly by the capsizing and obviously did not come clear of the ship. Only the boat's flotation inserts kept it above water.

Cusick approached the lifeboat warily. It was better to be inside anything than outside where he was. But getting inside the boat was no mean feat. Dozens of men have perished at sea, unable to get inside a boat or raft. And Cusick was badly fatigued now, and it was long past the time when many men succumb to hypothermia. The storm was still blowing very hard, with waves taking him for rides up as high as the roof of a two-story house and then down again.

How would he get inside the boat?

As Bob Cusick came near the boat, he grabbed the gunwale with one hand and kept hold of his oar with the other. Only when he was sure he had secured a good hold did he release the precious oar that had supported him for more than an hour. He grabbed the boat with his other hand. The oar bobbed for a moment and was swept away by the sea.

Now he took inventory. Clearly, he could not just hoist himself into the lifeboat. His water-soaked clothes weighed him down. His arms were like frozen legs of mutton. It was all he could do to grip the gunwales.

Earlier, he had toed off his water-filled sea boots. Now, with his stocking feet, he felt along the boat until he found a small toehold on a railing. He had his legs to help lift him. If there was any strength left, it was in his legs.

Then he studied the actions of the waves. Felt their surge and play against the boat. The waves might work in his favor. For the waves lifted both Bob and the boat together, but the boat would fall below him slightly as the waves slid out from them. If he could time it right, momentum generated by the wave and his weakened muscles might propel him up while the boat was sliding down and . . .

Bob Cusick would give it a try. If the waves knocked him silly? He had little to lose. He waited. A wave came. He and the boat rose together. Then the wave receded. As the boat fell below him, Cusick pushed with his arms and legs, adding momentum to the upward energy of the wave. He moved up and over the boat.

Then fell into it.

Chapter Five

THE SLOW SCRAMBLE

You have to go out.
You don't have to come back.

Unofficial motto of
U.S. Coast Guard Search
and Rescue Operations

3 A.M. / SATURDAY, FEB. 12, 1983 / MCCANN FAMILY RESIDENCE
ELIZABETH CITY, NORTH CAROLINA

Near the rescue station at Elizabeth City, North Carolina, Navy diver Jim McCann was fast asleep. McCann had been trained as a rescue swimmer—one of the hairiest peacetime operations around. If a Navy pilot ditched, McCann went in the drink after him. The fact was, McCann went into the drink after whomever whatever whenever the Navy told him to.

But now he was in deep clover. Had a plush job. Nine to five, five days a week. Whether he wanted it or not. McCann, in his early twenties, wanted action. And training other divers and rescuers and getting some training himself was not his idea of action. It was good for the family. But not for his goal. McCann had always admired his brother, one of the Navy's crack rescue swimmers. And he was following in his footsteps. Or wake, depending on how you looked at it. More and more, it felt like McCann would always be in his brother's wake.

On Friday, February 11, he got off work at five sharp. Like an office job. Tomorrow was family time. Kids and the wife. He had committed to getting a family picture taken on Saturday afternoon. And that was nice, having time to do something like that. Plus, it was free. They had won the session in a radio-sponsored contest. He went to sleep Friday evening with pleasant thoughts of the lazy day to come. Parts of this job weren't so bad, it was true.

Then the phone rang at three o'clock in the morning, and the family schedule went out the window. It was the rescue dispatcher. Not a Navy call, but the Coast Guard asking for help. A coal ship was in trouble off the coast, and the men were heading for the lifeboats. They were sending as many helicopters as they could. Would McCann round up a crew and report to the base? Yes, McCann said. "Be careful driving," the voice on the other end of the phone said. "The roads are slick."

There were quick kisses and promises. Yes, he'd do his best on the pictures, he said. Yes, he knew they were free. Yes, he knew he had promised. Love to the kids. I'll try to be there. Bye-bye.

McCann skittered down the sidewalk, and the words of the Coast Guard dispatcher came back to him. The weather was ghastly. Snow and rain pelted him. He slipped on the sidewalk again. When he got to the car, he put the key in and tried to open the door, but it was stuck. He reared back and kicked the door. Still nothing. He kicked again. The ice cracked, and he got into the car.

It was a short drive to the base, but McCann drove it with white knuckles. His car slipped and skidded frequently. On the base, he took a roundabout too quickly. The car literally came roundabout. Spun out. McCann sat in his car and exhaled deeply. Not even to the chopper pad yet. He rocked the car out of the snow and crept forward. A few minutes later, he was there. His crew wasn't. A few minutes after that, they arrived, and he was on the tarmac of the airstrip arguing with the pilot.

So far as McCann and the pilot knew, the crewmen of the *Marine Electric* were in thirty-man lifeboats. In stormy seas, but high and dry. The Navy pilot wanted maximum space in his chopper for the survivors. McCann wanted Bill Scarborough, an ex-Coast Guardsman, as crew, and he wanted another diver/swimmer—some help in the water alongside the boats if McCann had to go in.

So McCann ordered his crew onto the helicopter.

"Mister, get off my airplane," the pilot said to the second swimmer. "Get off my airplane now."

"Get back on that airplane," McCann shouted above the whine of the chopper's turbines.

It went on like that. A "hissy," as one of the men described it. Finally, they compromised. Scarborough would come. The second diver would not. Given the facts at the time—lifeboat evacuation in a howling gale—the decision was right. Given the true state of the mission—the pilot did not know that men were in the water already—the second swimmer could have been crucial to saving lives.

There'd been another hissy in the Coast Guard rescue station in North Carolina even before the phone call woke Navy swimmer McCann. Coast Guard diver Michael Carr had got wind of the *Marine Electric* emergency and volunteered his dive team to go out with the Coast Guard rescue helicopters. The Coast Guard had no rescue swimmers then, but Carr's team was superbly conditioned and ready to go. They were on standby and could literally jump into the chopper this minute. There was no need to wait for the Navy.

"No way," Carr's boss said. "You're talking about a Force 10 storm out there, and you guys aren't trained for this."

"What difference does it make?" Carr said. "We're all graduates of the U.S. Navy diving school, the best in the world. This isn't about rules. Let's go help those people."

"No way," his boss said. "Diving is one thing. Rescue swimming is another. You're not trained, and you're not going."

So Carr and his team sat there and steamed as the call went to McCann to roust his crew.

Elsewhere in the rescue operation, the process was just as rocky.

Where were the rescue ships? The rescue helicopters? En route to be sure, but not always by the most direct route. Twists of fate knitted complex strands of nuance and confusion. They all had to be untangled before the choppers could be airborne.

When the original distress call came in at 2:51 A.M., the position of the ship was reported as thirty miles south of the Delaware Bay. This placed the vessel just off the Delaware–Maryland coast. The Coast Guard has stations at Ocean City, Maryland, and Indian River, Delaware. The radio dispatcher in Ocean City notified the Indian River station and asked them in turn to notify the Coast Guard rescue station at Cape May, New Jersey—on the north side of the

Delaware Bay. But the Delaware station was having electrical problems and was running on emergency electrical support. Then, at 2:55 A.M., the *Marine Electric* radioed its position by latitude—37-51.8 north; 74-45.5 west. Ocean City realized the catastrophe was occurring in their zone, just nine miles from where the fishing boat *Theodora* had run into trouble, much farther south than originally thought.

Cusick and his men were still on the ship at about 3:15 A.M., when the cutter *Point Arena* was dispatched. At 3:24 A.M., the Cutter *Point Highland* turned from the *Theodora* at Chincoteague Inlet and headed toward the *Marine Electric*. The Cutter *Cherokee* was dispatched at 3:30 A.M.

But the cutters were still hours away from the disaster scene. Only the choppers could get there in time to do any good. The original order to launch the ready helicopter—CG 1471—came at 3:18 A.M. The crew made ready. Because the report at the time was that the ship was still afloat and needed pumps, heavy pumps were loaded on board. The chopper would normally have departed once the pumps were secured.

But the Coast Guard choppers had already been out in the storm that night—a storm the U.S. Weather Service said was the worst in forty years. They had flown over the *Theodora* and barely found her. Would not have found her without the sighting by the *Marine Electric*. And now the *Marine Electric* was in trouble, and there was no other ship to guide them in. They knew they needed more support if they were to attempt to drop pumps onto a bucking old ship at sea. They called for a fixed-wing C-130 to "fly cover for them"—to give them bearings and instructions and a backup in case they went in. So the C-130 had to be arranged for.

Then they learned that the *Marine Electric* was abandoning ship. So pumps on board the helicopter were useless. Worse than useless, because now the chopper would be attempting to fly out large numbers of men rescued from lifeboats. The mission had changed. Time passed as the pumps were off-loaded.

Then there was the weather. The unofficial motto of the Coast Guard was, "You have to go out, you don't have to come back." When they did not come back, the weather was often the reason.

The celebrated ditching of a rescue helicopter told famously in *The Perfect Storm* was caused in part by poor weather information. The aircraft simply did not have the fuel to beat its way back home against the stronger-than-expected head winds. And it had not received up-to-date information that would have allowed it to take alternative actions.

Moreover, the most dangerous missions flown by rescue pilots are at night or in blizzard whiteouts. The rescue crews this night faced both conditions, plus sixty-mile-per-hour winds. Over the past two years, two Coast Guard helicopters had been lost attempting to aid the crews of sinking fishing vessels. One chopper and its crew kissed a mountainside in fog in Hawaii. The other had encountered nearly identical conditions to this Force 10 gale on a mission off Portland, Oregon, and had had to ditch. Some of that crew made it. Some didn't. The picture of the Oregon chopper, downed right at the surf line, stuck in every pilot's mind.

The pilots heading out to rescue the *Marine Electric* wanted to make sure they had a shot at getting to the men. They were brave, but they were not foolish. Suicide missions did no one any good.

But it was pretty when the Coast Guard helicopter pilots went into action and beat the odds. For it was not a foolish dream Bob Cusick had about the Coast Guard pulling them out. These guys really did this stuff. It was what made them breathe. It was their heritage. It was their history, their glory, their tradition. There are dozens of tales of Coast Guard choppers plucking boaters from rocks, men from sinking ships, climbers from cliffs, downed fliers and doomed swimmers from the jaws of death.

Survey them all, though, and one case pops up like an Indiana Jones matinee movie.

The *Ocean Express.*

Gulf of Mexico. April 1976. The drilling barge rig *Ocean Express* was in big trouble. Towing lines to tugs had parted. A fierce storm was upon them. The captain of the vessel told his crew to abandon ship, but he stayed on.

Captain Hans Van deGraaf was trying to save his vessel. He asked the tugs to tow him toward shore—then cut him loose and save themselves.

The weather worsened, though, and the captain would either be rescued by a chopper or die. It was that simple. So when Coast Guard pilot Lieutenant Commander John Lewis called the barge captain from the rescue helicopter, the captain responded affirmatively. It was closing time. "Come get me if you can."

"Light a flare," Lewis told the captain. And he did.

The rescue would be nearly impossible. In high winds, with whipping lines, tall derrick towers, and froth snapping about, Lewis would have to pull off a miracle. To maneuver, a pilot needed to pin his eyes on a solid object. But in this maelstrom, there were no solid objects, just pitching oil rig and white foam everywhere.

"Here we go," Lewis told his crew and went in anyway.

The first pass was aborted. Turbulence made it suicide. He came back around again. Another chopper, flown by Captain Howard Thorsen, came on the scene, and Lewis reported: "I've been down there and couldn't do it."

He tried again.

Now the barge was heeling over at thirty degrees. There was little time left. One crew member in the helicopter leaned out into the storm and gave Lewis directions: "Come right . . . come forward . . . come left." The lights were going out on the barge, though, and Lewis could not keep his perspective.

From above, without warning, Thorsen, in the other helicopter, turned on his "Night Sun"—a bright light that illuminated the whole barge. Now Lewis was good to go. He saw the whole mess below. In the waves, the barge was bucking like a wild animal. He pulled out and away again. When they came back again to a hover, the barge was at forty-five degrees and on her way over. There was little hope, but Lewis laid the helicopter on its side and banked back in.

Below him, the barge was in her death throes. She was going over backward and sideways at the same time. Lewis's reference points were twisting and turning, and he experienced dizziness, a sort of vertigo. Saltwater hit the windshield of the chopper. Crewman Thomas was yelling now: "Up! Up!"

It was all they could do to pull up. The barge was sinking. No hope now.

In desperation, Lewis told the crew to lower the basket. Ensign John DiLeonardo was to monitor the altitude. Lewis went back in one last time.

"You're losing altitude too fast," DiLeonardo said at one point. "We're going down!"

In truth, the barge was rolling *up* toward the helicopter. It only seemed as if the chopper was going down. The barge pad, with the barge captain on board, was rising toward the chopper as the barge was rolling over and sinking.

Lewis gunned the engine and moved to escape. Down below, the captain waved his arms in desperation, trying to catch anything. Something swung his way. He grabbed it.

It was the rescue basket. Thomas yelled, "We got him!"

To Thorsen, in the helicopter above, all seemed lost. A sea of froth seemed to cover the rescue chopper. Then, he saw Lewis's helicopter surge, it seemed, out from under the curl of a wave, bank and roar away, safe to clear air. The barge sank a moment later. Captain Van deGraff came on board the chopper and asked, "How are my crew?"

When it worked, that's how it worked.

And nothing had changed in the seven years since. Rescues like that took lots of guts. And lots of luck.

But they also took lots of brains, preparation, calculation, and planning. Luck was the residue of preparation, the pilots figured. There was a lot of routine and organization behind such rescues. You *did* have to go out. You did not have to come back. But you wanted to make the right decisions before you went out. You did want everyone to come back.

In the case of the *Marine Electric,* there was one other twist to the thread that led to the dispatching of the choppers. Though the men were off the Virginia coast, slightly closer to the Delaware Bay and the Cape May rescue base of the Coast Guard, the Cape May unit had older, short-range, lighter helicopters—the HH-52 model. The station at Elizabeth City in North Carolina had the new HH-3 models. The differences were drastic. The old choppers carried only six men at a time; the new ones, fifteen. The old choppers had only one engine; the new had two. The old helicopters were eighty to 120 knots slower. They could move only at eighty to ninety knots. And they did not have the range of the new ones. The HH-52 had a range of only 400 miles—less in a raging gale, where the turbine had to fight strong head winds.

So, should the Coast Guard launch slower, smaller helicopters from New Jersey, which was perhaps a little closer to the scene? Or a faster, larger helicopter from North Carolina, 100 miles from the scene?

Their sense of the *Marine Electric*'s evacuation was that it had been orderly, that the ship was sinking slowly and the captain was abandoning ship methodically. The crew would be safe in the boats. So the big chopper from North Carolina would be sent, along with the C-130 cover plane.

Logs show that the Ocean City commanding officer was told that the *Marine Electric* abandoned ship at 3:14 A.M. and that a helicopter would be there in fifteen to twenty minutes. In fact, the helicopter did not get into the air until 4:13 A.M. in Elizabeth City. It did not have its C-130 cover as yet, but it was heading toward the stricken ship.

The *Marine Electric* was one hour away. The men were all in the water now, chilled, splashing, swimming, crying, dying. That part was simple. It was the rescue that would be complex.

Chapter Six

WHEN UP MEANS DOWN/
WHEN INCHES ARE MILES

I love you both, good-bye.

Report on the sinking
of the Lisa Lorraine

4:40 A.M. / SATURDAY, FEB. 12, 1983
IN THE WATER, NEAR THE *MARINE ELECTRIC*

For Dewey, it all seemed dreadfully unfair. He had been trying to help, doing the right thing, reaching out for the line from the lifeboat.

Then came the shudder and the jerk of the ship. The leverage of the rail against his leg was such that, without much of a push really, he toppled right over into the water.

The injustice of it all was lost in a second, for almost immediately he could feel the steel of the deckhouse pushing him down. He was young. He swam energetically. But the harder he swam, it seemed, the deeper he was pushed. He was moving up. His life preserver assured that. But he was moving up *against* the capsizing ship and deckhouse. They were pushing him down. In fact, they were moving much faster down, as the ship rolled, than he could swim up.

Against all intuition, he knew what he had to do. He swam down. Down, against the buoyancy of his life vest. Down, away from the sinking ship. He reached a railing on the submerged deck of the *Marine Electric*. He vaulted his body around it. Now the life preserver shot him upward. He broke the surface of the ocean and gasped for air.

As he swam away from the ship, in the dark he saw a shape. It was a life raft canister. He grabbed its lanyard and placed both feet against the canister. The raft promptly inflated. But in so doing, it pushed Dewey away. He mustered his energy and stroked back to the raft, which was floating high in the water. Other men clustered about it. Grabbed at its high rubber walls and held on.

Now, how did you get into this thing, floating so high up there? Nothing like this was covered in training or lifeboat drills. Safety was just three feet up. If they could just get in the raft. But how? The side of the raft was a sheer, smooth rubber cliff. You could not grab it. There was no purchase on those smooth sides. No ladder. No boarding net.

Earlier, Kelly had just seemed to slip into the water gently. It had just seemed to come up and get him. Then there was that vise, squeezing him mercilessly. Now he was very cold. Incredibly cold. But he had something else to worry about. The ship's huge stack still loomed above him. He looked up at it. He bobbed in the water. It was coming straight for him. He stared, transfixed, unable to move. The stack was coming for him, coming for him. He would be pushed down, like the men below him.

But then a hand reached for him, out of the darkness. The man must have been strong. He pulled Kelly away from the falling stack. Swam him out of there. Kelly was safe. He looked around to say thanks. There was no one there. Just total darkness. Just blackness. The harder he looked, the blacker it got.

Kelly swam. He reached a life ring. One of the life rings he had thrown out into the ocean. He had thrown it, and then he had caught it.

Richard Powers was in the water, too. Richard Roberts, a third mate, as well. And Albion Lane, the radio operator, Sparks, had made it. He saw what they all saw. Nothing. Pure blackness. Felt what they all felt. Pure distilled cold. Bone-chilling and bitter cold. They all looked around. Some of the little strobe lights on the life jackets had activated. They blinked. What light they produced just emphasized the darkness of the surging swells about them. They did not see

Captain Corl. They did not see Price. They did not see Wickboldt. They saw none of the men from the engine room.

In such conditions, men can quickly succumb to hypothermia— a condition caused by body temperature dropping too low. The official U.S. Coast Guard chart states the impact like this:

Water Temperature Fahrenheit	Exhaustion/Unconsciousness	Time of Survival
32.5 degrees	under 15 minutes	under 15 to 45 minutes
32.5 to 40 degrees	15 to 30 minutes	30 to 90 minutes
40 to 50 degrees	30 to 60 minutes	1 to 3 hours
50 to 60 degrees	1 to 2 hours	1 to 6 hours
60 to 70 degrees	2 to 7 hours	2 to 40 hours
70 to 80 degrees	3 to 12 hours	3 hours to indefinite
over 80 degrees	indefinite	indefinite

Charts lie, of course. Numbers lie. No numbers can tell what it's like to die slowly in cold water. No chart can explain what happened to the crew of the *Lisa Lorraine* near Half Moon Bay, California, or the impact that sinking had on the survivors and the victims' families.

The fifty-eight-foot dragger was headed toward waters twenty miles west of San Francisco, raising crab pots, in February 1988. The air was so clear the men could see the lights of San Francisco. Two men, Grant Coles and James Chew, both twenty-two, were on deck working an outrigger and block. They would load the crabs in pots weighing about 100 pounds. They already had seventy-four of them filled with crabs—a nice haul—stacked on the deck. Each man wore jeans and sweatpants, a cotton sweater, and down jacket against the chill. Over all of that, they wore rain slickers and rain pants. Deck work was hard and chilling. Keith Young, an old man on the boat at thirty-one, watched from the wheelhouse. Greg Hayes, a crew member, was asleep below.

The boat maneuvered to pick up pots and, top-heavy with crab, took a hard roll that placed the port railing below water. Hayes was tossed from his bunk but made his way up the stairs. He wore only jeans and a short-sleeve cotton shirt.

Coles went to help Young and get survival suits, but he was met by a solid wall of water rushing around the pilothouse. He looked for Young, even kicked out a window to see if he was trapped, but could not find him. Unknown to the men, the vessel had taken on water in its holds, and the sudden turn of the maneuvering was enough to destabilize and sink the boat.

The vessel rolled over completely, but the three men were able to climb over the rail and walk the hull as it turned. They were perched on the top of the overturned hull, huddled together. Young was nowhere in sight. Neither was the boat's life raft. It had all happened so fast.

They were high and still relatively dry, but to their horror, the hull began sinking. A four-foot hatch cover floated by, and they made for it. They grabbed the hatch cover and floated in the cold water. They talked. They prayed. Hayes was to be married soon to the daughter of the boat's owner. His own father had died in a fishing boat accident two years earlier. This could not happen to him. Not now.

But it did. After two hours, the men were cold and nearly delirious. But Hayes, in just jeans and shirt, was by far the worst. He gathered enough of his senses to utter one last sentence—"I love you both, good-bye"—and then let go of the hatch cover and drifted away. Chew watched helplessly as he saw Hayes's head go under and not come up. The two men were helpless, hypothermia had weakened them so. It was all the two surviving men could do to crawl painfully onto the hatch cover. Perched back to back, they tried their best to stay out of the water.

Finally, seven hours after the sinking, a twenty-two-foot pleasure boat spotted them, and they were rescued. With a water temperature of fifty-two degrees, the chance of death for a person in the water for three and one-half hours is 99 percent.

Only their heavy clothing, will to live, and ability to stay out of the water had kept them alive.

For the men of the *Marine Electric,* as they entered the cold, cold water in February 1983, the same rules applied as applied to the crew of the *Lisa Lorraine.*

All of the men felt a vise tighten around their chests when they hit the water, just as Kelly had. That passed in about ten minutes, and the other symptoms of hypothermia began.

Instinctively, the web of outlying capillaries in fingers and toes contracts. Already, their bodies were in triage mode, sending blood and precious warmth to the torso and the vital organs. This happens to anyone in a very cold situation, on land or sea. But in the sea, the process moves faster because water can conduct heat away from the body thirty-two times more efficiently than air alone.

Body temperature begins to fall. At ninety-seven degrees, the neck and shoulder muscles tighten as the entire web of capillaries on the body's surface tightens. Hands and feet start to ache from the cold and lack of circulation.

When the body temperature reaches ninety-five degrees, the threshold of mild hypothermia has been reached. Pronounced shivering begins. Muscles are trying, instinctively, to generate more body heat.

Heat continues to drain away. Through the armpits, the groin, the neck, and particularly the head, where 50 percent of heat loss can occur. Slowly, thinking erodes. For every degree drop in body temperature below ninety-five degrees, the cerebral metabolic rate falls by 3 to 5 percent.

Amnesia begins at ninety-three degrees. Victims forget where they are. At ninety-one degrees, an apathy takes over. They just don't care. Around ninety degrees, many fall into a stupor.

Falling to eighty-eight degrees, the body generally stops shivering. The blood is slow and thick, and the kidneys, working to eliminate waste, produce an overwhelming urge to urinate.

At eighty-seven degrees and counting, a victim cannot recognize a familiar face, and at eighty-six degrees, heart arrhythmia begins. Its pumping rate has fallen a full third. Hallucinations may begin. At eighty-five degrees, many victims feel overwhelmed by heat, perhaps because just before they lose consciousness the blood flows back to the chilled capillaries in a sudden rush.

Some try to tear off their clothes at this point—"paradoxical undressing" is the medical term. All, if they do not receive help and warmth, become unconscious.

And they die. They have not literally frozen to death. Their core temperatures are well above freezing. Their systems, particularly the heart and brain, simply cannot get the blood and oxygen needed for life.

And now, each of the *Marine Electric* men in the water began the phases of this journey as his core body temperature was slowly, slowly sucked away by this very cold sea and by the whipping wind above it.

Life and death depended on little things now. Would they turn left and find a life raft? Or turn right and paddle toward endless dark ocean? Would they come across a scrap of wood? A pallet? A splintered oar? A lifeboat?

Did they wear wool or cotton? Wool insulates well when wet. Cotton does not. Down is fine when dry, lousy when wet.

Were they skinny? Or chunky? This was one place where you could be too thin. A nice, comfortable layer of fat increased your chance of survival. And most merchant seamen on home-ported "good feeders" like the *Marine Electric* ran a bit heavy.

It was their one stroke of good luck against the odds. For the odds were very bad. They did not have survival suits—thick neoprene outfits like wet suits. The National Transportation Safety Board had been recommending them since 1978, after the *Chester A. Poling* went down. The suits had been used for rescues during World War II. But the Coast Guard did not require them. And the shipping line did not provide them.

The men wore heavy clothes, most of them, but nothing thirty-nine-degree water could not penetrate. Or winds that blew chills of fourteen below zero. Few of them would have a chance to get out of the water and aboard hatch covers or rafts. And rescue was at least one hour away.

Dewey and three other men clung to the life raft, safety so very, very close. Dewey was getting colder. His fingers were like dumb, unfeeling hooks as he struggled to get into the raft. He was still fairly fresh, but his strength was draining away rapidly. He rose in the water with all his might and hooked an arm above the inflated gunwale of the raft. Finally, after a twenty-minute struggle, he managed to hoist himself up and into the boat. It was a momentous, draining battle to get that far.

Now to get the other three men into the boat. One seaman was nearly motionless. Dewey, a newcomer, did not even know the man's name. But he would get the man inside.

Heavy seas washed over them. The man was near motionless, seemingly frozen. Dewey told the other two seamen to keep a tight hold on the line along the raft. Then Clayton Babineau, the second mate, swam over. He took charge. He was doing what he should be doing as an officer. Taking command. Bringing order to chaos. Going through the lists he kept in his mind.

"Find the ladder to the raft," Babineau said. He knew from the lists in his mind, from his training, from the drills. There was a ladder of some sort. "Get me in," Babineau said, "and we'll get the other men in as well." There had to be a ladder. It was on the list.

"Put over the ladder," Babineau called out. It was a good plan, and Dewey searched for a ladder. He found canisters of water. He found fishing line. But no ladder. A small piece of cargo net was the best he could do. He returned with great hope and draped it over the side.

Babineau tried to climb the net. But the netting had fallen very closely against the inflated raft. His fingers were numb. There was no room for his fingers. Dewey pulled at him, trying to lift his center of gravity over the raft's sides. Huge waves drenched them and turned the raft sideways. Babineau held tight, but this was not working.

Babineau and Dewey left their lists behind. There was no list now, nothing in the book to cover this, and both men thought quickly while there was still warm blood in their brains.

Dewey placed Babineau's numbed fingers in the net. That didn't work. Dewey doubled up the net, gathered it together so Babineau could get a grip. It wasn't working. The little capillaries had constricted, sending blood to his organs, making fingers useless.

"Get a foothold in the net!" Dewey yelled.

"I can't!" Babineau cried back.

Then Babineau hit on an idea. He swung about on his back and put up his feet. Dewey grabbed them and could get real purchase.

He was able to drag some of Babineau's weight inside the raft. But the greater part of his weight was still outside, and Dewey could not drag him all the way in. In that position, Babineau's head was underwater as well.

Nothing worked. They all held onto the lifeline around the raft. First one seaman drifted away. Then another. Babineau held on the longest, but then he, too, drifted away. Only his lists lived on, the last list, in the drawer for Mary, his wife, the list saying what to do when all the other lists ran out.

Dewey shined his $1.39 flashlight around, but he saw no one. *I've lost my guys,* he thought. All of them were gone. All dead. *I've lost my guys.* The thought would not go away.

Far from Dewey and the raft, Kelly and Roberts and Powers and Lane looked about, still clinging to the life ring. They sounded off by number and came out with six. The officers and two seamen named Joe and Harold. Kelly, the relief mate, did not know their last names. They were all pretty well stunned.

"There are ship lights," Powers said once. They all strained to see them. Powers used his powerful tankerman's light to cut the darkness. But they saw no ships. "There are ship lights," Powers said once again, when they were at the top of a wave. But the men, squinting, could see nothing. Only the twinkle of the strobe lights on the life jackets. And they could hear the cries for help. The men rose and fell with the swell of the sea, waiting for ships, helicopters, planes, lifeboats, anything.

They were growing colder and colder. They talked to each other with quiet encouragement. Hang on. Hang on. Daylight is coming soon, they said to each other.

Kelly was alert. He did quick mental calculations. Powers was chief engineer. But Kelly had his chief mate's license. Which made him ranking officer.

"Don't waste your energy," Kelly said. He remembered his North Atlantic survival course. "Conserve your energy. Don't yell for help. Don't scream. It drains your heat away."

Then they saw bits and pieces of ship debris float by.

"Grab that flotsam," he said. A pallet came near. "Grab it," he said. "Lash it to the ring. Let's make this larger. We got too many men on this little life ring."

So they did. They were all functioning. They fashioned a small raft from the flotsam and the wood pallet.

"Now let's get this guy up and out of the water. The air will be better. The water takes your heat away."

So they boosted the seaman up. Kelly, the relief mate, did not know his name. The man clung to the pallet for long minutes.

But it was not working. The gale ripped over the man, and the windchill must have been fifteen below zero. He was freezing faster up there. Had a better chance in the water.

"Okay," Kelly said. "Come on down."

And they floated there. Not all of them were directly on the ring. Some had to reach around others for a grip. "Help me," the men would say, "I'm cold," and Kelly began to lose track of time.

The face of his friend and fellow officer Richie Roberts, he saw, was pure white, startlingly white. And when he looked at one of the seamen on the ring, Kelly knew he was dead.

"Oh, I don't want to do this," Kelly said to himself. But another voice inside his head said, *You've got to. You are in command.* Kelly reached inside himself for reserves, forced his foggy brain to work, to form the words.

"Come on guys," Kelly said. "There's no room. We have to cast him loose. Let him drift free to make room on the ring."

The men fumbled over the dead seaman, pushed and tugged at him. He would not come free. Kelly saw that the dead man had an arm locked around the life ring. The corpse clung to the ring with a death grip. The men could not free him.

"Use leverage, guys. Pry him off!" Kelly ordered.

And finally the man was pried free. Kelly watched him drift off and thought, *Oh, Christ, what have I done?* But a living man took the dead man's place, and Kelly thought again that he had no choice. It was the right thing. The only thing.

He did not notice when the other men began drifting from the ring. First Harold was gone. Then they looked, and Joe had drifted away.

"How are you doing!" Kelly shouted to Richard Roberts, the other third mate.

"Okay. I'm cold. I'm cold," Roberts said.

Kelly did not know how much time had passed when he noticed that Roberts, too, had floated away. There was just Sparks, Kelly, and Powers now.

"How are you doing!" Kelly shouted to Sparks. *Keep up the spirits. Keep up the encouragement.*

Sparks was stiffening up. "I'm cold. I'm cold. Help me!" he said.

Powers had been shining the big two-handed tankerman's light up, giving the helicopters a reference point, looking for something, anything. Constantly he was scanning with the light.

Then Kelly noticed that the chief engineer's light was no longer in the air. He pivoted from the ring and gave Powers a slap on the back with his hand to get his attention.

Nothing. Powers was quiet. Dead still.

The tankerman's light began to float away from the dead man. Kelly grabbed it.

Then it was just Sparks and Kelly. They kept talking. We're going to make it. Daylight is coming. Hang on there. Hang in there. Kelly would not look at his watch now, because he was afraid his numb fingers would lose their grip. Any moment now, the rescue boats would come.

On his raft, Dewey was relatively secure. The canopied craft rode high on the waves. Few broke in. Those that did were fended off by the canopy. The raft had taken on only three to six inches of water. The canopy knocked back the chill factor. Dewey was trembling from the cold, but the relative dryness of the raft was comforting. The cold, cold ocean was not leaching away his warmth and strength as it was the others. He felt he would make it. He was confident. But the trembling would come and seize him, shake him as if he had malarial seizures.

Where were they? Where were the rescuers? Men were dying, and minutes made the difference.

Chapter Seven

THE AIR CAVALRY RIDES

No. It's scarier to fly for the Coast Guard than to fly in Vietnam. There's a lot of darkness out there.

> Coast Guard helicopter pilot
> when asked if it was "good to be home"
> from the Vietnam War.

5:30 A.M. / SATURDAY, FEB. 12, 1983
U.S. NAVY HELICOPTER, AIRBORNE, OFF CHINCOTEAGUE

Inside the big Navy helicopter, it seemed as if Jim McCann and his crew were all leaning into the head wind, all leaning forward into the beating they were taking, as if that would help the chopper. They were battering their way through the Force 10 gale, heading straight into it, flying blind into the blizzard.

But what was happening? And where was the game? It was all darkness.

Then McCann remembered that his crew chief was ex–Coast Guard. What frequency did they use? Scarborough tuned in. They could hear the give-and-take of the Coast Guard efforts. A Coast Guard chopper was already on the scene. And the Navy guys could tell right away. It was a cluster fuck. That's how they described it in the chopper. A mess. The men were in the water. The Coast Guard hailed the Navy chopper. The men are in the water! How many swimmers do you have? How many swimmers do you have? There was an urgency in their voices.

McCann's stomach turned. The Coast Guard had no rescue swimmers. They relied on the Navy. And the argument on the tarmac had cut the swimmers in half. One, the Navy helicopter pilots radioed back. McCann swallowed his bitter thoughts and did not blame the pilot. He had acted with his best information. Had the men made it to the boats, then the pilot would have been right. There is no data on the future. McCann shook off the bad thoughts and prepared for what lay ahead. It was about 5:15 A.M. now, still pitch-black. The Navy helicopter could see big ships making their way toward the site, ahead of the lights of the Coast Guard helicopters.

The Navy chopper came to a hover, and the Coast Guard and the Navy exchanged radio debates.

"We can't see anything," the Navy crew chief said, "and we should not put him in."

"They're down there, they're down there," the Coast Guard said. "Put him in. Put him in."

Him was McCann. And McCann wanted in. Insisted on it. So they rigged him up. He wore a wet suit, a cap, mask, and snorkel. A glow light—one of those incandescent cold lights—was strapped to his mask so they could see him in the water. They lowered him on a line with a padded strap and hook.

And there he was in pitch-black darkness, twenty feet down from the chopper and twenty feet up from the water. This is what he had trained for. How to dangle in a complete void and remain calm.

And he could see what the *Marine Electric* men saw. Nothing. Pure blackness. Only when the tiny navigation light under the chopper swept around could he see flecks on the water. The tape, the reflection tape, on the life preservers, was bouncing back the navigation light. There were men there. Flecks and specks of tape on the water.

Put me down! McCann signaled. And they did.

McCann hit the water and, wet suit or not, he was stricken, slapped painfully with the cold. He had been in ice water in training, but nothing like this. He could not breathe. For ten minutes, it seemed, he could only inhale. And cough. Thank God for the training. Thank God! If he did not know this reaction was normal, he would panic right now. He just needed to wait it out. Not do anything silly. Just wait. Just wait. It would pass. The waves took him up and down in twenty-foot swells. Up the height of a twenty-foot roof. Down the depths of a two-story basement. Don't panic. Wait until you get your breath. Even in this period, McCann could look around. In the waves, he could see shadows. Dark shadows that, at the top of the waves, looked like heads and shoulders. But he could not swim for them yet. He could not yet breathe.

When the Coast Guard helicopters first got there, the flight crews were elated. They turned on the lights. The angel was there. Just like the *Theodora* rescue. The lights of heaven had cast down from the skies, split the snow and rain, and were ready to beam the men up. And they could see the men below. They were waving their hands at the helicopter. Waiting to be rescued. The bad news was the men were not in boats, which is what the crew expected. But now the Coast Guard could do what it did best. Pull men from the water and certain death.

It seemed, at first, that the story would have a happy ending. They saw a canopied life raft, and there seemed to be a man flashing a light. The aircraft could handle up to fifteen men. The raft could hold at least that many.

Down below, Dewey knew he had it made. The chopper lowered its life basket. Dewey, shivering convulsively and chilled to the bone, leaned forward and fell into the basket. They raised him up to the hovering aircraft.

"Any more men in the raft?" the crewman asked Dewey anxiously.

"No," he gasped.

The crew covered him with blankets and turned an electric heater on him.

One down. Thirty or more to go, they figured.

But then the crews became puzzled. They would hover near a man. He would flap his arms for rescue. The crew would carefully lower their basket for him to climb into. These guys were good at this. They could put a basket right next to a man—and below him, too, so he just needed to lean into it to be rescued.

But now the men below were not helping at all. The basket would be right next to them, and the men would flap their arms in acknowledgment. And then do nothing. The chopper tried one man.

Then moved to the next. Then to the next. Like a mother bird nurturing lost chicks.

Then it hit them. The arms were flapping with the same rhythm as the sea. All the same. As if the arms of dozens of marionettes were pulled by one puppeteer. The men weren't flapping their arms. The ocean was moving them up and down. They bobbed motionless, lifeless in the sea, the waves pushing their arms up, gravity pulling the arms down. The ocean mocked the helicopter pilots.

But they could not tell for sure if they were all dead. For the Coast Guard did not have rescue swimmers. They did not have men equipped to enter the water to check. Some of the men might be on the verge of death, but still alive. Incapable of reaching out for rescue, but still reachable if only someone could get next to them.

For that, they needed a swimmer. For that, they needed McCann.

Chapter Eight

THE OPEN BOAT

And like the Mary Ellen Carter
Rise again!

Song by Stan Rogers

5:30 A.M. / Saturday, Feb. 12, 1983
Submerged lifeboat in the water a distance from the wreck

The lifeboat gave Bob Cusick shelter. But not much.

He found that sitting up did not work. The waves crested and broke. It was as if he were sitting at the shoreline in heavy surf. Tons of water would crash over him and push and pull him. It was all he could do to stay in the boat. He was determined to stay out of the water, but the wind was ripping him. The water was draining him.

But if he curled up in the bottom of the boat and braced himself sideways, half-wedged under the seat, he could hold his own. And it was less exposed, warmer down there. The lifeboat was filled with water, just barely buoyant. He could stay crouched down, with just his head out. The coat, Bea's coat, was tight at the sleeves and waist. He thought it might be functioning like a wet suit, holding the water there, warming it, giving him an extra layer of protection.

Jesus, though, it was still cold. Like the coldest martini. Like the coldest ice cream. Like the very coldest can of beer. Colder than when you were a kid and made snowballs without your gloves. He could no longer feel, it was so cold.

And the waves still rocked him. Every eleven to fourteen seconds a huge breaker would wash over him. He would have to press against the boat. Hold on with the frozen meat hooks he had for hands. And hold his breath, hold his breath. It took much longer for the waves to clear off the boat than it had when he was just holding the oar. Being in the boat was worse than swimming in the open seas in that sense. It was exhausting.

The cycle repeated. Over and over again. The water would clear and suck away from the boat, and Cusick would gasp for breath. He would hyperventilate. He could feel the dip of the boat and know the next wave was coming. He would thrash his arms and legs in this interim, trying to keep the circulation going, trying to keep any warmth. Then he could feel, in the way the boat was rising, that a breaker was on its way. He would see the crest, gasp for one big gulp of air. Hold it. Hold it. Hold it. Hold it. Hold it until his lungs were bursting. The water would clear and suck away from the boat, and Cusick would begin thrashing about again.

There was a way out of this. He was very tired. He was very sleepy. If he just relaxed and relented. He would just . . . let go, really . . . breathe in the water . . . take one deep breath of it instead of the air and it would be much simpler, like going to sleep. He was going to sleep now, and all the cares and worries would be done, he knew. One soft prayer and he would be gone with the others. No reason not to, really. He was the oldest. No one would expect him to survive. No one would blame him. Just breathe in the water, a quiet voice said.

From somewhere inside Bob Cusick, a spark kindled. He thought about his old friends lost at sea. I'm still here, guys. I'm still here, he thought. And a song came into Bob Cusick's mind from nowhere, and he could not get rid of it. It was a tale by the Canadian folk singer Stan Rogers about a ship—the *Mary Ellen Carter*—that had been sunk due to a careless owner's cheapness, and how the crew went back to raise it from the depths. How did the chorus go? Rise again? Rise again! Like the *Mary Ellen Carter*, rise again! There was a memory of banjos and a rousing, strummed guitar. It was what he had. The song. The memory of his old friends. The vision of the Coast Guard. His family. Bob Cusick flipped through them like playing cards, rotating them in his head. Out of nowhere, in the dark, from a swamped lifeboat, a voice roared back at the waves. It was more hoarse shouting than singing.

> *And you to whom adversity*
> *Has dealt the final blow*
> *With smiling bastards lying to you*
> *Everywhere you go*
> *Turn to and put out all your strength*
> *Of arm and heart and brain*
> *And like the* Mary Ellen Carter
> *Rise again!*
> *Rise again!*
> *Like the* Mary Ellen Carter*!*
> *Rise again!!!*

It seemed like hours to Cusick that he bellowed that song, then held his breath and thrashed, then bellowed the song again. He thought he could see hints of dawn, traces of light to the east. It gave him hope. The hope, the thoughts, the song. They all fought the urge to sleep, the voice that told him to breathe the water.

And he thought about his life. It wasn't the flash-before-your-eyes thing. It was slow, leisurely, reflective.

The small things he had not done. Never told Carol, his daughter, this. Never told Bea that.

And why not? Little fears. Inconsequential when you looked at them from where he was now.

And he said to himself, swore to himself then, *In all of Christ's land, in all of Christ's land, if I get out of this, if I get out of this, I will not care, will never be afraid, will say these things, will do these things.*

It was not bargaining with God. It was a solemn personal oath. *If I survive . . .*

All the time, the vision had stayed in Cusick's head. *The Coast Guard will come out and get me.* He literally visualized how it would be. *The Coast Guard will come out and get me.* There would be a helicopter. A basket. A line. *The Coast Guard will come out and get me.*

But there was none, and the would-be rescuers, when they came, looked nothing like Cusick's vision. While the helicopter taxied McCann in its basket over the wave tops from body to body, the two merchant vessels in the vicinity did what they could, looking for bodies, looking for survivors.

At daylight, the Norwegian tanker *Barranger* saw a strange sight. A swamped lifeboat, international orange in color. It carried one man. He seemed to duck down as the waves broke over him. Then it looked as if he were shouting. Or singing.

The *Barranger* moved closer. Jacob's ladders and nets were thrown overboard. Crewmen braved the pitch of the ship and the sweep of the waves and went down the nets to give Cusick a hand.

Below, Cusick still had his faculties. He knew the danger of this sort of rescue. Rescue was just a few feet away. It was so tempting. Grasp for any rescue. Any chance was better than none.

But waves were cresting at up to twenty-seven feet, he calculated, judging from the length of the lifeboat. There are abundant stories of men who died just inches from rescue because their boats were crushed against the hull of a large ship. Cusick knew this. So did the captain of the *Barranger,* as the two veteran seamen stared at each other across the waves.

The simple fact seemed absurd, but there it was: Even the most modern technology did not save men in this situation. The problem of getting men out of a lifeboat and onto a rescue ship has eluded the industry and the experts.

The history of lifeboats in the twentieth century was hardly a success story, and this was true even in contemporary times. Lifeboats were fine if your ship sprung a leak in calm seas and you had time for an orderly evacuation.

But if you had rough weather, if you had mounting seas—and most maritime disasters had both—then the fact was you might just as well call them death boats as lifeboats, because your odds of dying were at least as high as living. The word "life" in lifeboats may give seamen comfort of sorts, but the record of marine casualties shows that they are difficult to launch in bad seas and just as difficult to get out of alive once you have gotten into them.

The same storms that batter thousand-foot merchant ships to a point of abandonment play havoc with a twenty-five-foot lifeboat. The boat may be launched. The men may get in it. But what exactly does one do when a small lifeboat in storm conditions approaches a monster of steel that is the modern maritime vessel, there for the rescue?

In dozens of cases, the answer has been that lifeboats founder, splinter, crash, and sink. Many men who manage to abandon a ship die within yards of safety as they attempt to board the rescue vessel. It can be as if the boat has been blown onto a leeward shore against rocks or a seawall.

In the 1970s, clever engineers thought they had solved the problem with lifeboats by designing the "rescue pod." And for a while, it seemed as if they might have succeeded. They even succumbed to the hubris of calling the capsules unsinkable. The pods looked like flying saucers. They hung from oil rigs or merchant ships, ready for quick boarding and instant drops into the sea. They contained comfortable seating and a motor for steering and powering the ship to safety.

Then came the wreck of the *Ocean Express* in 1978, when the captain was snatched from the sinking oil rig at the last possible moment. When the *Ocean Express* seemed certain to go down in the Gulf of Mexico in a Force 10 storm, the captain had told his men to take to the pods.

One capsule slipped away without a hitch. The forty-horsepower engine zipped it away from the sinking barge. The colored, egglike pod carried fourteen men and was working the way it was designed to work.

The first capsule motored to a nearby survey ship, the *Nicole Martin,* and slammed hard up against her. The men inside the pod then faced an interesting question. As one writer of the time put it: "Capsules are wonderful, *but how do you get out?*"

The pod slammed against the rescue ship time after time. There was no way to dock it. Or lift it from the water. At one point, a crew member in the pod yelled, "Get away from us! Get away!" He feared the constant slamming would sink the pod. But the distance between the pod and the ship was only eight to ten feet. Timing the rise and fall of the waves, the crew of the *Nicole Martin* hauled the pod people to safety. One by one. Everyone got out alive. The only injuries were bumps and scrapes.

But that was luck, not engineering.

On board the second pod, nineteen men huddled around the interior as the diesel churned through the storm. Men grew seasick and headed for the toilet. One man steered by a stubby tiller. Everyone was comforted by the knowledge that the pod could not sink or capsize. They were certain they were safe.

They faced the same problem as the other pod. Ships steamed to their rescue. But then what? On board one of the tugs, a rescuer said he could see the pod on the crest of a wave, high, high above him, one moment, only to have the tug rise and the pod sink, putting the pod far, far below him.

One man aboard the pod, a driller named Tommy Loftin, opened the hatch and threw out a line attached to a floating strobe. The other end of the line he tied to the pod's lowering hook. Someone on the tug caught the hook. But then what?

The pod crashed fiercely against the tug. Loftin's finger was smashed badly—a part of it just gone. Waves kept hurtling him down the hatch. Others below yelled at him: "What's the matter, man! Why don't you get out?"

He could not. One moment, he was two stories above the tug. The next moment, the tug was two stories above him. The pod kept slamming the tug.

"We're safer here," someone told Loftin. "Tommy, go up and tell the tug to pull us to shallow water, then get away from us."

Loftin did. From the tug, a voice came back over the waves: "Ain't no way we can tow you."

Loftin closed the hatch.

Then it happened. Was it a particularly steep wave? The strain of the line to the tug? The men without seat belts were thrown against those still belted in. One side was suddenly weighted very heavily. The capsule flipped to that side. Then it flipped completely upside down.

The lights went out. The motor stopped. There was no flashlight. The men now were huddled at the ceiling or hanging from their belts. They could hear the throb of the tug's engines as she maneuvered to try to save them. The capsule jerked a few times. But the weight of the men, nearly two tons, was like lead in the keel of a sailboat: It kept the little craft floating upside down. As they struggled silently, the men could see a strange green light through the windows. *It's the tug's searchlight,* the tool-pusher, Boudreaux, thought. *We're seeing it through water. They'll get us yet.*

Boudreaux squirmed. Then he felt water. His foot had gone through a window. Water came into the pod. The pod jerked again sharply. Another jolt, and the main side doors of the capsule fell open. Boudreaux leapt. And made it through the doors. Five others followed him. Men on the tugs fished them from the water with boat hooks. They got the five. Only Loftin was injured. They were poised. At the ready. Waiting for the others. To gaff them from the water and onto the safety of the deck. They waited.

But there were no more. The others went down with the pod. Trapped in an upside-down world where unsinkable capsules sank, ceilings became floors, and lifesaving devices became tombs.

By the time the *Marine Electric* went down, in 1983, leaving Cusick to fight for his life with rescue just yards away, there still was not an easy way, no new technology, for lifting men from lifeboats to the decks of ships.

If anything, Cusick was in worse shape than most. His boat was swamped, and he could not steer it. If by chance he came near the ship, he could not grip anything authentically. His hands were dumb weak hooks.

The odds were that a wave would pluck him up against the steel wall of the ship and throw him, broken, into the sea. He was too weak now to survive that. Too exhausted and fragile to fight the waves and the currents.

The lifeboat would almost certainly be smashed, dumping him into the water and his death, he thought. It was a sucker's bet. Cusick had been at sea long enough to know it.

The Norwegian captain realized it as well. He saw Cusick in the lifeboat. The old mate was waving him off. He was saying thanks, but waving him off. The two officers' eyes met. They understood.

In the lifeboat, Cusick was thinking, *Better this way. There was a better chance this way.* The vision came back. *The Coast Guard will come out and get me. There will be a helicopter. There will be a line. There will be a basket.*

The chances of that happening were growing slim.

Chapter Nine

THE DAY OF THE SWIMMER

If a man is in need of rescue, an airplane can come in and throw flowers on him, and that's just about all.

IGOR SIKORSKY
developer of the modern helicopter

6:30 A.M. / SATURDAY, FEB. 12, 1983 / IN THE WATER, NEAR THE WRECK

After minutes that seemed like hours, McCann started breathing normally, but still he faced twenty- to thirty-foot swells and minus fourteen degrees Fahrenheit windchill temperatures with forty-mile-per-hour winds. He was outfitted in a four-millimeter neoprene wet suit with socks and gloves, neo cap, small flotation device, fins, mask, and a chemical light attached to his mask so the boys above could see him.

But the mask quickly froze over. So he popped it to the top of his head and faced the wind and spray barefaced. Then he found he could not swim on his stomach. The action of the waves was such that his flippers almost always came out of the water. He needed to turn on his back, knees bent, to get traction and torque.

And then there were the swells. He rode them up. He rode them down. Two stories up. Two stories down. Every eleven to fourteen seconds, he made that trip. At the top of the swells, he looked for survivors. Then he would kick out for them.

This was not terribly efficient, however, and, communicating by hand signals, the Navy swimmer teamed up with the Coast Guard helicopter. The Coast Guard helicopter dropped its basket near McCann. He got in it. Then the chopper air-taxied him over the swells. They tried to find the *Marine Electric* survivors from the bounce-back of light from the reflector tape on the life preservers.

McCann was not sure what he was finding. The men were cold and motionless. He taxied up to them, jumped in the water, and swam them to the basket. Sometimes the basket was on top of the water. Most times, it was partly under water. So McCann would float the man to the basket and hoist him up so that his waist was on the rim of the basket. Then he would reach down, grab the man's pants leg, and heave. In such a manner, he loaded man after man. The chopper hoisted them up and then returned the empty basket to McCann.

He spied a cluster of men in the water and began floating them to the basket. One man gripped a floating wooden pallet so tightly that McCann could not pry loose his hands. It was a death grip. McCann had no choice. He left him in the water.

But at least one man was alive. McCann did not know it then. Never knew how many dead men he sent up. But one man in the cluster still clung to a life ring.

Gene Kelly and Albion "Sparks" Lane were still on the life ring. He kept talking to Sparks. Kelly could see the helicopters. Once they passed over but did not stop. Twice. Three times. They did not see him. He saw ships now, too. He tried to flash the tankerman's light at them. Tried, but he could not aim it. He did not have fingers and toes. He had no arms; that is how it felt. He would shiver for a minute, then be still for ten seconds, then shiver again. Over and over, like convulsions.

When he heard the chopper again, Kelly tried to wave the powerful tankerman's light straight up. Not aimed anywhere. Just straight up. With all his might, he willed unresponsive arms and fingers to function. He did not even see McCann in the water next to him. Did not even know the swimmer was helping him. All he could see was the basket descending from the helicopter. Descending from heaven.

"Sparks!" he said triumphantly. They had made it! They had made it!

"Sparks! They're here."

But when he turned, Albion Lane was already gone. McCann found Kelly alone on the life ring. The ring that he threw from the *Marine Electric* had supported six men, but saved only one. Kelly never even saw the swimmer in the water, and McCann didn't know Kelly was alive. Kelly never even knew there were hands on him. He just saw the basket, and then he was in it, heading up.

Kelly went up by himself, but saw as he was going up in the basket that a swimmer was in the water. As the winch pulled and he slowly ascended above the waves, one thought flashed through his mind, over and over. A thought of great regret, of remorse.

I should have taken the light. I should have saved Powers's light.

In the chopper, Dewey was still freezing and trembling. Kelly was sobbing uncontrollably now. His pants were down around his knees. He was vomiting seawater and oil. Both men were covered in oil. The crew gave them blankets and turned up the heaters. Kelly looked over and saw three corpses. One had its eyes wide open. Kelly pulled up a blanket over his own eyes, to keep from looking at the dead man.

Jim McCann looked up from the water and kept his eye on the Coast Guard helicopter. He desperately missed that second swimmer, because, wet suit or not, he was growing colder and colder. Soon, he knew, he would have to come out.

Then he became aware of a different danger. The crewmen above him were staring with great intensity, not at him but at the water. They hovered a short distance from McCann in the dark and seemed to be following something. Then Jim's mind told him what it was.

Sharks.

He was certain the crew had spotted sharks and were marking them, following them closely, just a few yards from McCann's position. As he rode up the waves, he looked for fin tips cutting through the water. Adrenaline propelled McCann's body now as he turned his head, trying to spot the predators.

But then he became aware of a different danger, one more

profound. For the crew and the chopper were sliding away. They didn't seem to know where McCann was. Clearly they did not, as they slipped farther and farther away, staring intently down, looking for his glow light. Hell, they weren't looking for sharks, they were looking for *him*.

Suddenly, the tables had been turned. McCann the rescuer was in the soup. Lost with the rest of them. Destined to become as cold and motionless as the men he had been hauling to the basket. They must not see the light. Without the light, he was lost. There were no swimmers to come get the swimmer. He groped with numb fingers for his mask and the chemical light fixed to it.

Gone. Everything. No mask. No light. Nothing. Adrenaline popped McCann's senses again, but he did not panic. The training, God bless the training. His mask had a cord. The cord was attached to him. If he found the cord on his waist. . . . There. He reeled it in. From beneath the dark waters came the mask, its light still attached and still on. Hand over hand, it came back to McCann.

He put it squarely on his head, light up, clear shot to the chopper. *See, I'm still here. See, like a big-eyed puppy dog,* he thought. *I'm still here.*

The chopper drifted a bit more. Then someone saw the glow light, and the machine side-slipped back to Jim. The McCann Air Taxi Service was back in business. He went from crewman to crewman. All motionless.

It was still dark. As McCann swam, he saw lights on an approaching ship in the distance. The helicopter hovered directly over McCann. And now the *Tropic Sun,* a supertanker, was steaming to the rescue as well. But in its earnest mission of goodwill, the tanker was steaming directly toward the helicopter—and directly toward McCann. The chopper and the swimmer held their positions, hopeful that the tanker would turn back. There was no clear radio channel on which to warn the tanker. But they all felt the tanker would turn.

And then something dawned on McCann. *These tankers can't turn on a dime. Even if they see me, they'll still hit me.* There was no time to swim to the rescue basket and be taxied away. McCann was going to be crushed, swept under and chewed up by the prop, unless he swam hard right now.

It was a cliché. McCann's life passed before his eyes. Every good thing, every bad thing. He saw it all as he swam the race of his life. The tanker loomed large now, just yards away. McCann stretched for every ounce of strength. He kicked and heaved for air and swam and swam some more.

A large swell picked up McCann and carried him above the level of the deck of the ship, just five to ten feet from the side. McCann suddenly saw a crewman on the ship. Could almost reach out and touch him. They were eyeball to eyeball, each as startled as the other at such an encounter. McCann had never seen anyone that close in his life. The man was burned into his memory. He wore a dark wool watch cap. It was blue. The man had dark brown hair. Scruffy, with a beard. A lumberjack red shirt. Blue jeans with dirt on his knees. He looked at McCann like, *What the hell are you doing out there?* And McCann looked at him like, *Why are you trying to kill me?*

The scene held for a few seconds, almost in freeze-frame, both startled men gaping at one another. Then the ship moved forward, and the wave receded into a trough.

McCann realized he was not out of the woods yet. The prop was coming soon. He could be dragged under by the powerful pull of the propeller. He struck out again and swam for all he was worth. Pounding strokes and kicks over the swells and down the swells as hard as he could.

Seconds later, he had made it. The wash of the prop hit him and hit him hard, but no harder than the waves he had fought for more than an hour. He was home free. No sharks. No hull. No prop. He was back to being a rescuer.

But he was a very tired and cold rescuer. His crew called him in for a rest. He rode the basket up to the Coast Guard helicopter. In the rear of the aircraft, he could see seven mannequins. That's how he thought of them. Seven dead crewmen, frozen. Some sitting, some lying sideways. They looked like mannequins, but beside them were two men huddled in space blankets. They had the heater turned on them full blast. They looked like they would make it.

McCann himself looked more like a survivor than a crewman. He was shivering. A wet suit works by holding a fine layer of water against the body. The layer is heated by body temperature and helps keep the swimmer warm.

Up in the chopper, McCann had lost his heated layer of water. He was growing colder and colder. But he also wanted back in the game. This is what he'd asked to do, trained to do. This was his job.

The crew relented and let him go back down. Instantly, McCann felt the cold again. He was quickly overwhelmed but willed himself to go on. He swam to a body and loaded it. He was shaking. Badly. He knew that if the crew saw him shaking, they would jerk him up. He gripped the basket with all his strength. If he could grip it hard enough, he could stop his body from shaking.

But hell, the whole basket was shaking. He was flagged. Get back up in the helicopter, they said via hand signals. And he came back up. Had to. The chopper was low on fuel anyway. They were ready to leave the scene. Had to.

Daylight came. The freighter *Barranger* radioed that there was a lifeboat with a survivor. A very weak survivor. The chopper was headed back to base but turned, fuel low, for one last rescue.

They hovered over the man. He was just standing there, looking up. Very unsteady. He could not grasp the basket. He could not get in it. Once they tried, and the man failed. Twice, they tried, and a wave nearly took him over the side of the lifeboat.

McCann looked down, still shivering. "Put me down there!" he yelled at the Coast Guard crew. He was hammering the side of the helicopter now. "Put me down there now!!! Put me down, put me down!!! Put me back down there in the water!!!"

Chapter Ten

CLOSING TIME

IF I am going to be drowned—if I am going to be drowned—if I am going to be drowned, why, in the name of the seven mad gods, who rule the sea, was I allowed to come thus far . . .

Steven Crane

"The Open Boat"

6:55 a.m. / Saturday, Feb. 12, 1983
Submerged lifeboat, a distance from the wreck

More than an hour had passed since the helicopters had reached the scene. Cusick had drifted far from the other men. He had turned down the chance of a ship rescue.

Worse, both the men and the helicopters had been put through the mill—and the mill was winning. McCann, the swimmer, was suffering from hypothermia himself now. He could bang all he wanted and demand to be put back in, but the Coast Guard would not do that. Could not. McCann had barely enough strength to make it back into the rescue basket and be hoisted up the last time. Low on fuel, with McCann out of action, the pilot made the call about 6:30. They would run Dewey and Kelly to a hospital now.

The other Coast Guard helicopter was having similar problems. Petty Officer Gregory Petch had no wet suit or training, but he volunteered to man the basket as CG 1434 moved from body to body. He did his best, but a big wave battered him and the basket. It nearly threw Petch into the sea, and it damaged the winch on the chopper, so its basket was out of operation.

As McCann's CG 1471 turned to leave, the *Barranger* radioed,

"Need assistance for a man in a lifeboat." This was right after Cusick had waved off the ship rescue.

Now what were the choppers to do? CG 1434 had some fuel left but no winch. CG 1471 had no fuel but did have a winch. Well, there it was. *"You have to go out. You don't have to come back."* The pilot banked McCann's chopper and circled toward the *Barranger*. It was closing time. They would go for one more round. By the looks of the fuel gauge, though, closing time had already come and gone.

Cusick was still taking cresting seas. Still thrashing about. Still holding on. Still shouting into the storm. *Rise again! Rise Again!* Still visualizing. *The Coast Guard will come out and get me.* Still seeing the helicopter. Still seeing the line. The sun had just crested over the eastern horizon and . . .

Then it was there. For real. He knew it was for real. There was a tremendous backwash from the helicopter blades. The chopper seemed just inches off the water. A basket was coming, coming. But the seas were heaving, and the wash of the blades was pushing Bob Cusick around, staggering him.

The basket was there in front of him. Attached to the line. His vision. Cusick stood up. Or tried to. His legs were not there. Just numb pegs. The basket was there, and Cusick fell forward and . . . missed. He fell square back into the lifeboat.

From above, the crew could see Cusick lying there. They made another pass. The basket came in. Cusick struggled. He braced against the seat. He struggled to his feet. His legs were worthless. Worse than drunk. The basket came, but so did a big sea. It washed completely over Cusick. The men above could see him covered by the wave. He vanished from view. Then the old mate poked his head through the waters. He was still there, still clinging to the boat with hands like ice tongs.

The crew thought it hopeless. The gauges all said, Go. Leave. They were low on fuel, but the backup helicopter had no winch. And McCann was banging away like a madman, yelling, "Put me down. Put me DOWN!"

So they would give it a last try.

The basket came over again for a third pass. Cusick still had trouble getting up on his feet. He had no strength. No feeling.

Dumb wooden stilts. He would stumble again. He would reel like a drunken prizefighter. He would die in this boat and . . .

The song that had sustained him in the cold came up within him again. *Rise again! Rise Again!! RISE AGAIN!!!*

Robert M. Cusick, chief mate of the *Marine Electric,* tried to stand up. He extended both arms. He could not rise. But the Coast Guard, the guys on the winch, they were good. Sweet Jesus, they were so good, they just laid the basket in the boat. And when the basket came by, this time he rose just enough to roll into it. Had just enough spark to rise and roll.

The Coast Guard will come out and get me. The Coast Guard will come out and get me. Only now the vision was from a different angle. Cusick looked down. The international orange lifeboat was getting smaller. And smaller. Just a toy, really, far, far below him.

When Cusick was brought into the helicopter bay, the pilot gunned the engines and banked toward land. Jim McCann looked back at the seven dead men and compared them to Cusick. There wasn't a lot of difference in how they looked. He looked at Cusick again and thought, there's one near death. Dewey and Kelly looked at the new arrival and looked at the mannequins. Dewey and Kelly wondered. Was he with them? Or the dead.

Hands were working on Cusick. There were blankets. The electric heater. Still, they could not tell.

"What month is it!?" Coast Guardsman Verner kept shouting into Cusick's blank face, looking for signs of life. Cusick remained silent, frozen in time.

What month? What month? What month is it? Can you tell me what month it is?

Cusick stirred. He vomited a great belch of oil and seawater. *What month was it?* He could answer that.

"February," Cusick said. "It's February."

As the helicopter headed for shore, the men on the *Tropic Sun* were steaming to the rescue of the others.

The crewmen on the big tanker never knew they had caused such anxiety for McCann, the diver. They were on a rescue mission and steered with all earnestness and sincerity to save their colleagues. Rules and custom require that course, but there is something much stronger at work as well, the brotherhood of all seamen. Schedules, production pressures, personal plans: All are thrown away on a decent ship when another is in distress.

And now the *Tropic Sun* crew and officers were excited, charged with anticipation. They could see men in the water ahead, closely grouped. The first light showed their orange life jackets clearly. And they were animated in the water, waving their arms at the ship. All of them.

Get some hot soup and blankets, Jim Walsh heard his officers call out on the *Tropic Sun*. They were exuberant. "We're taking them on board!"

Walsh was filled with a joy, a good feeling, and overwhelmed with happiness. The feeling was primordial. They were members of the pack, saving a pack. The men were energized as they prepared to snag their brothers from the sea. It could be them out there. This was more than compassion. It touched their very hearts and souls as no one else could understand.

Then, as they came in closer, they noticed that the long line of men in the water waved their arms in a sort of rolling rhythm. Almost as if a puppeteer had all their arms on the same string and was keeping time with the roll of the ocean.

Now the men in the water were next to them. The big waves carried them up to deck level.

Walsh thought they looked as if they were leaning back in easy chairs, watching television, very relaxed and peaceful.

The men on the *Tropic Sun* watched the dead men float by just feet away, raised up by the waves to deck level. The live crew looked at the dead crew. The live men put away the blankets and turned down the heat on the soup. The dead men drifted on with the waves. The big ship made a lazy turn and prepared to help the Coast Guard in its grim and mournful task of recovering the bodies.

The inverted hull of the *Marine Electric* bobbed for several hours as the big waves rolled over it and the wash of the waves sucked at the hull. Rescue helicopters buzzed about and then headed for hospitals with the survivors and the dead. Television choppers reached the scene, flitting about like dragonflies as they jockeyed for a good angle, scampered to another angle, moved on.

No one was on the scene later, when she sank around 12:30 P.M. No one had her final position. Rough seas had kept the rescue choppers away from the deadly hulk. And now they did not know where she had taken her final roll to the bottom. Rescue planes buzzed about, looking for Captain Corl—the only man clear of the engine room whose body had not been found—but came up with nothing.

The men in the engine room went with the *Marine Electric,* 130 feet down, in a fluttering descent, much as a toy boat, swamped, flutters to the bottom of a bathtub. Cadet Wickboldt, Price, Browning, Charles Gidden, the third assistant engineer, Anthony Quirk, the engine mechanic, Howard J. Scott, the second assistant engineer. All six were with the ship, at 130 feet. With their dreams of marriage, a family compound, an auto repair shop, a steady berth on a new ship, of wives and children.

The ship torqued as she bobbed and sank, they said later, and the new midsection, most of it, wrenched loose and floated free, to its own grave. All 24,000 tons of coal lay strewn on the ocean floor. The bow and stern of the old T-2 tanker, built in wartime, were thought to have danced along the bottom, bow down, before settling upside down on the starboard side, a stubborn strip of metal joining the sections, a mile or more from the midsection.

Above, the waters closed routinely around where the hull had bobbed, as the waters routinely have closed over thousands of ships for thousands of years.

The blizzard itself had moved out, heading north toward Greenland, where it would finally dissipate. The National Weather Service called it "the worst East Coast storm in forty years." The Mariner's Weather Log bulletin dubbed it "Monster of the Month." Ships reported waves of up to fifty feet.

New York City was socked in with twenty-six inches of snow, Washington with twenty-six. Philadelphia, with twenty-one inches, had not seen such a storm since 1909. Airports were closed. Along the Eastern Seaboard, snow shovelers were clearing walkways and plow crews were scraping roadways. Big-city political futures hung on whether the plow crews could efficiently push the snow from the streets into the rivers and seas that surrounded them.

So on land, the action was frantic.

But there was a clean cast to the air now, thirty miles out to sea off Virginia, and a quietness to the sea.

Saturday looked as if it could be sunny.

Part Two

ON LAND

*When a man suspects any wrong, it
sometimes happens that if he be already
involved in the matter, he insensibly strives to
cover-up his suspicions even from himself.*

*And much this way it was with me. I
said nothing and tried to think nothing.*

HERMAN MELVILLE
Moby-Dick

Chapter Eleven

THE SURVIVORS

. . . and they covered him with clothes, but he gat no heat.

First Book of Kings

11:00 A.M. / SATURDAY, FEB. 12, 1983 / PORTSMOUTH NAVAL HOSPITAL
PORTSMOUTH, VIRGINIA

The day of the rescue, Jim McCann lay in the Naval Hospital at Portsmouth, Virginia, layered under blankets, monitored by nurses, watched by doctors for core body temperature and signs of the little tricks of hypothermia, when he told the nurses, "Get this thermometer out of me or I will. I've got important stuff to do. I feel just fine, and I'm leaving."

The nurses did not believe him at first, but when he threw back the covers and threatened to yank the temperature sensor from its indelicate spot, they began to take him seriously. Hurried conferences were held. The doctors agreed that McCann was well enough to be discharged, and two and a half hours after arriving, he was hurrying back to his car at the helicopter rescue center, the silly hospital gown dumped in a puddle on the bed.

It was almost noon. He drove as he had early that morning, fishtailing on the ice and slush, and he nearly spun out again on the base traffic circles.

And then he was home. Through the door.

"Come on!" McCann said. "Get ready! Let's go, go, go." He was already digging out his dress clothes. "We've got pictures to get taken. We've got an appointment!"

Forty-five minutes later they were in the photo studio. On time, as promised.

. . .

It had not gone so well for the *Marine Electric* survivors and the families. At first, no one knew for sure who had survived. Even the men in the chopper were not sure.

"Is that the chief mate?" Kelly had asked Dewey when they were still in the helicopter with McCann.

"No," Dewey said, as he looked down at Cusick's oil-covered face. "I don't know who it is. I don't remember any black people on board with a beard."

Then Kelly smeared some of the oil off Cusick's face, tried to put two and two together, but still was not sure what it added up to. Yes, this man was probably Bob Cusick. Thick black bunker oil covered his beard, hair, face, body. He did indeed look as if he were a black man wearing a coal-black parka. It was tight at the sleeves and tied tight around his head. It looked like a hooded wet suit. Kelly did not know it was Bea's silly coat, too good for a dirty old coal ship.

So Kelly could not tell if it was Cusick. Kelly was only the relief third mate, and he did not know everyone. Neither did Dewey. They huddled in blankets near the heaters and thought about the "unknown seaman" in front of them.

But Cusick did not think anything. He remembered saying "February" when asked by the Coast Guardsman, and the man leaning forward gleefully, after so many disappointments, after stacking so many dead bodies in the rear of the chopper, and yelling, "Hey! I think this one's going to make it." And he remembered Dewey saying something about not remembering any black men on board with beards. Then Cusick was gone. Lost in blackness.

He revived when the helicopter landed near the hospital in Salisbury, Maryland, and remembered them jostling him onto a carrier. Into the ambulance. The jolt of the ambulance. He was conscious for a moment and felt an overwhelming need to turn on his side. He struggled. The urge seemed like life or death to him. He had to be on his side! He levered himself, smiled, and felt great relief, but he did not know from what.

Then the darkness came again. There was a stop at the hospital.

A transfer to the gurney. Hallways. Lights. Hospital smells. Then darkness. He could feel someone cleaning his face, wiping off the oil, someone in white. Then darkness again. Nothing.

This was a time they could lose him. Treating hypothermia is not so simple as just "warming a person up." Severe cases should be barely stirred, never shaken. Many amateur rescuers make the mistake of rubbing the limbs or forcing the person to walk. Their thought is: *Get the circulation going, warm this guy up.* They accomplish the former but not the latter. Upon walking, cold blood from the limbs rushes to vital organs. The heart, working fine at rest with regionally warm blood, is flooded with a sudden rush of cooler blood, while the warm blood rushes to the limbs. Blood pressure tanks. The heart is overwhelmed and fibrillates. The person can die right there—take a few steps, feeling fine, do a header and die. In 1980, sixteen Danish fishermen were reported rescued after being in the water just one and one-half hours in the North Sea. Hale and hardy, it seemed, they graciously thanked their rescuers and then walked below for hot drinks and soup. All sixteen died right there.

So the medical specialists were careful with Bob Cusick, now in a critical stage between life and death. There were many modern methods of treatment. Warm intravenous fluids could be pumped into him. Electrical pads could be applied carefully. They could soak him in a warming tub. There were new techniques for warming the air in his lungs, too.

But for the most part, they used an ancient cure. Dr. Elton Adams, a Montana physician who specializes in survival skills and treatments, is fond of quoting the First Book of Kings in the Old Testament, to illustrate just how far back this goes.

"Now King David was old and stricken in years; and they covered him with clothes, but he gat no heat."

And essentially, this is what they did for Cusick. They covered him with warm blankets. And Cusick gat heat. It was simple, ancient, effective. And it avoided rewarming shock through a gradual, gentle, natural warming. Cusick's core body temperature rose gently and steadily, a degree every twenty minutes or so.

As all this was happening, far to the north, in Scituate, Massachusetts, in the Cusick home near the bay, Bea did not know if Bob was dead or alive, and her temperature was rising twenty degrees, it seemed, every minute or so.

She had been called by Bob's sister early Saturday morning with the grim news that her brother, Bea's husband, was dead. The radio reports, the first ones, said the *Marine Electric* was believed lost with all hands. Bea was devastated. Her emotions were at the surface in normal times. When she talked of something only slightly sad, her voice seemed as if she would burst into tears. On the threshold of sobbing. She would reverse course, if she heard something funny, and her voice verged on laughter. Always this was the case, her feelings just under her skin. All of it was balanced, controlled, endearing. Bea would be right there, in the moment, fully attentive, feeling your thoughts, your emotions, almost as you did. Sometimes before.

But Bea had been a nurse. She was accustomed to death and the news of death, and that gave her a steely center. One part of her was petrified, terrified, already grief-stricken. Another part was acutely functional, nurse-ready and operational. She knew the word was not yet final or official. The news reports said *believed* lost. And besides, the media often got it wrong. Her hope was that it was wrong news, not bad news. This hope moved her to action.

She called Bob's friends in the officers' union. She reached Pat King, the head of the Masters, Mates & Pilots union in Boston. She could not believe Bob was dead, she said. Would not. What did they know? Was it true? She would believe it only when it was official. Could Pat call, Bea pleaded, could he just call and find out? She had to know.

"Okay," King said. "But Bea, don't hold your hopes too high."

King and Charles Johnson, both friends of Bob Cusick, were nearly as devastated as Bea. But King recovered and called immediately. He threw his union weight around at Peninsula General Hospital in Salisbury and found a union rep there. "How many survivors?" "Just three," they told King. "Kelly, Dewey, and one unidentified guy. Nobody knows for sure who he is."

The unknown seaman was still unconscious, the union rep said. "Describe him," King said. "Tell me what he looks like. The guy we're looking for is Bob Cusick. He's about fifty-nine, gray hair, gray beard grown in the seafarers' manner. An older fellow. Go look at the guy. Do it now!"

The union rep was back in minutes. "Hey, really sorry. Not your man. The guy here has thick black hair. Pitch-black. Black beard. Looks like he's maybe thirty-five years old. Sorry, guys."

No way that was Cusick, and now King had to call Bea. He turned to Johnson, a closer friend of Cusick. "You do it," King pleaded. Johnson thought about it. *Bob Cusick dead! Ahh, geez.* He could not do it either. "Who can we call?" he asked.

They agreed on Captain Walter Beatteay, Cusick's old master on the *Albatross*. They had served together for years. He knew Bea well.

Beatteay was shocked and saddened by the news, reluctant to make the call. "You were his *captain*," Johnson argued. "It doesn't matter if that was years back. You still are his *captain*. You should do it." Okay, he would make the call. He hung up on King and Johnson and slowly tapped out the numbers on the key pad.

"How did you say it? Our guy didn't make it, Bea? He's gone?"

Bea was burning up the phone lines, so Beatteay's dreaded call found only a busy signal. Bea was calling them all. Family. Friends. Captain Farnham.

Farnham.

The first time she really knew what was happening, what would happen, is when she reached the regular master of the *Marine Electric*. Farnham and his wife had occasionally stayed with Bob and Bea at their home. Had eaten the "awful waffles." They knew each other well and were friends. Bob had sailed for years as Farnham's right-hand man. "Captain Farnham," she said when she reached him at home, "I have to know what's happening, whether Bob is alive or dead."

"I haven't heard anything," Farnham said, and Bea thought his voice seemed cold, distant, dead. And she thought instinctively, *he's lying.*

"I need the number of the company," Bea said.

"I don't have it," Captain Farnham said. And right then, Bea *knew.* Of course he had the number. All captains did. She knew Farnham had signed on to the other side. Knew for the first time there *were* sides.

And if he were on one side, then Bea was on the other.

Bea Cusick's awful epiphany was based on more than superstition, sea stories, or a prejudice. The tendency of Coast Guard Marine Boards of Investigation to absolve owners and blame officers is grounded in fact and history.

Cynics said it this way: First, the Coast Guard heroically rescues officers from sinking ships. Then they line up the officers in front of Marine Boards of Investigation. And summarily shoot them.

The glib generalization was far too sweeping, of course, and no one was literally shot these days. But the tradition of marine boards taking action against an officer's license, or laying the blame for a casualty on the officer, or even suggesting criminal prosecution, has traction in truth. Many officers brought before marine boards may well *wish* they had been shot, and how that could happen is the story of an old warhorse of a ship that had sailed from Texas only a few years back.

The SS *Smith Voyager* was overage when she loaded her first-ever cargo of grain at the port of Houston in 1964. Her operators, Earl J. Smith & Co., Inc., of New York, had contracted with the U.S. government to carry bulk grain to India. The vessel had been built to carry war materiel, not bulk grain. Nevertheless, the owners ordered the ship converted, with Coast Guard approval, in a mere ten days. They installed sheets of plywood that were supposed to make certain the grain was loaded evenly and kept from shifting. Tons of shifting grain at sea is a nightmare for any master.

After inspections, the Coast Guard let the *Smith Voyager* sail, even though her freshwater condenser did not work well and there were big gaps in some of the portals and doorways that were supposed to be weathertight. Numerous other systems on the old ship were marginal, susceptible to failure or just plain not working.

Frederick W. Mohle, the captain and master, loaded the ship in Houston with about 10,200 tons of winter wheat bound for Calcutta. Under such a load, the vessel sank low in the water, down to its legal marks.

But the owners, a court later said, had directed Mohle to do something they all knew was wrong. The ship *seemed* to meet its load levels in Houston. But without that freshwater condenser working correctly, she would have to take on additional freshwater en route. A few days after leaving Houston, Mohle put in at Freeport, Grand Bahama Island, and loaded up with freshwater and additional bunker oil, which lowered the ship nine inches *below* its load line.

Should Mohle have refused to do that? Yes, by any code of masters of the high seas. But in the modern world, Mohle was more a mid-level corporate go-fer than the true master of his ship. He had the job security of a migrant worker. If he were to refuse, he would be fired. If the union objected, it would be replaced by a rival. The story of owners overloading ships was an old one, dating back more than a century, to the days when Samuel Plimsoll in England crusaded for load levels and created the load marks that came to be known as Plimsoll lines.

Moreover, when Mohle's crew had attempted to load legally once before—going light on the cargo to allow for the extra water needed—the operator's agent had pressured them not to. Captain Mohle expressed concern about the overloading, but his fears were dismissed by the company. Reviewing this trip many months later, a federal court even found that the operators had *ordered* Mohle to make sure he dumped off some fuel and water on the far side of the trip. That way, he wouldn't get caught when he docked in India, as another of the company's ships had. So the operators not only knew, the court said, they encouraged the captain to be clever so that he and the company would not be caught.

So Mohle sailed. He sailed using the clever plan of the company.

The Atlantic Ocean, of course, has a talent for unraveling clever plans. "The sea will find a way," a British marine engineer once said. And in the *Smith Voyager's* case, the corners of this plan rolled up one by one, like a badly laid carpet as all the little tacks wiggled and popped loose. Each unraveling seemed minor. All, when summed, were catastrophic.

Four days at sea, they ran into real trouble. The weather turned bad and the seas rose to twenty feet, covering the bow.

Little failures, inconsequential in themselves. The rudder packing had leaked, flooding the steering engine room. One engine was shut down, then the backup burned out. The steering went down entirely. Holes were burned to drain the engine room floods. The storm came.

Little failures, one on top of another, were common in old ships. And on board the *Smith Voyager*, the failure chain continued unchecked.

Next the sanitation pump failed. As an electrician struggled to fix it, an engineer discovered a leak in the main condenser, which fed stored freshwater to the steam engine. Not only could the condenser not create enough freshwater, it could not even pass it through to the boiler.

The engineer and his chief used a low-tech approach to this problem. They fed sawdust into the main condenser. And that leak was plugged.

Meanwhile, the main steam line sprang a leak. With such a serious leak, the engine room was cleared. Now the ship was powerless. The master could neither steer nor propel the ship, and the *Smith Voyager* was taking waves broadside when she was already nine inches below her legal load line. The waves were breaking over the hatches, pounding them severely.

A short time earlier, the officer on watch had reported that the ship was listing to starboard.

Pump water and fuel to port, the master said.

But the steam leak had emptied the engine room. No power, no pumps. No propulsion. No balancing of ballast and fuel.

Now the list was ten degrees. An ominous tilt. Somehow, the grain must be shifting.

About twenty minutes after the engines stopped, there was an increase in list. The hastily installed "grain feeder boards"—the plywood designed to keep the grain stable and in place—gave way under the awkward rolling of the ship. The partitions just seemed to disintegrate, and tons and tons of grain rolled to the right side of the ship.

Now the list was twenty degrees. Beyond ominous. The storm continued to send huge waves crashing against the ship. A disassembled door on the main deck, no longer watertight, was allowing tons of water into the ship. The holes, burned earlier to let water *out* of the steering compartments, were allowing water *in*.

Then the ship took another big roll in the waves and stayed at a perilous thirty- to thirty-five-degree angle—a third of the way toward capsizing at ninety degrees.

The radio officer needed help from a colleague to hold his chair in place. Otherwise, it slid to the far corner of the radio shack, with the radio officer in the chair. The ship was rolling farther with each big wave, now, righting only to the thirty-five-degree mark.

The electrician, busy on the sanitation pump, noticed smoke coming from the main generator's panel. He went behind the switchboard and found water spraying with great force through a crack in the hull of the old ship.

The ship hoisted distress flags. The radio officer was hailing ships far and wide, asking them to stand by. The *Smith Voyager* was in real trouble. Even with help, Sparks could not keep his chair at the radio from sliding.

About 1 P.M., Captain Mohle saw a big bulge in the number-four hatch—a sign to him that the grain had shifted and might be swelling. He had intermittent power at best and a thirty-five-degree list, abeam to big rollers, with the situation getting worse. Like Corl, Mohle looked at his cards. A responsible electrician had reported water spraying with pressure through the hull. He was on a nineteen-year-old ship that had poor maintenance and worse operators. More than thirty lives were at stake.

It was enough. He sounded the general alarm, a ten-second blast on the ship's horn, then told the radio officer to send out the SOS and the crew to launch number-one lifeboat.

And then the deaths commenced in the usual manner.

A lifeboat swamped. The men clambered in anyway. A nearby cargo ship, the West German *Mathilde Bolten,* had steamed to the rescue. The men paddled the swamped lifeboat to the sheer wall of the big ship. Cargo nets and rescue lines were draped down. Men jumped to the nets of the big ship. The first batch timed the waves just right and made it.

The second effort was a catastrophe. Men grasping for the cargo nets outweighed the men trying to balance the lifeboat. The boat capsized.

And, as ill-timed and inevitable as could be, a huge wave carried the swamped lifeboat—heavy with tons of water inside it—and flung it against the hull of the *Mathilde Bolten*. And against the fragile men who had fallen in between.

The ocean is ever egalitarian in such times, indiscriminate of rank or department. The chief engineer, the third cook, a steward, and an oiler all were crushed to death.

The ship itself survived for days and was taken under tow, still listing, before she sank on December 27, 1964.

In retrospect, the fact that only four men had died seemed a minor miracle, given the rust, overloading, leaks, and equipment failure. Other masters had fared far worse under similar situations.

The courts ruled later that the old tub was clearly unseaworthy and should never have gone to sea. And that the owners not only knew the ship was sunk below her marks, but had ordered it and then sought to cover it up, a judge wrote.

The Marine Board of Investigation told a different story. Initially, it recommended that the owners be investigated for knowingly sending the old ship to sea in an unsafe condition and that the captain also be investigated for knowingly loading the ship beyond load limits and for "prematurely abandoning the ship." The swollen number-four hatch? That was just the billowing of a tarp, not swollen grain, the board said.

Mohle should have kept his cool and could have saved the ship if he had. He should be investigated to see if his license should be stripped.

But there was no reason to fault the Coast Guard, the board said, ". . . or any personnel of the Coast Guard or any other government agency or any other person . . ."

Yet, the facts of the report itself seemed to document clearly how the ship was allowed by inspectors to sail with a condenser that didn't work, with doors that weren't weathertight, with a rudder packing that leaked, with a grain-storage system that failed catastrophically, with a hull that sprang leaks, with a sanitation pump that did not work, with bilge pumps that did not work, with a condenser system that was inoperative except when fixed with sawdust, and with a main steam line that sprang leaks. At various times, the captain had no power, no steering, a thirty-five-degree list, shifting grain, twenty-foot waves, water over the hatches, and a radio operator who was sliding around the ship like a punk skateboarder. And *despite* that, he saved all but four of his crew. In any other line of work, he might have been a hero.

As in all marine boards, the commandant of the Coast Guard has the final say and can overturn conclusions of the board that seem ungrounded.

And to his mind, he did just that.

Forget prosecuting the owners, Admiral W. J. Smith ruled. You haven't shown they really knew, and besides, "The first and primary responsibility for the safety and seaworthiness of an American flag vessel must rest with the Master and the vessel's officers."

Concentrate on Mohle, the commandant said in effect. Not the owners. Not the Coast Guard. Nail the captain.

The *Smith Voyager* case was not atypical. Old, unsteady ships were being sent to sea under great pressure from owners, and the masters really had little control, if they wanted work. Yet, it was not the owners who were blamed or the old, infirm ships themselves. The operational managers—the officers—were blamed for the sins of the system.

Years later, Dr. Charles Perrow, a Yale University professor of sociology, would write a book entitled *Normal Accidents* and find that this behavior was typical in the maritime system, a system that alone among major industrial bureaucracies was actually organized to *induce* errors, not correct them.

An enterprising Perrow student, Leo Tasca, had painstakingly examined four Marine Board of Investigation cases and their findings. Then he took the same cases and analyzed how they came out in courts of law. In each case, the owners and operators were found clearly liable and paid handsome sums. Yet the heart of each case was essentially ignored by the marine boards. The results were so clear-cut, said Perrow, who previously had viewed the Coast Guard as above reproach, that he could only conclude the Coast Guard was "highly biased" toward owners.

• • •

Bea did not know any of this at the time, of course. She simply knew the folklore of how officers were blamed and what the tone of Farnham's voice meant.

His voice was toneless, dead. She hung up on him. Sharply. Slammed the phone down. It was the rudest thing she had done in her life. She just had no time for him, if that's how it was.

She began to pick up the receiver to make another call, trying to bring back her husband from the rumors of his death. But her phone rang first. It was Corl's wife. Phil is dead, she said. I know he's dead. Oh, Bea, I wish I had taken the trip. I wish I had gone down with him, Bea. I would give anything to have gone with him.

Elsewhere, the wives and parents of the crewmen played grim variations on this mournful tune. Relatives, close friends, and colleagues all were getting the news, some of it wrong, most of it dreadfully correct.

S. I. Pirtle, a woman officer the crew called Sam, had sailed on the ship a few months earlier. She tried but could not deny the pictures she saw in the *Atlanta Constitution*. There were her old friends in grainy black and white.

Pete Delatolla looked back at her, his face round and blank, she thought, showing nothing of the good man she knew, so full of emotion and energy. Pete's right-hand man, Jose Fernandez, dressed up in the photo. Hands always full of tools in real life. Robert Harrell and Robert Hern, ordinary seamen so close together in life, the refrain was always, "Where are Harrell and Hern? Go get Harrell and Hern." Together now, side-by-side in the newspaper.

Charlie Johnson, Edward Mathews, Jose Quinones. All her friends, older men who were so kind to her they left Madeira wine, homemade birthday cards, and a gaily colored wicker basket in her cabin on her twenty-third birthday.

Sam Pirtle's hands shook so hard they rattled the newspaper. All her wonderful friends were dead, all her dear friends from her very first ship.

Mary Babineau could not find out anything and would not for two days. Even then, the story was unclear.

Still, she knew Clayt was dead, felt it, and knew she was going to have to do it. Walk into his den and office. Open the file he had told her about. She hated him for those damned lists! And when she opened it, all she could think of was, *Oh, Clayt, I love you so. The one thing I hated about you, those lists, they're all I have now.*

Everything to do was there on his list. The lawyer to call. The insurance. Instructions on how she should reject the first offer, no matter what.

She was overwhelmed. *Give it to God,* she thought. *You cannot handle it. Clayt is gone. Give your grief to God. And follow Clayt's list. Follow the list. It is a gift. The list has given you six months of Clayt, six months of him.*

Marsha Price awoke at seven that morning, about the time the choppers were carrying Cusick back to land. She looked outside and saw snow in three-foot drifts.

Well, she thought to herself, *no Girl Scout meeting for Heather today.*

Then she flipped on the radio for the weather report and heard the news. An unidentified ship was lost off the Virginia coast.

A shudder ran through her as she thought, *Oh, no, it can't be him, it can't be Mike.* They were having dinner with George Dolak tonight. *Don't be silly,* she thought, and then the news said the ship was carrying coal and flew an American flag.

Heather watched her mom sob, then pace back and forth. "What's wrong, Mom?" she asked.

"Mommie is just having a bad day, honey," Marsha Price said.

Heather was only eight, but she knew that wasn't true. It was something else, she thought. Adults were funny sometimes.

Friends came over and relatives, too, and her mom seemed to cry even more. "How could this happen?" they asked. "It can't be so." And when Heather asked what was happening, her mom told her, "Daddy's ship has capsized, honey." And she thought, *Hmm, that's a word I don't know,* capsized.

They told her *capsized* meant "sunk," and she filed that information away and learned a new word and thought, "Okay, but where is my Daddy? He should be home on Saturday."

Her mother and relatives and friends were in the other room

when the television news said the ship was the *Marine Electric* and all on board were lost. Heather was not sure at all what was going on, but there was a sudden surge of moans and cries in the other room, and then her uncles and aunts and friends glided from the room with strange, concerned looks on their faces. They stood around Heather, very close to her, and put their hands on her shoulder and head. The eight-year-old thought, *They are sheltering me.*

She had no idea why. It was silly to think her Daddy was not coming back. She was used to him being gone at sea for days, weeks, months. Of that she had no fear. This circle of adults, though, frightened her. To her, the circle was . . . ominous.

Marsha Price had never felt such emotions and conflict. Moments after the radio news, she felt a deep cutting blade of grief slice through her, emotions with an edge and depth she did not know existed. They cut deep, deep within her, and freed sounds and moans she had never heard before from anyone.

Then she would tell herself, *No, wait. You don't know. You don't know it's his ship.* And when she learned about the ship, she said to herself, *No, you don't know if he's dead. Mike will survive. This is* Mike *you're talking about. He's too stubborn to die.*

And when they said all the men had been lost, she still did not believe that. The company called, tried to be helpful, but said their people were trapped in the blizzard, too, so the news was slow getting to them.

When the company did send news, it placed Marsha Price in a horrible purgatory worse than hell, and in there with her were the other relatives of the engine room men.

The engine room guys, the company told her, were unaccounted for. There was a slight chance they were trapped below. Don't count on it, but Mike might still be alive. They all might be trapped down there. There were reports of noises down there. The company was going to send down divers.

Steve Browning's father, from the hills of West Virginia, would tell friends, "My boy is going to be fine. The company is a-goin' to save him. He's down there in a air pocket, and they're gonna save him. The company told me so."

The engine room men might be down there. They might not.

But for certain, some of the families, their loved ones, were trapped in a small air pocket of hope. They gasped at that hope, as if it were precious oxygen, and fought against the grief and sorrow that surrounded them. Every hour with no word meant less hope for them to breathe, but they could do nothing else but crowd into the small bubble of hope.

The Wickboldts were not among those hoping for a miracle. Early Saturday morning, Catherina and Richard Wickboldt were out together shoveling snow off the sidewalks. The grief of the loss of their son on the *Golden Dolphin* nearly a year earlier had slowly subsided.

Inside, the phone rang and rang. Catherina stomped the snow off her boots and went to answer it.

Mrs. Wickboldt, a man's voice said, I am from Marine Transport Lines and it is my unfortunate duty to tell you that the *Marine Electric* is down and your son George Wickboldt is dead.

Catherina Wickboldt laughed to herself and could not believe how mixed up bureaucracies could become.

"No, no," she said to the man patiently. "You're making a mistake. We lost a son at sea last year, but his name is Steven, not George, and the ship was the *Golden Dolphin*. You've got it all mixed up."

I'm sorry, Mrs. Wickboldt, the man said, but I'm talking about George Wickboldt on the *Marine Electric*.

Mildly exasperated at the man's denseness, Catherina Wickboldt called to her husband. This was like the cable guy messing up the service or the mechanic not knowing what was wrong with the car. They wouldn't listen to a woman. Her husband would straighten him out.

"Richard," she said, cupping the phone. "It's some fellow calling about Steven, but he's got the names all mixed up. You tell him, I can't make him understand."

Catherina was ready to go back outside to shovel more snow when she saw her husband's face change. He did not have to say a word. She knew. It could not happen again. They could not lose another son to the sea.

But they had. Their Georgie was dead. Steven and George, just nineteen months apart, had been almost like twin brothers. Catherina Wickboldt looked up one day to see Steven, just four, walking on the back of the couch, hands out for balance. Climbing up behind him, just a little over two, was Georgie, making the same dangerous trip down the thin ledge of couch. Now they both were gone.

Friends were coming over to the house again, and their sons and daughters gathered about them. The two remaining sons were maritime professionals. There's no way he got out of the engine room, they thought. So when the company man called to tell the Wickboldts there might be someone down there alive, none of the Wickboldts believed it. He had drowned, or been crushed, or struck by the superheated steam, or succumbed to hypothermia.

But they knew he was dead. They knew Georgie had again followed Steven, just as he had as a young boy, and that the two brothers were together now. The grief was unbearable, but to them the fact was believable. They all had too much experience in learning about death at sea.

Julie, Gene Kelly's wife, learned of her husband's death early Saturday morning, when Gene, in fact, was lying back, quite alive, in a warm steel tub in the Maryland hospital. All hands were gone. The news said so. Friends told her so.

She was a widow. She was a widow with a seven-month-old beautiful baby girl. She began the slow, tearful process of accepting that fact, letting the emotional hypothermia slowly suck any feeling of happiness from her. Gene was gone.

Then, at 10 A.M., the telephone rang.

Chapter Twelve

THE FROG

What the eye does not see, the heart does not feel . . .

Samuel Plimsoll

nineteenth-century maritime reformer

10:00 a.m. / Sunday, Feb. 13, 1983 / *Philadelphia Inquirer* newsroom

By 10:30 on the Sunday morning after the sinking of the *Marine Electric*, Eugene Roberts, executive editor of the *Philadelphia Inquirer*, was calling editors and reporters at their homes. There seemed no plausible explanation for why he was doing this. Roberts was not a morning man, for one thing. He preferred working late into the evening as the newspaper drove toward its final edition deadline.

Moreover, few *Marine Electric* crew members were from his circulation area, and Philadelphia was 102 nautical miles up the Delaware River from the sea. So there was no strong "local angle" to mobilize his news staff.

Roberts himself cut no swashbuckling figure that made you think of a hero or great newspaper crusader dashing into action. In fact, if there was an un–McCann, an exact opposite of the pumped-up and heroic Navy diver, the un–McCann would seem to be Gene Roberts. Ben Bradlee, the famous editor of the *Washington Post,* once was said to have the bearing of an international gambler. Roberts seemed more a small-town Southerner come to the big city. Long ago, his staff had affectionately nicknamed him "The Frog," based in part on his apparent laconic manner.

And all of it was deceptive. Gene Roberts was one of the most formidable, driven journalistic forces in America in 1983, and he was about to set a team of investigative reporters upon a world that was rarely covered by the American media.

Samuel Plimsoll, the great maritime reformer of the nineteenth century, had explained it succinctly. "What the eye does not see, the heart does not feel . . ." More than 100 years later, the great collective eye of the media still saw little of the suffering of seamen, and the heart of the public therefore felt little.

But Roberts had. He had seen it and he had felt it. And now he was about to do something about it.

In fact, there was a fierce crusader behind Roberts's down-home exterior. Deconstructionists said it came from his boyhood in segregated North Carolina and one incident in particular. Roberts and his friends were swimming in a river when they heard shouts of alarm. A teenager had gotten into trouble in the water. He was pulled out and could have been saved if only the ambulance had come on time. The ambulance never came. It was a white ambulance. There was no black ambulance. The black kid died, right there, with Gene looking on in disbelief.

Some swore the young Gene Roberts figuratively was standing on that riverbank watching every time the adult journalist wrote or edited an exposé. When he was a reporter in Detroit. Then metropolitan editor. Then a reporter for the *New York Times* on the civil rights beat. Then Saigon bureau chief of the *Times,* and then national editor. Then editor of everything at the *Inquirer.* With the best reporting, with the best writing, with the most intelligent research and context, he would find and attack systems of injustice with a great ferocity.

In the case of the *Marine Electric,* another part of his past came into play. Long ago, early in his career, he had covered the waterfront for a Norfolk paper. Alone among senior editors in America, he knew both the heartbreaking nature of the business and its potential for good stories. He was convinced Philadelphia needed a maritime writer, even though the city's days as a great port were fast ebbing. For years now, he had been attempting to get a reporter to fill that beat, and only recently had he succeeded.

Now he had his maritime writer on the phone, and Roberts's directions were as clear as they were sweeping. Figure out what it is you need in terms of travel, people, editors, photographers to get the story. You'll have all those things on Monday. Whatever you need. I want you to go heads down on this with Larry Williams. He'll be your project editor. Come talk with me when you're ready to go.

It was a lot for Roberts to say, because his most effective communication many times was silence. He'd first seen the merit of silence selling Bibles door-to-door in his younger days. He would knock on a door with a bag of Bibles in his hand and say "Hey!" when the door opened. Then he would remain perfectly quiet. Inevitably, the sales target would say, "What you got in that bag, son?" and Roberts would be through the door.

Silence could open a lot more doors than fast talking. As a reporter, he found that a studied silence often pumped out information from people far more effectively than questions. He used the same technique as a manager. He simply stated an acutely focused goal and was silent while his reporters and editors talked and talked around the goal until they had it right.

So he had said few words this Sunday on the phone, but everyone on the line knew that each word weighed a ton, and they were about to do some journalistic heavy lifting.

Roberts and his staff would win a string of seventeen Pulitzer Prizes in eighteen years, and most of them were a result of the man's willingness to commit huge resources on investigative projects. Now they were about to mount a classic *Inquirer* investigation into the sinking of the *Marine Electric,* and they all knew the upside and downside of such a venture. The upside was the best working conditions anywhere in the world for serious investigative reporting. Some of Roberts's reporters had worked for two years on projects, and their series covered pages and pages of the newspaper for days on end. This sort of commitment earned Roberts a reputation among many as the best newspaper editor of his era.

The downside was that any number of excellent journalists had worked months and months on some projects, only to see the stories killed because the story, it turned out, simply was not there. Roberts had learned that lesson about silence, too. Newspapers that were new to investigative journalism often were filled with stories that were not so much "in-depth" as "in-length." When they had half the story, they made up for that by running them twice as long.

Roberts demanded the whole story. Or nothing.

On Monday, his maritime writer was in Roberts's office, giving all the wrong answers. It was clear even from the initial wire reports that the old ship had had her share of repair problems. The reporter wanted to chase them down, hit the hiring halls, talk to seamen. The reporter had covered an earlier sinking of an old ship, the SS *Poet,* but never really nailed the story. This time, the story would pop open.

But Roberts suggested a change in tactics and pace. Most reporters were sprinters. On projects, Roberts wanted marathoners. Don't go chasing after the seamen in the hiring halls, he told the maritime writer. They aren't likely to talk right away. They will talk with time.

This time, don't go broad. Go deep. If the system is rotten, it had a beginning. Lay out a statistical case that is bulletproof. Go back through the files and find where this started. Go all the way back to World War II if you need to. You've got the time and the resources.

Go back in time. Drill down. Find out how it all started.

Then people might talk on the record for a change, he said. And we can nail the whole system—not just one bad ship. Go for the whole system. If it's as bad as we think it is, change the whole system.

The reporter was obstinate and unrelenting. Roberts drifted away. His head bobbed down and then up, nodding up and down slightly, for all the world like one of those toy dog figures in the back windows of automobiles. The reporter was running on and on about the better way to cover the story, and Roberts let the reporter run on. He looked up and to the right at a ceiling tile in the corner of his office. He was far, far away. Silence served him well in management. Once, after a prolonged bout of silence, a reporter had asked him, "Gene? Are you there? Did you just take a walk around the block in Saigon?"

But now the reporter had vented and come around without Roberts uttering a word in argument or direction. "Gene, what the hell am I doing?" the reporter said. "You were *talking* to me and I wasn't listening. I got it. You're absolutely right. We'll do the system. Can I fly down to Washington instead of driving?"

Oh, Roberts said, with a smile and eyes that laughed at them both and flashed with a fierce intelligence. You can do anything you want. You've got anything you need.

And soon the team the *Inquirer* had gathered began to show just how bad the system was. Roberts heard the progress in weekly reports.

A week later, Larry Williams, the project editor, got an excited call from one of the reporters digging through files.

The class of ship to which the *Marine Electric* belonged was structurally unsound.

It always had been.

The T-2 tankers, built during World War II, were serial sinkers. Some even sank at dockside. They were built of "dirty steel." They contained "tired iron." By one count, more than 500 men had died on old ships in accidents that never should have happened.

The *Marine Electric* may finally have sunk on February 12, 1983. But it had begun slipping beneath the waves four decades earlier.

As Roberts shuffled through the notes, he was a lot more reserved than the reporter. It was a good start. What it wasn't yet was a story.

It might never be.

Chapter Thirteen

WHY YOU?

Richard Bishop, the Fitzgerald's *first cook, lives a haunted life,
unwilling to talk about the ship or the men who die in her, refusing to
share his pain with even his closest friends or his family. . . . And in
his dreams he still hears the same bitter question other shipwreck
survivors have heard before him: Why you?*

ROBERT J. HEMMING
Gales of November, The Sinking of the Edmund Fitzgerald

9 A.M. / SATURDAY, FEB. 12, 1983 / PENINSULA GENERAL HOSPITAL
SALISBURY, MARYLAND

In the Maryland hospital, a doctor was working on the "unknown
seaman." Pitch-black oil coated his beard and hair and made the man
look younger than he was. Hair looked like a passable dye job.

Would love to know how low the man's core body temperature
had gone, the doctor thought. What a case study! Almost three
hours in the water. It did not happen. Now his body temperature
was above ninety-eight degrees. Looked like he was going to make
it. Things here you had to watch for. A lot of cold blood out there
in the limbs. Little tricks of hypothermia. Let's do this slowly and
gently. Keep the crash cart handy. Heartbeat a little irregular, but
strong enough. Pulse a little spotty, but good enough. Actually, he
was doing better than the younger guys a few beds over.

Bob Cusick awoke, saw the doctor with the stethoscope, grabbed
the doctor's arms in a firm grip, and said:

"My name is Bob Cusick. My telephone number is 617–545–
9378. Call my wife.

"Tell her I made it. Tell her I am okay."

The doctor's voice was calm. He took Bob's hands away and rested them gently on the bed. "All in due time," he said. "All in due time."

Cusick looked about him. There were bills, ones and fives and tens, hanging on a line near the bed in the hospital, like sheets from the washer. Drying, he thought. They are mine, he thought.

He turned his head again. His Seiko Navigator wristwatch was on the bedside next to him, the one he had bought in Hong Kong in the 1960s when he was making Asian runs.

Mine, he thought. He focused in on it. Still ticking. He could see the second hand moving slowly, and the red hand he could adjust to Greenwich Mean Time. It was a good watch. Strange, the whole time in the water he had never looked at it.

In due time, the doctor was telling him again, we will call your wife. All in due time. First we take care of you, and he methodically continued his exam and care for this person who said he was Bob Cusick, married to Bea.

And Bob Cusick relaxed. In all of Christ's land, he knew two comforting truths.

He was alive. He was warm. Cozy. Toasty. So very warm.

Up north, Captain Beatteay tapped out the call to Bea another time. He still did not know how to say it. He did not know who the survivor was, just that it wasn't Bob Cusick. The line was busy. Saved again from this awful errand for a few short seconds. He hung up and dialed again. Now, God help him find the words, the call was going through.

Bea picked up. She seemed unnaturally ebullient, given the givens. Maybe hysterical. Bea, I'm afraid I have bad news, he was going to say, when she interrupted him and said, "Oh, Captain Beatteay, it's okay! I just got off the phone with the doctor in the hospital. Bob is alive. He just had oil in his beard. They didn't think it was Bob. Even Kelly and Dewey didn't know who he was."

Beatteay called King and Johnson, and the two of them

whooped in celebration. Their old friend was back from the dead. Resurrected from the body of a black-bearded thirty-five-year-old.

A similar script played out with Julie Kelly. They had put Gene Kelly in a steel tub with warm water to bring his body temperature back. Soon he was officially okay, and they said he could make a call. At home in Massachusetts, Julie Kelly had learned she was a widow early Saturday morning and was still adjusting to that, crying, looking at their seven-month-old daughter, so peaceful and innocent of this worst of all developments.

At 10 A.M., the phone rang. Already the calls of condolence were coming. Soon they would bring food over. Gene Kelly's widow picked up the phone.

The voice on the line was Gene.

She paused. He was dead. He was alive.

"I made it," Kelly said. "I made it."

"They told me everyone was lost," she said at last. Her tone was distinctly dubious.

"I don't care what they told you," Kelly said. "I'm alive, hon. I made it."

And the tears came again, grief and happiness, all mixed together.

In Maryland, Cusick's warm glowing moment had passed, and now he felt considerably older than thirty-five. Older than fifty-nine. A nurse had asked him: "The oil isn't coming out of your beard. Mind if I just shave it off?" "Sure," Cusick said. Bea would like that. She hated the beard. And when the nurse carefully shaved off the beard and the oil in it, he looked even younger. Baby-faced. But he felt like the oldest man in the world. His core body temperature had warmed to normal after a few hours under blankets and pads. Bea was on the way. All that was good news.

But the other news was awful. The nurse told him that only he and two others had made it, and it still had not hit him. She tried to tell him more, but her supervisor came in, angry because she had shaved off Bob's beard instead of cleaning it. "It's okay," Bob Cusick said. "I asked her to. It's okay." But the bedside nurse was in deep trouble with her boss now and was telling no more tales.

Only when Dewey, Kelly, and Cusick were together in the same room were they able to piece it together. They had seen several helicopters out there. And several ships. They assumed that others had been fished out alive and were in other hospitals. They hoped they were.

"No," said the doctors. "You three are it. No one else survived."

Cusick's first reaction was to think, *You're kidding. Come on. It's a bad joke.* Then he thought about it. Of course it was true. The engine room guys never had a chance with stuff falling all over. He had heard this tremendous racket, a screeching of iron and steel as the ship tipped. The boilers probably exploded. If not, then the cold water killed them, or they drowned.

The others? How close had Cusick come? The deckhouse falling on top of them all. Cusick just managing to swim down and up. Finding the oar. The strange pull of the line. Finding the lifeboat. Of course they all were dead. It was a miracle he was alive.

And then he thought more. *"Are we going to make it, Charlie?" "No, Mate, we're not."* Charlie Johnson from Alabama, the best bosun you could want, was gone. Charlie with his young kids. Charlie, always there for him. His strong, strong right hand. The cadet was gone, too. Wickboldt. And Price, with his wife and daughter. Heather was the daughter's name. And Price's dreams. The dreams they had talked about for quiet hours. All gone.

And he, Cusick, fifty-nine, a full life lived already, was alive.

Why?

What was the reason?

The question first struck him in the hospital. Like the spotlight of the chopper on the *Theodora,* it was a cone of light, a ray, fixing him, freezing him.

He could already feel the families of the dead men asking that same question. Why my husband, father, brother, lover, son? With his full life ahead of him. Why him and not you, old mate?

Cusick's exuberance at surviving was quickly carried down, like the men trapped under the main deckhouse as it sank, pushing them down. He felt his spirit falling, pushed down, down. He clawed and scrambled in his mind, trying to escape the feeling. But it was always there. Why? Why him?

A psychologist might have diagnosed it as survivor's guilt, might then have identified the subgenre "existential survivor's guilt" as the strain infecting Robert Manning Cusick.

And a psychologist who was at all familiar with maritime hierarchies and responsibilities would have quickly noted that there was little or no evidence of "content guilt" in Bob Cusick's demeanor.

Content guilt kicks in when the survivor—justified or not—concludes that something in the "content" of the disaster was caused by him. Or that he could have done something to prevent the disaster, but did not. People who have, in reality, absolutely nothing to do with the accident or death frequently blame themselves. Oh, if only I had not invited Aunt Mabel for Christmas, she would not have gotten on the plane that was hijacked by terrorists . . . that flew into that unpredicted storm . . . that was struck by lightning . . . that crashed after the seagull was sucked into the jet engine. It was all my fault.

Kelly, in fact, soon felt this sort of content guilt, however baseless in fact. He had stood the eight-to-twelve watch, the one before the foundering. What had he missed? It all had been so quiet. Normal. He must have missed something. Not heard something. He was a good officer. But he must have missed something, sent all those men to their deaths.

No one then or since has suggested he did anything wrong or that he missed anything. But the thoughts and the guilt were relentless. The nagging question hit him first in the hospital, and they checked out with him as well.

Dewey, too, seemed to blame himself somehow. "I lost my guys," he would say of the men near his raft. "I lost my guys."

But those particular furies did not dog the chief mate. Cusick knew for certain that something had gone wrong with the *Marine Electric.* If she had been whole, a ship her size would not have sunk in this storm. Scores of vessels, many smaller, had survived the storm.

And he knew for certain that the company had done a pretty awful job of repairing the ship and that something in the age of the ship, the repair of the ship, had caused the sinking, had caused the deaths. That the hatch covers were more holed than whole. That the vessel was riddled with cracks. That the iron was tired, and "tired iron" lost its life and ability to flex.

The idea that he might have blown the whistle flitted across his mind. But only briefly. The system worked the way it worked. As an officer, his duty was to report the items of disrepair to his captain, who in turn was to report them to the company, who in turn was to report them to the Coast Guard and repair them.

Cusick knew he had reported items to the captain, had in fact thoroughly documented the ninety-some holes in the hatch covers, the hole in the hull he had patched with a coffee can lid, the cracks in the deck, the watertight doors that were missing, the hatches that would not close correctly, the hatch braces carried on board but never installed.

Did the captain then bump that upstairs to the maintenance managers in the company? Cusick thought Farnham had. Was sure he had, in fact, on some of them, because Cusick had discussed it with the corporate guy, James Thelgie, the Fleet Director. But it was beyond Cusick's charter and rank to do more. He had done his job. He was not a Crusader Rabbit who insisted that repairs be made and I mean right now. That was not his training. That was not how chains of command worked. Always the chief mate, never the master. The number two. That is who he was.

And what if he had called the Coast Guard? Babineau had done so, with no impact. And the inspectors could not miss what was wrong anyway. In one case, a crack in the deck was circled in white paint and chalk so that no one would trip or got a shoe caught in it. The inspectors literally had stepped over it.

He had done what he could do. And done it well. He knew that and was not going to beat himself up over it.

So it was not that sort of guilt—content guilt—that was pressing him down, drowning his spirit.

It was the other. What the survival psychologists called existential guilt. And in some ways, this was the more deadly variety. A psychologist would say that existential guilt dealt with the very meaning of life and forced sufferers to confront a question they had not explored. Or had comfortably answered, but could not now.

If I survived, why? If I survived, there must be a meaning, a reason why. Something I am supposed to do.

But what? Many survivors never find it. They stare into the abyss and are unable to create a meaning for themselves. They founder, wallow in depression, leave families, jobs, dream of trading places with the dead, become suicidal, and remain profoundly saddened their whole lives.

On the Great Lakes, they call it the "why you" syndrome. Some people shake it. Some are ruined by it. And it means even the survivors of gruesome shipwrecks could have a part of their lives claimed forever by the tragedies. That they only partly survived.

So it was for the sole survivor of the SS *Daniel Morrell,* which made its last voyage some seventeen years before the *Marine Electric* tragedy.

The ship was sixty years old—christened before the original Great War—when it was sent into the gales of November in 1966 from Buffalo bound for Taconite, Minnesota, on the Great Lakes. It was scheduled to be her last voyage of the season. It would be her last voyage, period.

Soon gale-force winds whipped up waves of twenty-five feet. Watchman Dennis Hale went to bed about 11 P.M. on November 28 and awoke about 2 A.M. to the sound of a loud bang. The "loud report" so familiar to marine board reports on the old ships.

Then there was another bang. Hale watched in horror as the books on his shelf fell onto the floor. They had never done that before, because the books were mounted fore and aft and were not subject to wave action. The fact that they fell meant the ship was somehow bending in two, rocking fore and aft, not left to right in the wash of the waves.

Then the general alarm sounded, and Hale grabbed his life jacket, forgetting the books, forgetting, in fact, his pants. He rushed back to find them but in the darkness could not, and he ended up leaving, virtually bare-ass, wearing only his woolen pea coat and underpants. Then he dashed to the deck and ran to the forward life raft.

Now it was clear the ship was splitting in two. A close knot of his fellow crew and officers stood around the raft.

"Get on the raft and hold on tight," someone said.

No attempt was made to launch the raft. They would just let it float free. The master, the first mate, the second, all sat in the raft, as if in one of those inflatable backyard splash pools, waiting, waiting, watching sparks from the two halves of the vessel as they grated on each other. The ship's hull had severed most of the way through, but not entirely. Perhaps the ship would hold together. Maybe they could get out of this with no butcher's bill to pay in a currency of dead men.

Then the vessel broke cleanly in two. Waves crashed over the men on the bow in the raft and dumped them and the raft willy-nilly into the raging lake. All of this—the initial crack, the general alarm, the final split, the big wave, the men hitting the water—took only eight minutes.

Hale, wearing the pea coat, his undershorts, and a life jacket, clambered from the waves back into the raft. Everyone else had been thrown clear as well. Two deckhands, Arthur Stojek and John Cleary, Jr., were already in the raft, and Charles Fosbender, the wheelsman, reached it soon afterward.

They saw no one else. The officers were just gone, all of them.

The men shot off flares. No one answered. The men lay on the raft, hugging each other to keep warm. They had no radio. No one knew where they were in the dead of night, in the heart of a snowy, gale-blown blizzard on Lake Huron, in subfreezing winds that blew the waves to twenty feet. No one even knew the ship had sunk.

They clung to one another for more than seven hours. Cleary remained conscious right up until he died about 6 A.M. Stojek died right after Cleary.

So it was just Hale and Fosbender. Robert J. Hemming, an author who researched the wreck, told what that was like.

Fosbender grew weaker and complained that his lungs were filling with ice. Hale told him, "Crawl near me." Fosbender did, but rose up as he was crawling and said he saw a ship through the snowy blizzard.

But there was none. The men huddled together through the morning. No rescue. Then it was 2 P.M., a full twelve hours after the ship had sunk. No rescue. And then it was 4 P.M. The men had been dunked in the water and had floated in an open raft for fourteen hours.

"Denny," Fosbender said to Hale. "I'm going to throw in the sponge."

And with that, Fosbender turned his head and died.

Hale buried himself beneath the bodies of his frozen colleagues, seeking any refuge from the gale and the windchill that sought to steal his body heat and life. All that night, he thought he could see the lights of farmhouses on shore. But he knew he could not walk if he washed ashore. His feet were just not there, had no feeling. He moved back and forth between consciousness and darkness.

He made it through the night, then felt suddenly hungry and began eating chips of ice. Then an apparition appeared, Hemming wrote, an old bearded man with a milk-white complexion and commanding eyes. Don't eat the ice, said the vision.

Hale blacked out again. Woke up again. Blacked out. Woke up. Started eating ice again. The vision came again and, Hemming wrote, lectured Hale sternly:

"I told you not to eat the ice off your coat! It will lower your body temperature and you will die!"

Hale dropped the ice and lapsed into a stupor.

Late Wednesday afternoon, nearly twenty-six hours after the ship had sunk, a Coast Guard helicopter pilot spotted the raft with nothing but dead bodies in it. He landed on what were now quiet waters and began loading the corpses onto the chopper.

Then Hale's right arm popped up from among the dead men, and his eerie pale white head followed. Hale had severe frostbite but otherwise was okay.

Physically, he was okay.

Physically, he had survived. Emotionally, like Cusick, he was deeply wounded.

As Hemming wrote, "He suffered a greater form of torture as a result of his nightmare on Lake Huron . . . The 'why-you syndrome.'

"Hale never went back on the lakes. He works as a machinist in Ohio, never wanting to discuss his memories or relive his nightmare."

And it was the same, later, when the *Edmund Fitzgerald* went down on Lake Superior in 1975. Richard Bishop, the *Fitzgerald*'s first cook, was in port, off duty when the whole crew was lost on the *Fitzgerald*. Hemming says he "lives a haunted life, unwilling to talk about the ship or the men who died in her, refusing to share his pain with even his closest friends or his family. . . . And in his dreams he still hears the same bitter question other shipwreck survivors have heard before him: "Why you?"

After the *Marine Electric*'s sinking, Bea could already feel that Bob was headed that way. And Bea was heading to the same space. She could reflect emotions from across the room. In a tight moment, a real moment, she was right there, those antennae searching, reflecting back what you were feeling.

And now she could feel what Bob felt. Her antennae were so acute. Too acute now. Families of those who did not survive wanted to talk to her. To find out: What was my husband doing when Bob last saw him? Tell me how he met his end. Did he suffer? Did he say anything about me? Tell Bob anything for me? Tell me something.

She was kind, and they were kind. But she could feel the *unasked* questions they all had. Oh, you are so lucky, Bea, they would say, with a strange inflection in their voice, a wondering inflection. Or so she thought. Later, none of them would recall such thoughts, did not think they had them. What they meant, Bea knew, when they were being kind was really, why *your* husband and not mine? Why did Bob Cusick survive?

And Bea, so sensitive, felt very bad. It was true, she thought. Bob and she had had a good life. Had a full life. And these young people, these poor, poor young people. One with a young daughter.

Some just married. Some just about to be married. She knew all the ship's stories. It was not fair. They were right. How did God make such picks? She cried at their loss. And at her gain. And her guilt.

And then she thought, Wait. Bob has a life, a wife, a daughter. We didn't make this decision. We didn't have a choice.

Bea thought of Carol, her daughter, a college junior in Amherst, and realized she must think her dad dead. She called Carol's dorm room at the University of Massachusetts. No answer. No roommate.

Carol Cusick in fact was enjoying a normal day at school. In no way, manner, shape, or form did that involve piling out of bed early on a Saturday to listen to the news. And any friends who did listen certainly did not know that her father was chief mate on the *Marine Electric*.

So she was out, heading toward a dinner with friends. Only later, in her dorm room, did she understand that something was amiss. Phone service was out at Carol's place, disrupted by the storm. Bea had called the state police. A trooper agreed to find her, tell Carol that her father was okay.

A little later, at Carol's room, there was a knock on the door. She opened it to see a uniformed trooper standing formally before her.

"Ms. Cusick, I am here to tell you that your father is okay and alive. He is one of the survivors."

Carol's face dropped, and her body shivered.

"Survivor of *what?*" she said.

"Why, the wreck of the *Marine Electric,* ma'am." the trooper said. "His ship sank this morning."

And Carol slumped back in a chair. The officer gave her the basics. Many dead. Your father survived. A short time later, Carol was walking through the snow, trying to find a phone that worked.

The media were pounding Bea regularly now. A reporter for the *Boston Globe* called several times, a polite young woman who apologized but said her editors said she had to keep calling even if Bea said the reporter could not talk to Bob Cusick. Another just waited in the driveway, sending in a note that he would wait there. They were polite, actually, but oh-so invasive. How could she promise that her husband would talk to them when he was in the shape he was in? She had talked to him on the phone, and in just that brief time knew her Bob was no longer the same Bob. She had never heard him talk like this, about the ship, the seas, the oar, the boat. He was not . . . right.

She flew down to see Bob and the other survivors, and just before landing in Norfolk, she looked out the window toward the sea and said to herself, "It was out there."

At the hospital, Bea was let straight through. The company representatives were kept waiting, though they badly wanted to talk to the survivors. First, the Coast Guard had interviewed the survivors. Then the union. Then the union attorneys. Families came finally as they trickled in from the airport.

She was ushered into a room where all three survivors were perched on a bedside. "Like magpies on a wire," Kelly would say. They were wearing short, flimsy hospital gowns. Bob's face was blank. That staring-into-the-abyss look. His face looked rounder and younger without the beard.

"Well, I want to thank the nurse for that," Bea said when she saw her clean-shaven husband.

Then Bob's face crinkled into a smile. The look said he had seen God's Green Pastures and understood God's Great Cosmic Joke.

"Well," he said, gesturing at Dewey, Kelly, and himself. They were all bursting out of the gowns. "Well," he continued. "You can see one thing in common all the survivors have." He pinched his midriff, and they all laughed.

Bea hugged him for a long time. She was laughing and crying, a little of one, a little of the other.

But Bob. Bob Cusick had told the one joke and then faded. He was back now staring into the abyss. Her Bob was not her Bob. Gone from her, the bright wit and warm smile. The light had gone from his eyes, as if a candle had been snuffed out, and there was not even a whiff of smoke to remind Bea of the light and energy that once danced in his eyes.

He *could not shake it*. What did it mean? Why did he survive? There must be some reason. Some good reason. He could not fathom what it was.

"Bea," he said, "I do not know why I survived. I only know I cannot go back to sea. Not after this."

"Are you sure, Bob?" she asked. Knowing his love for it, knowing it had been his whole life. "We'll do what you want, but think about this some, get stronger, then decide."

"No," he said. And later, while he was still in the hospital, he resigned from Marine Transport Lines.

It was not a swipe at the company. He just wanted to stay away from the sea, never to go back. He was a company man and did not mean the company harm. But in resigning, the company man had left the company. And so far as the company was concerned, you were at this moment either with 'em or against 'em.

Those were the sides, when it came down to it in a Coast Guard Marine Board of Investigation hearing. Officers who survived could make the choice. They could choose sides but not the consequences. And the consequences for any surviving senior officer often involved blame. Who was responsible for a disaster at sea if not the senior officers?

The law was clear. The company was liable if the *company* knew unseaworthy conditions existed. But if the *officers* knew and did not communicate that to the company, well, case law was clear there, too. If the company paid at all, the sum was millions less. They had no "privity" of the knowledge that the ship was unseaworthy.

As it turned out, Farnham was *with* them. So Cusick must be against them.

And just that quickly, Bob Cusick was back in the drink. He was imperiled again, though he did not know it at the time, by waves of lawyers and gales of testimony and courtroom questions so chilly in tone they could make the North Atlantic in February seem like a hot tub.

And he could do nothing. For this *thing*—the *why*—still had him by the throat.

It was unlike anything he had encountered before. He had never had to think about why much—only what and where. He was a man of the sea, called at an early age. Blessed at age fifteen with the knowledge of what he would do with his life. Now that was gone.

He had been *spared*. He did not know why. He was humble enough not to think God had some great cause for him. No voice spoke to him to save lepers in Zimbabwe.

No voice spoke to him at all. It bore him down into deep depression. He could not eat or sleep.

He could not swim down in order to swim up.

He just sank lower and lower.

There was no answer.

Chapter Fourteen

THE COAST GUARD CAPTAIN

If you can't get more boats, then sell less tickets.

JOSEPH CONRAD
on the wreck of the Titanic

10 A.M. / WEDNESDAY, FEB. 16, 1983
COAST GUARD MARINE BOARD OF INVESTIGATION
PORTSMOUTH, VIRGINIA

With a crisp formality, the Marine Board of Investigation into the sinking of the SS *Marine Electric* convened in Portsmouth, Virginia, in the chambers of the City Council on 16 February 1983, just four days after the ship went down.

The official intent of the inquiry was "to the fullest extent possible . . . obtain information for the purpose of preventing or reducing the effects of similar casualties in the future . . . to determine if there is any evidence that any incompetence, misconduct, unskillfullness or willful violation of the law . . ." had taken place by licensed officers, the Coast Guard, or others.

As those solemn words were read, three Coast Guard officers, in their blue, gold-trimmed uniforms, sat down behind desks, comprising the board. Two members of the National Transportation Safety Board, who were convening their own inquiry, sat with them. In the audience were a handful of lawyers and dozens of journalists and family members of the crew. Strobes flashed, video cameras whirred.

The media captured the formal demeanor of the board, which spoke of competence, tradition, and procedure. The media caught the uncertainty and fear of the young seaman, Paul Dewey, as he made his way toward the stand to tell the board of his ordeal in the raft. Dewey, the first man in the water, would be the first man in the witness stand.

The cameras could not capture what was going through the mind of Captain Dominic A. Calicchio, one of the three Coast Guard officers on the board. He got the call about the *Marine Electric* on Saturday and was told by the board chairman, Captain Paul Lauridsen, from Washington headquarters, that the sessions would begin in Portsmouth, near Norfolk, early next week.

"Sure," Calicchio, said, and then added: "You know, most of the crew was from the Boston area. Any chance we can move the hearing there?"

"Well," Lauridsen said, "that may be so, but all the loading information is near Norfolk, and that may play a major role. Besides, it looks like the ship just ran aground, so this could be a quick one."

"But the families could really *use* the hearings," Calicchio said. Not really arguing. Reasoning. "You know, they won't be able to attend all the hearings in Virginia if this goes long. We could cover the coal loading in a day or so, then convene in Boston."

"No, it's set," Lauridsen said. "We have the City Council chambers booked, and we don't have a place in Boston."

Calicchio's mind examined what he had just heard. It's not right, was one thought. The families needed this to heal. He had seen it before. They needed to know, to come to closure on it all. Don't have a place in Boston? Give him a phone and two minutes. You'll have one. Coal loading? He could not remember when coal loading ever was a factor in something like this.

What was going on in the real world here? He did a mental printout of the factors. It's how his mind worked when he heard something that wasn't quite right, didn't have the proper ring. What were the factors? Motivation? Truth? What hard reality was dodging at the edges here, just out of sight?

A hearing in Boston? Big media. Sobbing wives and daughters on the nightly news. Great visuals. The liberal Kennedy political powers. If the hearings went long, a constant stream of outcries would be broadcast on the nightly news. That would lead to the network news, and this eventually could be a big hot button in Washington.

Portsmouth? A smaller town in a military region that knew how to bury its dead and move on. There would be a gaggle of media types. A few days of hot lights and sound bites. And then nothing.

"Well, it would be better for the families in Boston," Calicchio told Lauridsen. "But I'll see you in Portsmouth."

Ahh, this isn't right, Calicchio thought, and that was just the first phone conversation, before it really even started. Calicchio wondered, not for the first time, if the Coast Guard command knew what it was doing by putting him on this Marine Board of Investigation. He had questions most officers in the Coast Guard did not. They should know that, but did they?

Dom Calicchio was not a particularly imposing man. He had the bearing of a kind uncle—Yogi Berra with that puppy dog look. But those who had seen him in action knew he could morph in the merest of moments. One second he was the kind uncle. The next, his face would narrow, his eyebrows knit close together, and he would zero in on a fact, a question of seamanship, a wrong assumption, an error in reasoning. And the kind uncle would change to predatory inquisitor. He could look like Yogi Berra one instant, Rudy Giuliani on a very bad day the next.

So which did they think they had?

Maybe they saw him as the token. The expert merchant mariner who rounded out the Coast Guard board and made it invulnerable to outside criticism. Or maybe it was his turn now to show he could be a team player if he wanted to advance in the Coast Guard—his second chance after the Miami incident, when he'd been seen by some of the brass as a troublemaker and by the rank and file as a hero. He did have a guardian angel in HQ, an admiral who had gone to bat for him before. So maybe the guardian angel was saying, "Dom's okay. Give him another chance to show he's a team player."

Most likely, they figured this one wasn't going to be much. And maybe it wasn't. That was okay, too. He really wanted to get to the bottom of whatever happened. Not make something out of nothing.

When they all met down in Portsmouth, the NTSB guys were saying they thought it would be open and shut. It certainly sounded as if the ship had gone in too shallow, trying to rescue the fishing boat. The company had issued a press statement saying the ship wandered into shallow waters when it attempted to rescue the *Theodora*. Tragic, but these things happen. Pete Lauridsen, a poised, pipe-smoking officer, the board chairman, nodded thoughtfully in agreement.

"Let's not rush too far down that path," Calicchio said gently. "Fellas, let's not come to any conclusions just yet. Let's hear the facts."

The only facts so far were that the permanent master James Farnham, the captain who had been on leave during the ill-fated voyage, was almost sure this is how it happened, Lauridsen told Calicchio. *Well, of course, the permanent master might want to say that,* Calicchio thought. *There is no blame in such a tragic accident. Ship runs aground in effort to rescue fishing boat. This guy is in pain and certainly wants to believe that.*

And then Calicchio thought to himself, *But what if there was something wrong with the ship? What would Farnham say then?*

A layman might think the permanent master would be the first person to blow the whistle. Calicchio knew better. He knew the informal and unsaid rules. He knew the Merchant Marine Officer's Dilemma and the informal code of silence.

He knew these things from experience, because he had been a merchant mariner, a good one, for twenty-three years. So had each of his brothers, the older one, Michael, and the younger one, Alfred. The "Sailing Calicchio Brothers." All three were masters with their own ships at one time, and each had their own code that allowed for damned few moral dilemmas.

Their code was the Old Man's Code. Their father had never been to sea. *"Only on the boat ride over from Naples,"* Dom would tell anyone who asked. But the father had taught his sons, all three of them, a strict code of behavior as they grew up in East Boston. You did what you *knew* was right, not what anyone told you. You thought for yourself and did the right thing. You listened to people, but in the end, you were your own man, and any compromise with something you knew was wrong violated the Old Man's Code.

The Old Man's Code. That is what had got Dom into the soup in Miami, for sure.

Calicchio was Coast Guard but not *Coast Guard* when he went to Miami. He had spent years as an officer in the U.S. Merchant Marine, had started as a kid during World War II and moved up to become a captain on ships of U.S. Lines, the pride of the American fleet. Shipping was slow in 1957, and he joined the Coast Guard for three years under what was labeled the "219 Program." He began at junior grade and made lieutenant in three years. Then he went back to the Merchant Marine. But every year thereafter, he did his turn in the Coast Guard Reserve. Each year during his reserve duty, his commanding officer encouraged him to reenlist full time in the Coast Guard.

So eventually he did, in 1968, as a lieutenant commander. He was asked to come in because the Coast Guard needed him. The Coast Guard knew rescues. It knew drug interdiction. It knew safety regulations and small boats. It did not know the big ships well, however, and Calicchio's recruitment was designed to help plug that deficiency. Years back, the Bureau of Marine Inspection had run ship safety programs. The bureau was composed in part of ex-merchant mariners who knew their stuff and cared about what happened out there. The Coast Guard took over the function in World War II, and most mariners thought it never had been the same, that the Coast Guard looked at the "book"—all those regulations—and not the true state of the ship. The mariners now viewed the Coast Guard inspectors, most of them, as just passing through. Or they were so young and green they could try their best and still not get the job done.

Well, Calicchio thought, *I can do some good here.* Who do seamen have? Who looked after them? They were an odd lot, many of them, a mixture of loners and losers, winners and leaders. But they had one thing in common. No one looked out for them on land, where the regulations and inspections ruled.

He would think of the sweet old guy on one of his early ships who was all but useless in many ways. Too much booze. No family. Still, he tutored Calicchio, loaned Dom a sextant, taught him how to take a position the old-fashioned way. Read the stars.

Or take Paul Dewey, the young man who was being sworn in as the first witness as Calicchio and the others started the inquiry into the *Marine Electric* disaster. Dewey was the seaman—a kid, really, at twenty-nine—who had the luck to make it into the raft. Calicchio listened intently, the kind uncle's face urging Dewey to feel comfortable in these unfamiliar circumstances. The young man literally shook in the witness stand as he told of men dying so near rescue.

The seaman had no one, Calicchio thought when he signed on full time with the Coast Guard. He could help here, add something. Balance the Coast Guard by using his knowledge. Not giving the seamen unfair advantage or an edge. But by doing what was right. It was with that idea he entered service full time. Not to pick a fight with the Coast Guard. Not to tilt at windmills. He wanted to protect men in peril at sea by making sure their ships were sound when the peril came. And, as the Old Man had told them, to do the right thing.

He had loved that time of his early service. He was in Europe for four years. In New York City, too. Then to Miami. Dream assignments, really. He was officer in charge of all ports in Florida—Jacksonville, Tampa, Port Everglades. And Miami, where forty-eight foreign flag passenger ships docked.

In Miami, he had taken a look at passenger ship safety and been horrified. First, there were not enough lifeboats. There were these elaborate, elaborate formulas for figuring out how many lifeboats you needed. Cubic cabin space, volumes. Regulation upon regulation!

They made Calicchio dizzy, because the plain fact was right in front of you. *There weren't enough lifeboats.* And they could not be loaded fast enough. For the formulas had left out common sense. For one thing, the formulas were based on "average human beings," while other regs required that the average human beings wear fat lifesaving vests.

The Coast Guard and the international committee charged with fostering guidelines for safety at sea were tied into knots by the passenger shipowners. They had debated the matter for eight long years. They did not seem in a rush to add new boats and mechanisms, but Calicchio embarrassed them into it.

He staged a passenger loading drill using a lifeboat and 100 crew members on a sparkling white cruise ship. It took forty-five minutes to load the passengers into one boat in ideal conditions with ship-savvy crew members—far past the safety standards of half an hour. And the boat was so crowded that its engine could not be started. The passengers in their vests could barely breathe. They were crammed in like sardines. Imagine what would happen when more than a thousand terrified senior citizens—the most common passengers on cruise ships—stampeded toward the boats.

"But the boats met the requirements," said the shipowners. "There are 100 people in here."

"Don't make an issue of fifteen minutes," they seemed to say to the lieutenant commander.

Calicchio smiled and turned to the packed lifeboat.

"Okay," he said. "Now let's all do a little rowing!"

Of course, they could not, and his point was proved beyond doubt. Now the safety establishment was shocked out of its eight-year reverie and embarrassed into applying the informal "Calicchio Standard" worldwide. The big cruise line companies shelled out millions. And wrote dozens of letters of complaint. Inevitably, some in the Coast Guard were embarrassed as well, and Calicchio was seen as something of a pariah among those whose business it was to meet in Switzerland to forge international rules over grand dinners.

But Calicchio did have fans. There was the guardian angel in HQ, Rear Admiral Clyde T. Lusk, the Washington head of the Coast Guard's Merchant Marine Safety office. Dom broke the international deadlock on lifeboat safety when it needed to be broken, Admiral Lusk wrote in a letter to the top Coast Guard brass.

"This as well as other issues have been debated to the point of analytical paralysis," Lusk said. ". . . Calicchio's actions converted this question from one of academic speculation to one of real life urgency.

"Commander Calicchio took an unpopular stand, stuck to it and was proven to be correct. I thought I'd share with you the concern of a number of my senior staff that his diligence may have damaged his career."

So there were people in the Coast Guard—Lusk and his staff—who gave a damn.

Even with Lusk's letter, Commander Calicchio could not *buy* a promotion to captain. It was 1981 in Miami—thirteen years after he'd joined as lieutenant commander. This wasn't right! He had had to threaten suit to make them promote him to captain. And then they transferred him in 1982 from his command of all Florida ports to be executive officer of the Port of New Orleans. Effectively, he was promoted in rank and demoted in responsibility. He went from overseeing all Coast Guard functions for all ports in Florida to assisting the commander of one port.

More likely, they wanted to bury him. Later in 1982, they changed his role again. He was made a Coast Guard judge. He had his own little office, and he was a sort of quasi-judge, sitting on cases involving violations of navigation and pollution laws. Who had discharged oil in the harbor in violation of what government regulation? Who turned left when he ought to have gone right? Who should be fined how much? Well, at least that minor position had honed his skills on the bench and prepared him for this job. He learned how to handle lawyers, and his skills at questioning were razor-sharp now.

But how did you use those skills to make things better? To try to change a very bad system?

"They're trying to make things so safe it's dangerous," Calicchio was fond of saying.

What he meant was that they made all these rules without looking at the real system. This was not new to the maritime world. More than 100 years earlier, C.M. Norwood, a member of the British Parliament, said drily, "I can assure you that we require on board our large ships a barrister even more than we require a doctor. There are so many acts under which we conduct our business that it is impossible for any ship's captain to know how to act to keep within the four corners of the law."

By 1983, there were hundreds of rules and regulations governing a passenger ship, and *none* of them actually got to the real problems. In fact, so many rules meant that any of them might be ignored at any given time.

"We are making things so safe, it's dangerous," Calicchio would say again and again. "There are a million manuals and a million rules. They are trying to take thinking away from people, so that people cannot do their jobs using common sense."

Mostly, he thought, the proliferation of rules was designed to cover the ass of the brass and then assign blame to people who weren't *really* to blame at all. A thousand passengers died because they couldn't get to the lifeboats soon enough? They would call a Marine Board and cruise through a buffet of regulations to see whom they could blame. You could bet the captain and the officers would go down on something like that. You could bet there would be more rules and regulations, when the simple fact was right in front of you: There weren't enough lifeboats.

The system didn't solve maritime problems. It seemed to create them.

In fact, this was roughly the same conclusion that Dr. Charles Perrow, the Yale sociologist, would come to. Calicchio had a high school degree and no other formal training, just years of experience and an open and perceptive mind. "Self-taught," he would say simply.

Perrow used formal research and the principles of sociology and found in his book, *Normal Accidents,* that the maritime system was "error-inducing." There were many reasons for this, he wrote, but one was that accidents were blamed excessively on the ships officers. There were also incredible "production pressures" on the ships and new technology that meant the officers sometimes took imprudent risks and relied excessively on radar or auto-pilot systems.

Complicating this from the American standpoint, he said, was the fact that nearly forty percent of the fleet was composed of aged World War II ships far, far past their prime and normal scrapping age.

So, sitting in Portsmouth, listening to Seaman Paul Dewey explain how he had lost his guys on the little raft, Calicchio was heir to a system that had been adrift for decades.

He had little hope of completely reforming such a system. He just wanted a fair board.

Or maybe this case was just open and shut. He doubted it. He heard Dewey describe his voyage. No big thump in the night when the ship went to the fishing boat's rescue. No loud reports or cracking sounds.

And Calicchio thought to himself, *This grounding didn't happen. The 25,000-ton coal carrier bottomed out on shoals? Slammed down hard*

on the bottom in twenty-foot waves? Then took hours to sink? And then the
tides and the currents carried the ship miles to the deep water where it now
rested? Not in this world. Not on this planet.

Every fabric of his being understood the situation of the officers
on the *Marine Electric.*

Calicchio was not surprised that Farnham was cooperating with
the company and had even blown off his union lawyers for a company lawyer. Farnham said he was convinced that the ship went too
shallow, and he may even have believed it. People were funny. Denial was funny.

Make enough regulations and rules, pile one on top of the other,
and you could always bang and hang the officers.

But that did not absolve the officers. They had responsibilities,
too. Calicchio never believed the converted warships could not sail
as seaworthy ships, if there were good inspections and proper maintenance. The officers *did* have a role in that.

And the officers here almost certainly made some errors. Early
on in the hearing, Calicchio fanned out the inspection records and
reports he had received.

There were drawings of the hatch covers by the chief mate that
Calicchio could not believe. More than ninety holes in the hatches.
Fractures in the deck? No wonder Farnham was with the company
lawyers.

And a hole in the hull? Patched with a coffee can lid and cement? Who the hell had done that? Calicchio searched and saw that
it was the chief mate. He looked for the name and found it. Robert
Manning Cusick.

Could that be Bob Cusick from Boston? Roxbury? It had to be.
From the Sea Scouts? Fella who hung out with Mike, Dom's big
brother, when the Calicchios lived in East Boston? Had to be. A
very smart fellow.

Mike Calicchio was going to sail with his fellow Sea Scouts after
the war started back in 1941, but Dom's mother had a premonition.
The ship, the *Major Wheeler,* would sink. "Don't go," she said. "Please
don't go."

"Oh, Mom," Michael Calicchio said, "I gotta. All the other guys
are."

But she persisted, even became sick. She held him by his shirt and begged, don't go, son, please. And he relented, concerned for her health, not his at first, but finally just plain spooked by this extraordinary display. He told his Sea Scout friends about his mom's premonition. Then some of them got spooked, too, and Joe Trudeau and Jean Dakin, his buddies, signed off as well.

But a lot of his friends went. The *Major Wheeler* was torpedoed in the maelstrom of 1942. Much of the crew was lost, many of Mike's friends among them.

And Cusick, years later, when the mourning was past, would say with a sparkle in his eyes whenever he saw one of the Sailing Calicchios, "Dom, (Mike, Al,) always, always, *always* . . . listen to your mother."

Calicchio had sailed with Cusick on one trip years ago, and the guy had seemed okay, a good guy. Knew his stuff.

Well, not the first time that a good guy from the old days had gone a wrong way, Calicchio thought. He would disclose the indirect relationship to the Coast Guard, but it meant nothing to him in his job. If Bob Cusick was patching up old ships with tin and cement and not reporting it correctly, he was going to have to survive more than the North Atlantic. Because Dom had listened to his mother, for sure. But he always, *always* listened to his father. The Old Man's Code did not allow special treatment for an old acquaintance or the friend of his brother. Serious matters were at stake here. *Thirty-one men had died.* You *had* to do the right thing. How could you not?

Fact was, Calicchio thought, Cusick may be at ground zero here. Calicchio had seen it before. Right or wrong, he could see it happening again.

Corl, the relief master, was dead, and Farnham had gone over to the company side. Kelly? No one could blame anything on the relief third mate, and besides, the guy was completely straight and blameless. That left Cusick as the goat. If there wasn't some sort of natural explanation for this. If the shallow-water theory did not hold up . . . they all would be coming for Cusick, Calicchio included.

The chief mate was responsible if the hatches were bad and he had not told the master.

If there was a hole in the hull? Chief mate.

If the coal were loaded improperly? Chief mate.

If the anchor slipped during the storm and holed the hull?

Mr. Cusick, front and center.

Well, Calicchio would do what he had to do. Old Man or not, he also had to at least consider his own career. He couldn't just throw that away. Maybe Lusk *was* giving him a second chance. Saying "Join the team, Dom. Here's your chance."

He was only one man on a three-man board, and he knew for certain he was alone in his view of maritime safety. Probably he would stay completely alone here. Paul Lauridsen, the chairman, seemed like a typical career man. A candidate for flag rank. Real admiral material, they all said. Murphy, the young lieutenant commander, seemed like a good kid, but he was green on this sort of thing. He was Coast Guard all the way, not bluewater Merchant Marine.

Dom would see how it all played out. He would move carefully.

And he would see how Cusick played as well, soon enough, for Dewey was nearly done on the first day, and Bob Cusick was next.

Chapter Fifteen

THE DREAM

*Thoughts of eternity thicken. He begins to feel anxious
concerning his soul.*

HERMAN MELVILLE

Mardi

7 A.M. / TUESDAY, FEB. 15, 1983 / CUSICK RESIDENCE
SCITUATE, MASSACHUSETTS

Bob and Bea Cusick returned to their comfortable home near the
bay in Scituate on Sunday, and there he encountered each night
what they came to call The Dream.

Night after night, he was in the boat again, convulsively shivering. The seas were breaking over his head again, crushing him,
rolling him out of the boat. He was on the ship in her last moments.
Are we going to make it, Charlie? No, Mate, we're not. Clayt Babineau,
the second mate, asking Cusick the same question. Then Cusick was
shivering again, muscles contracting against the cold sea. Thrashing
out, kicking the covers. Saying something in his sleep, a coarse,
hoarse sound that seemed almost a mumbled song.

Each night, Bea would wake him and say, "Hon, you're having
nightmares again. You're kicking the covers. Bob! Everything is
okay. It's just The Dream. You're safe. You're safe. We're back home
in Scituate, Massachusetts. You're in your home. You're in your bed.
You're okay."

Only he wasn't.

They came asking "how"—the families of crew members and
dead friends. How did this happen? How did the ship sink? How did

Clayt, Rich, Joseph, Charlie, James, my lover, my husband, my son, my father, my brother die?

They asked, "How?" He heard, "Why?" He even suspected it of Mary Babineau. Though she came right out and told him not to feel guilty. Told him that . . . told him many things . . . told him he should know she sure wasn't blaming him . . . made him laugh with her stories of Clayt.

He wanted to apologize. To say, I am so, so sorry I survived and not your husband, lover, brother, friend, partner, parent, son.

What role for him now? He was a dead man. Then he was spared. So why?

The media were bombarding him, trying to mine this for all it was worth. They were true furies, dogging his every step.

When would the pack leave? is what Bea and Bob wanted to know. The calls were still coming in three days after the sinking. Some were spreading rumors that the engineers were still alive, tapping out messages, pleading for rescue. What did Cusick think?

Late in the afternoon on Monday, Bea opened the door and saw another one of them. Bob had slipped out to fill prescriptions. "I'm sorry," Bea told the man, "he's not here and he couldn't talk if he was. Please don't bother us, please respect our privacy." And she began closing the door.

"Ma'am," the man said. "Mrs. Cusick? Bea? I'm George Dolak, the night engineer, the best friend of Mike Price. Friend of your husband, too? I worked on the *Marine Electric,* and I'm wondering if I could talk to your husband about what went wrong. I don't mean to disturb you."

Bea looked at him. He was an emotional wreck. Dolak looked as if he had broken down somehow. The fact was he had, in a way. Instantly, Bea's manner changed, her antennae working. She was a nurse and knew what grief and a broken heart looked like. This guy had both.

"Oh, God, you poor guy, come in," Bea said.

Dolak pointed toward the driveway. "That's Mike Price's truck," he said. "Marsha Price, his widow, asked me to pick it up from the power plant, and I was driving it and all Mike's things were in it like he was coming back and I . . . I just couldn't handle it. I had to stop, couldn't go on, couldn't keep driving the thing, and you are the only people I know here. . . ."

Bea and George talked for more than an hour, Bea just being there, listening, letting him talk, getting it off his chest, talking about Mike, about his friend's young daughter, about the ship and what a rust bucket it was.

Then Bob Cusick came home. He saw George and gave him a bear hug, the man who was going to be Price's partner. The guy in the car business, who would alternate with Price, one of them working in the repair shop, the other shipping to sea. Then switching off. By the luck of the draw, Dolak was here and Price dead. By the luck of the draw.

"Well, not quite," George said. "That was Price's dream, but it was my nightmare. The repair business, you bet. It was perfect, and they could do it. But the ship part? No way." He *told* Price, *warned* him: "That old tub is unsafe." "Look, Mike," George had told him, "I've been on the *Poet,* the *Golden Dolphin,* the *Silver Dove. They are all at the bottom of the sea!* It's not worth it. Lying awake at night, listening to the vibrations of the ship. Waiting for a wrong pitch, a wrong hum. Wondering if it means your life.

"Don't sail on these old tubs anymore! They will kill you." The only place Dolak would set foot on the *Marine Electric* was at the dock, where he was night engineer, tending to the ship's needs at dockside. Where you could swim off it when it went down. Not *if* it went down, *when* it went down. That's what Dolak had told Mike, but he was so stubborn. So stubborn. He was going to just stick with it until the new ship came in. Then it was a dream job. Once he had an idea, a job, he just stayed with it. Wouldn't give up. On a dream, on a job. That and the charm of the guy. He could charm anyone.

"He was in the engine room at the last," Bob told Dolak. "Price was manning the pumps and didn't leave even after the orders. He stayed to secure the engine room. Kelly yelled at him: 'Get out of there now! We're going down!' "

"So *stubborn,*" Dolak said. "It's why you loved him. What made him a high school football star on the defensive line. That's one of the reasons they won the Class B State Championship back in '66.

What let him make it in a closed small Massachusetts town as an outsider. Why we would have made it in the auto business together. He had the talk, but also the walk. Always got the job done."

Dolak said he was leaning hard on the Marine Engineers Benevolent Association to send divers down to cut into the engine room. *Claim the bodies,* Dolak thought, *and put an end to the suffering. Let the wives bury their men in the ground properly.*

The two men sat in comfortable chairs, talked and sipped whiskey. Outside, a few blocks away, the bay waters lapped gently at the Scituate shore—the same saltwater that had wrenched Cusick and the ship so violently just days before. Like a lake now. A pond. The waves hardly broke the surface tension. The water just rose and fell, rose and fell. Heaved ever so gently, like the chest of a child at sleep. Looking out the windows, the two men might have been on a ship's bridge, talking shop, talking about the song of the sea they both once had heard. Only now, neither was going back. Cusick did not hear even the quiet little song the little waves played on the shores of Scituate. That song was gone.

"The hatches," Cusick said, "are what did the ship in."

Almost certainly that was it, Cusick said. The hole in the hull patched with cement gave way first. Or that old World War II bow gave way. Farnham was oh-so careful about how he treated that old bow. They had strengthened it, but in dry dock Cusick had seen the welders, seen how the bead of the welds seemed wrong. Or maybe it was the dilapidated dry cargo hatch. Whatever it was, something gave way somewhere to lower the front of the ship in the water, to bring the head down.

Then it was just a matter of time, Cusick told Dolan. The water came up over the lowered bow and then boomed over the hatches by four feet or so. Boom. Six feet of water. *Tons* of weight. There was nothing to the hatches. Tape and epoxy held them together. Spit and chewing gum. The hatches gave way, and the ship filled and capsized.

"Yes," said George, "if they were pumping like crazy and getting good pressure, as you said, that made sense. Only they wouldn't have had a chance of pumping out the cargo holds."

"Why not?" Cusick asked.

"Well, they put solid plates over the drains so the coal wouldn't get into the pumps. They disabled the drains and the pump system to save the pumps."

"That's right," Cusick said. "And the hatches, well, they never worked right after the 1981 dry-docking in Jacksonville. Never worked *right?* Never worked—period. Forget the patches for a moment. You could not get the hatches closed so they were never really watertight. Then they skipped the last dry dock due in January because the coal was needed, and the Coast Guard said 'fine.' "

Well, it was all wrong, they both agreed. Something should have been done by the company. They should not have skipped the dry dock. Should not have taken the ship out on the North Atlantic in winter. The company could have barged the coal around just as well without missing a contract.

"You know they'll come after you," Dolak told Cusick. "You know that's how it works." Cusick nodded that they might. Knew his admiralty law. Hell, the loading records had gone to the bottom. He had nothing to prove the cargo was loaded sound and firm.

And then the real question Dolak had.

"How did you make it and the others did not?" George asked. And Cusick was still thinking more *why* than *how*. The *how* was preposterous. Swim down to get up. Find an oar. A thin piece of wood in a whole vast ocean. A single toothpick. Get tangled in a line. It drags you to a lifeboat. Your wife buys you a coat you yourself would never buy. A waste of money. It's tight at the wrists, long at the waist, with a hood. It acts like a cheap wet suit. You listen to a song that saves your life. A last-chance helicopter rescue snags you. All of that bizarre tale Cusick related to Dolak in great detail, reliving it again. Getting it up and out.

George thought the tale might be even more bizarre. Cusick had said the water in the lifeboat seemed warmer when he entered it. Probably, the superheated steam escaping warmed the water in Cusick's lifeboat. Not likely, Bob thought to himself. Too much water coming in and out. But, hell, the whole and utter fact of his survival was unlikely. The escaping steam was Mike Price's last gift, George Dolak said, and he choked saying it. The steam that killed him helped save you. So why not, Bob Cusick thought. It was no more bizarre than everything else, and he did not contest it with Dolak, just listened and mourned with him.

The two of them could only figure out that the sinking never should have happened. None of it. The ship should not have gone to sea.

For days after the wreck, Bob Cusick would rise in the early-morning hours and end his sleeping nightmare. But then his waking nightmare would begin as he grappled with the intangible question of his survival and an overwhelming feeling of guilt. He had lost all of his men. All good friends. All like family. At times, Bea and Bob would just hold each other. Just hold each other and sob.

What was he to do? He was the son of a butler who had served. He could have gone captain, could have been master of his own ship, had he been more aggressive. But he would have had far less time with his family. Far less flexibility to sail when he wanted, where he wanted. And he would have had to take that old tub across the North Atlantic on its grain runs. The last thing in the world he was or wanted to be was a crusader. Something should have been done about the *Marine Electric,* but, hell, that wasn't his job. Not his charter. Not his rank or mission.

Kelly did not have the "why" problem. His guilt was different. What should he have done? What could he have done? Up there on the bridge, eight to twelve?

The why was pretty clear to him. She cried and needed her diapers changed regularly. He had a seven-month-old daughter at home and a loving wife. His purpose in life was clear.

So when he left the hospital, Kelly prepared to support the family, picked up the keys he had jammed in his pocket back on ship, and hitched a ride to the parking lot at Brayton Point, where he had left his truck. Climbed in. It started right away. All his day-to-day odds and ends were in the cab. As if nothing had happened. The lot itself looked normal. Across the way, he saw the truck of Albion "Sparks" Lane, sitting there to the side alone, waiting for the radio operator to return.

Sorry, Sparks, he thought. *You almost made it.*

But there was no lingering thought about why. The furies of "what" filled his head, but never why me and not Sparks.

Cusick had the "what" down well enough for now. He knew he had to appear at the Marine Board of Investigation in just a few days in Portsmouth, Virginia. It would have been nice of them to hold it in Boston, where most of the crew had lived. Would have been nice of them to give him a few days to recover. But the board had asked him to appear on Thursday, less than a week after the wreck.

He felt drawn to the inquiry by a string pulled by the dead men. Pulled there just as if by the line that had wrapped round his leg. "Don't let him do this," his friends told Bea. And he told Bea, "I have to." "He can go," the doctor told Bea, "but watch him. There are still weird patterns in the heartbeat. His ears aren't quite right yet."

Bea asked him to postpone it.

But Bob just pursed his lips and said, "We've got to go. I can't explain it. I have to go now. I have to tell what it was like for my friends who died. They have to know how the men died. I owe my men that."

Even Grant Connelly, one of Bob's best friends, could not dissuade him, and, phoning from the West Coast, accustomed to the command authority of a master, ordered Bea to stop him.

"Goddamn it, Bea!" Connelly bellowed. "He can't do this! They're going to go after him, and he's not well. Those lawyers will tear him into little pieces!"

"Well, you stop him, then," Bea said, "because I can't. You're going to have to physically stop him, because I can't. He's got to get this out of his system."

"Now you listen to me, Goddamn it!" Connelly began.

And Bea hung up on the second person in her life. She loved Connelly like a brother and was sorry they were fighting. She couldn't do anything, and neither could Connelly. The next day, Bob Cusick was shaving for the plane trip south to Norfolk when he looked in the mirror, paused, and was convulsed in deep, wrenching sobs. Bea said, "Let's not do it, hon. You don't have to go now."

"No," he said, it was something he had to do.

"What are you going to do there?"

"I don't know. I just have to go. Have to tell them what happened."

And again, later, after they had cleared the boarding gate, when they were walking down the covered runway to the plane door, Bea saw Bob's whole face grimace, then set itself in a determined rictus. He sobbed, his face breaking into tears. He was choking off the sobs. They came out anyway, as if he were attempting to expel oil from his lungs. Sob after sob. Primordial. Unstoppable.

"Don't want to go, don't want to go," he gasped between the sobs.

But Bea noted that he never stopped walking toward the plane. She clung to his arm. "Let's go home," she said.

"Can't," Bob Cusick said. And by the time they reached the plane door, he was dry-eyed and controlled. A little red-faced was all. "It's okay. I've got it out," he said.

But it was clear to Bea he hadn't. That evening, they ate dinner overlooking Hampton Roads with their attorney, Henry Howell. Howell was a Southern gentleman, the former lieutenant governor of Virginia, hired by the Masters, Mates & Pilots to represent the officers. In his sixties, tall with a full mane of white hair, he was a gracious and endearing host. The three looked out through the big windows at the panoramic view of the mouth of Chesapeake Bay— a great harbor of a great naval power.

The testimony would begin tomorrow, and while Howell dwelt on it as little as possible, he had to prepare his witness. He cautioned Cusick that they might go after him, particularly if it wasn't a grounding. The Coast Guard and the Marine Transport Lines attorney might be ruthless.

"No way it was a grounding," Cusick said.

"Well, if it wasn't a grounding, then if I were their attorney, I would try to shield the company by saying that, well, I would go after you, Bob Cusick. Try to show how you had screwed up by not telling the captain, not telling the company, about problems on the ship. Or by not loading the coal properly. Or by screwing up the anchor.

"So say as little as you can. Do not volunteer. Do not lie! But do not give them anything to go on. Yes and no answers—or I don't recall, if you feel you're confused. You will be amazed at what they can do to the simplest fact, attorneys. How they can embroider well-meaning words and deeds into culpability."

Howell made it clear to Bea and Bob. You can make a lot of money here, he said. You should make a lot of money. Pain and suffering. You've sure had that! Loss of income. If you're disabled? Can't go back to sea? Wear a brace on your neck if it hurts. Tell how you suffered out there in the water? I'm not saying that to chase your business. But you should know. That was the gist of his short "pitch."

Cusick knew all that. Knew his admiralty law from officer's school and training. Knew the legal concept of privity and how it could hurt him badly. If they could show that he hadn't reported correctly to the captain, well . . . the company was home free by not being privy to the poor condition of the ship.

That's not what he was worried about. He had done what was right. He felt no guilt of that sort. Let the attorneys hammer.

Make money off it? Bea and he had talked about it. *Make money off it?* It was profane even to consider that. Oh, we don't need that sort of money, honey, Bea had said. All those men dead. We're okay with the money we have. We have to do what is right.

Bub Cusick picked at his food, hardly touching it. Bea never saw the smile reach his eyes. He had that 5,000-yard stare into the void. His eyes were as dead as Farnham's voice on the phone. The old Bob was gone, lost at sea, and Bea was not sure she would ever see him again.

"Is there a port chaplain?" she asked Howell quietly. There was, and his name was Clifford Olsen, a chaplain for the port of Norfolk. He had visited the *Marine Electric* many times. Cusick remembered meeting him.

Bob Cusick was not one of God's most attentive servants. He believed in God. Skeptically. But he believed. "Bury me, don't cremate me," he had always said with a mischievous and intelligent smile. "I don't know that it's true, but just in case there is a second coming . . . just in case all those things the Bible-thumpers say are right about Revelations, I want to come up out of my grave, you know . . . rise again. Doesn't cost you anything, really, so bury me in the ground."

He did not believe in a God who sent the lifeboat, the oar, the line, the coat, the 'copter to save Bob Cusick and just Bob Cusick.

But there had to be a why here. Had to, and if Clifford Olsen could help him, yes, he would go with Bea.

It was a short meeting. A short prayer. Cliff Olsen did not tell Bob that there was some great purpose exterior to them all. God often acted from within a person, not from the top down through a Charlton Heston voice piercing berayed clouds.

Don't go looking for a pillar of fire or a burning bush here, Bob. There is a reason you were saved. There is an answer to why. If you are not seeing it "out there," then look inside. The answer is inside. It is within *you*. You will know the reason. When the time comes that God wants you to see the reason, you will know it.

And that made sense to Cusick. *Look within.*

What was it Clayt Babineau's widow had said? He had talked to her. She had tried to calm him. Tell him it was all right. Told Dewey, too, that she knew they did everything they could to save Clayt. It was okay.

"But I don't understand, Mary, what it is I'm supposed to do now," Bob Cusick told her. "Why I was saved."

Mary Babineau's eyes sparkled with humor. She was highly religious but had this streak of black humor.

"Why you damned fool," Mary told him with laughter in her voice. *"I know why you were saved, if you don't! You were the only one on that ship that knew every hole, every patch, every ding and chip in that old rust bucket!"*

And that was true, he thought. Very true.

It came back to him as well, a part of his time in the water. A thousand thoughts had come to him as he drifted, freezing, singing, praying for hours. A slow slide show of his life. The good, the bad. All the little things he had not done or said that could have made life better. They came and went. He hadn't told Bea this. He hadn't let Carol know that. All the important little things unsaid.

And for what reason? Fears or concerns that seemed so petty and needless. The cold, cold water distilled his reason and the feelings of his very soul into a pure dense substance of resolve. All the little fears of his life. He saw them for what they were, and he was not proud.

In all of Christ's land, he swore to himself in the water back then, *in all of Christ's land,* I will not let those fears stop me, if I live. *If* I live, I will not care about anything that will stop me from living life fully and genuinely. Of helping, of loving. I will care about nothing that stands between me and living life.

He was not bargaining with God. He was promising himself. Administering an oath. Resolving. His life, if he lived, would not cater to petty fears, because he could see, there in the water, how those fears killed a man a little at a time, took pieces of his life, made it less than it might have been.

In Norfolk, Bea and Bob were staying with Bill Long, the retired officer who still helped at dockside with the loading and who was a good friend.

He showed them their room, then said, almost sheepishly. "Bob, I don't know why I kept these. You know I always throw them away. If they're of any use to you, here's your loading records, show you did the job right."

And something was released in Bob Cusick in those days and nights before the hearing. The sum of it all. Bill Long. Mary. Cliff Olsen. George Dolak. Kelly. Dewey. Charlie Johnson. The dreams. Bea. Carol, his daughter. The time in the water. The line. The boat. The chopper. The distilled reasoning wrought by the cold water.

It was there all along. It was inside him, not out there somewhere. This store of information. This detail. This horrible experience he had been through. This promise he had made to himself out there. Finally, they all fell together like the tumblers of a well-oiled lock.

He'd known all along what he was going to do, it seemed. He just wasn't letting the new thoughts out into the front part of his brain and out of his mouth.

He was unafraid now. There was no way to explain it.

He decided he would not hem and haw and say "I don't recall" at the hearing. He would not be a crusader, either.

There was no way he would make money off this. Wear a neck brace.

He would simply say what was in his heart and mind.

That was it. He knew now why he was alive. He would simply tell the truth. About it all. The good and the bad. He would bear witness. Straight down the middle.

A burden dropped from him. The furies disappeared.

In all of Christ's land, the company man was not afraid. Utterly and absolutely, Bob Cusick was fearless.

Chapter Sixteen

THE BOARD

To die for commerce is hard enough, but to go under that sea we have been trained to combat with a sense of failure in the supreme duty of one's calling is indeed a bitter fate.

JOSEPH CONRAD
on the Titanic

10 A.M. / THURSDAY, FEB. 17, 1983 / MARINE BOARD OF INVESTIGATION
PORTSMOUTH, VIRGINIA

The Marine Board of Investigation had listened to Paul Dewey tell his heartrending story of rescue and loss from the life raft, of Clayt Babineau's valiant effort to climb the sheer walls of the raft with only ice hooks for hands.

Now it was Robert Manning Cusick's turn.

The executive officer of the board stared at the audience and called out, "Mr. Cusick, will you please stand, remain standing, raise your right hand; I'll administer an oath."

Bob Cusick had signed his own oath the night before. This one would be no problem.

He walked quickly and a bit stiffly, bent forward almost as if the top half of his body were in a race with the bottom half. Any faster, and he would be jogging.

The chief mate sat in the witness chair and faced the audience squarely, as if he were at the bridge of a ship. Looking out at the unknown. The future. But confidently. Almost heartily. With a relaxed face and a near-twinkle in his eye. From the audience, Bea beamed back at him.

"Glad you can be here with us," Lieutenant Commander E. F. Murphy said with a soft smile.

"Thank you very much," said Bob Cusick in a confident voice, with just a little ironic grin. "I appreciate it greatly."

The audience laughed gently and cautiously. And Calicchio thought: *Well, Cusick still has his sense of humor, at least.*

Lotte Fredette sensed something in the air. *What was this fella doing?* He did not have the twisted, worried look of other officers she had seen take the stand. He didn't look as if he had just taken a bite of something very sour. He was comfortable in his skin.

Lisolette "Lotte" Fredette, the leader of the mothers of the dead crew of the *Poet,* could not easily afford the trip from Philadelphia to Portsmouth for the Marine Board hearings. Nor could the other mothers, Anne Bradley and Barbara Schmidt. But none of them could afford to stay away. Their sons had died on an old ship three years ago. Now more men had died.

They had come to witness. They had come to see men lie. Or at best tell just one part of a truth. That is how the mothers saw it. That is what happened during the *Poet* hearings. They were sure it would happen again here, at the *Marine Electric.*

In 1980, her Hans had boarded the SS *Poet* at a grain pier on the Delaware River. The Philadelphia Phillies were playing in the World Series nearby, and they could see the glow of the stadium lights and hear the rippling waves of cheers. She had driven him there, and at the end, after seeing the ship, had begged him not to go. But she knew that if Hans was missing his beloved Phillies to sail, nothing could stop him. And then, when he laughed and kissed her good-bye, she handed him a sweater. It was the last time she saw him. The old troop carrier, refitted to carry grain, sailed down the Delaware River and into a storm. End of story. Full stop.

The hearing on the *Poet* seemed to them more intended to hush up problems with the old ships than drive toward some discovery of why the ship sank. For years, the owner, Henry Bonnabel, had run a string of badly maintained trampers. Some of them sank. Others nearly did. None of them was under thirty years old—ten years past the time when most ships were scrapped.

Now Lotte Fredette and the others were watching to see how another disaster inquiry would play out. It seemed to be going the same old way. Farnham, the master, sat at the company's table, and Henry Howell, the union attorney, turned to him in front of the audience and said, "Captain Farnham. Aren't you at the wrong table? Don't you belong over here with your brother officers?" But Farnham remained silent and turned away.

It *was* different in one sense. There were survivors, and two of them were officers. But Hans's friends had explained the rules about that. Even if the old ship was a rust bucket, the officers could not say so. If they did, they could be prosecuted, blamed, no matter what the truth. It fell to them no matter what.

And then the board officers slowly walked Bob Cusick through testimony about his career and his experience at sea, right up until the point of the last trip of the *Marine Electric*.

No, he told them, the company had never pressured them to overload the ship.

And how were they trained by Captain Farnham on lifeboat drills?

"I would like to clarify that, to bring out the story that Captain Farnham is a very competent master, and he ran his vessel in such a way that the crew was exceptionally well trained."

Straight down the middle. He would tell the truth. The good part about Farnham.

In rapid succession, the board asked Cusick about the hatches. The hull. The drains.

And the chief mate replied that the hatches were in horrible shape. They had never fit since a 1981 dry-docking. He had sketched more than ninety repair areas in the holds. Weaknesses. Would the board like to see the drawings? He had copies.

Also, there was a hole in the hull he had fixed with cement and a coffee can lid, and it had never been fixed properly by the company, though they knew about it. And the drains in the cargo holds were covered to prevent coal from jamming the pumps.

Calicchio could not believe this last one.

"How would you pump the water out of the cargo hold, if you had any?"

Captain Lauridsen told the stenographer: "Let the record show that Captain Cusick shook his head negatively."

Robert Hughes III, a crack admiralty lawyer for Marine Transport Lines, shuffled papers at his table. This part could not be good for MTL. This guy did not seem to be intimidated at all, and he seemed to be animating Calicchio. The Coast Guard captain seemed literally to lean forward in his seat and was totally engaged with Cusick. They were playing off each other.

From the company standpoint, the sinking of the *Marine Electric* was the worst possible event at the worst possible time. Marine Transport Lines was no sleazy little tramp ship operation, and it was not hard at all to make a case that the company was among the finest, most innovative of American ship lines.

Now, the lawsuits were upon them, tarnishing all that. Soon, the family members and surviving crew members would file $100 million in suits against the company. The company would file a petition in New York to "limit liability" by proving the ship was seaworthy. If the company could do that—show they were not at fault for the sinking—then liability would be far less.

The best way to do that, and it was the company burden, was to show that this was an awful tragedy brought on by nature or accidental grounding. If that failed, then their best bet was to show that a member of the crew or the officers did not perform their duty properly and the company was unaware of this negligence.

But the economic impact could be even more horrible than the legal. The timing of it all, it had to be said, was just awful. Could not, in fact, have been worse.

They had been close, so very close, to replacing the *Marine Electric.*

Marine Transport Lines was building a new modern bulk carrier, the *Energy Independence,* to replace the *Marine Electric.* It would be finished before the next winter.

So close, so very close. If only they could have made it through one last winter with the *Marine Electric.* They felt they had to, just had to send the old ship out to sea, and it was the worst luck, the worst luck that the old girl did not make this one last winter.

Compounding this bad luck was the fact that on the very day the *Marine Electric* sailed, it had been announced that Marine Transport Lines was being spun off from its huge transportation company parent, GATX. GATX stockholders would receive one share of MTL stock for every five shares of GATX they owned.

And GATX? Well, for starters, it was finally rid of the sluggish maritime company that ate capital and bled red ink. The official story was that MTL could better seek financing on its own, rather than relying on GATX, where capital investment more frequently went for trucks than for ships.

Now MTL could raise its own capital, build its own ships. James Rand, the MTL chief executive, had plans to compete head-on with the Japanese and build modern vessels, a first in years for American merchant shipping. The spin-off gave MTL the ability to be innovative, with capital to back it. They could replace their tired-iron ships.

The spin-off, in short, freed MTL to steer its own course and build new ships. Few other U.S. ship companies were so innovative. And then, the very day after the spin-off, on the very first full day of the new corporate course, one of its old ships sank and threatened to sink all their plans.

Now there was only damage control. Captain Farnham had "signed on" with the company defense team. He reviewed the Coast Guard radio tapes, listened to the whole *Theodora* incident, and concluded that the big ship had been directed into shallow waters, and had bottomed out in one of the troughs of the big waves and slowly, slowly taken on water and sunk.

It was a possible explanation. And for the company, it was one of the best. There was no blame here, no negligence. Just heroism and tragedy.

• • •

Maritime law was a funny animal and it could bite any hand that fed it.

It was most famous for biting the owner's hand. A longshoreman or seaman who slipped and fell at sea or dockside might receive checks for the rest of his life for lost wages and pain and suffering—and still bowl regularly.

A whole industry of "slip and fall" cases powered a niche of American lawyers, and both sides in these matters acknowledged informally that there was widespread, well, *leniency.* A Lloyd's of London syndicate spokesman once noted wryly that American seamen, of all seamen in the world, seemed to have the weakest backs, because more than half of all the bad backs paid for by claims against Lloyd's were American backs. Either that, he said, or the U.S. had an outrageous tort system.

But there were times when the law turned against the mariners, as well. Seamen who *died* on ships that sank could receive damages limited to the amount of cargo carried, capped at $60 per ton, and the salvage value of the ship.

So the whole crew of the *Marine Electric* might receive a total of about $1.4 million from MTL. That amounted to about $40,000 per man. That number would balloon only if the crew and the families and their attorneys could show that the *Marine Electric* had not been fit to go to sea and the company knew or should have known. Then, the gates would swing wider. But not much wider. The last verdict against MTL was for the loss of the *Marine Sulphur Queen* in 1963. There, the court ruled against the company and said the ship sailed in an unseaworthy condition. But the total award was still small by American civil court standards, only about $15 million total for all the dead men. In contrast, a New York jury would set a record in the year 2000 by awarding $19 million to one man who dove off a pier unmarked by shallow water warnings.

In the case of the *Marine Sulphur Queen,* the court declined to award punitive damages, and this explained the relatively low awards. But if ever a maritime case could result in punitive damages, the *Marine Electric* was it. If the company could not prove that its ship was seaworthy, even admiralty law judges might be moved.

All of that could happen unless legal steps were taken by Marine Transport Lines, and the company was taking them now, as aggressively as it could, in this first skirmish line at the Marine Board.

The main battle over liability would take place in a formal courtroom, but the Marine Board was a trial heat for that courtroom. Evidence would first be presented in the Marine Board. The context would be set there as well. While the Marine Board operated under its own quasi-judicial rules, and while its rulings carried no legal value for damages, the investigation was, in a sense, a pretrial hearing. It could make or break the company, not to mention badly damage its reputation and, therefore, shareholder value.

As important here, the board also served as a sort of grand jury because it could recommend criminal investigations and actions as well.

Still, there were differences from a trial. There were no accused parties, only "parties of interest"—men such as the captain and the owner, the survivors and the families of the dead—who could be expected to have a stake in the outcome. Moreover, there were no impassioned opening and closing statements.

Still, the battle lines were drawn. Each attorney for a party of interest could examine witnesses, and these examinations and cross-examinations could be as brutal as in any courtroom.

Thomas L. Rohrer, the New York-based chief counsel to MTL, prided himself on protecting companies against "runaway juries" when cases reached a trial. At first, this one *seemed* controlled. An accidental grounding. Tragic. End of story. What would change that story? It was logical. Conceivable. Believable. No log existed.

It was the perfect defense. Everybody won. Certainly the surviving officers would not contradict it. Why would they? It got them off the hook and a nice-enough "no-fault" settlement as well.

If it weren't grounding, then the survivors were in a no-win situation. If the ship were deemed unseaworthy, then the officers, particularly the chief mate, were responsible for the condition of the ship. If something were wrong and they had not told the company or Farnham, the permanent master, then the blame lay squarely on the officers. Specifically, the blame would fall on the shoulders of Robert Manning Cusick, the chief mate.

Conversely, if Cusick and the other officers showed in testimony that Farnham and the company *did* know the ship was in bad shape, then Marine Transport Lines was in bad shape.

Rarely had that happened, however. In dozens of Marine Board cases since World War II, only a few had concluded that owners and operators acted poorly. It was stated policy to hold the officers first and foremost responsible.

Rohrer was the big gun of the legal defense team and worked the home office side of matters, talking to officers, reviewing records, checking diving reports, and surveying the chess board for strategic moves.

Hughes, the crack admiralty lawyer, was one of Rohrer's knights on that board. He was a partner in a Norfolk law firm and had been hired as the local MTL counsel on the spot. He had worked for MTL before, and on the *Marine Electric* as well. "I represented her in her first wreck and her last," he would say years later.

Hughes would do his job. He was an advocate for Marine Transport Lines. Period. It would be unethical for him to be anything else. He would give MTL 100 percent of his professional and highly effective effort.

But privately, he was thinking he could only posture. It seemed clear to him that the company had sent a very old ship out into the North Atlantic in February, into the teeth of a Nor'easter.

Hughes knew that his best hope was to show the ship had grounded, but now Calicchio was bearing in on the condition of the old ship, drilling down mercilessly on MTL's defense.

"You made mention that the covers were thin, words to that effect," Calicchio said in follow-up. "How did you arrive at that?"

"Oh," said Cusick. "You could run across some of the hatch covers, and they would bounce [pieces of hatch cover and rust] up and down like playing tiddledywinks on the ice of a pond."

"What hatches especially?"

"Number four was very bad. Number three."

"And what was the condition of the ship when she left the shipyard supposedly after having repairs?"

"The condition of the hatches was very bad. . . . Somewhere along the line, it was decided, for whatever reason I was not privy to, to change . . . to a gasket that was . . . considerably shorter [than the original hatch cover gaskets].

"The hatches were put on at the last moment, at the last day. I spent the whole night trying to get them to open and close. They were in much worse condition as far as opening and closing the hatch covers . . . because this particular gasket, this short gasket, wasn't even reaching, in many cases, to the sealing bar. . . . We left the shipyard without the hatches being repaired."

"How about the dogs? The hatch fasteners?" Calicchio was leaning farther forward in his seat now.

"The dogs were there, but they didn't all work properly. Only about half."

"The metal itself of the panels was in a deteriorated condition. They had done—there was still a lot of very thin metal in it everywhere. There were doublers [big metal plates] put here and there. But basically the hatches were in very poor condition at that time, I thought."

"Well," Calicchio said—and this was not a friendly question at all—"did YOU at anytime inform the Coast Guard of these deficiencies?"

"No," Cusick said. He would carry the knowledge of that inaction forever. But it was not how the system worked, simply to ring up the Coast Guard like that.

Hughes made notes on his paper. If Calicchio had not covered this, Hughes sure would. Cusick would not get off so easily just laying these things out as if he were some tourist on the Love Boat. These things could be seen as his responsibility, and if the company could show that he had not informed the permanent master, liability did not attach. The company did not have "privity."

Calicchio, knowing the same thing Hughes knew, drilled down on the mate:

"Did you at any time during this period make your concern known, if you did have any concern, as to the hatch covers, to the master or any other company official?"

"Yes," Bob Cusick said. He paused. "I made it clear to the master. He knew very well what they were. He was just as concerned about them as I was. . . . He was very insistent that I get these latest sketches done and get them passed in. . . . He was hoping that they would fix them up."

"And the general condition of the vessel?"

"As far as the main deck was concerned, the outboard part of it was in excellent condition," Cusick said.

"The areas between the hatches, that is fore and aft between one hatch and another, was not in good condition. In fact, there were areas that periodically over the last two years holes would appear in the deck due to the thinness of the metal and rust away. . . . We had a couple of them recently, and we put some epoxy—put what we call Red Hand over them and submitted them to the chief engineer. . . ."

"What would you grade the general condition?"

"The general condition, I would have to grade as . . . poor. The hatches were very poor. The main deck area between the hatches, poor. . . ."

Lotte Fredette was whispering to the other *Poet* mothers and scribbling notes. All the things that had not happened at the *Poet* hearing . . . *were* happening here. An officer was telling the truth. A Coast Guard officer was asking for the truth.

Hughes continued jotting notes. Well, this wasn't good. But there was the cross.

Then Calicchio asked Cusick to describe the sinking. The chief mate told the story again. At the capsizing, he sobbed involuntarily and shuddered. The audience was hushed as he told of his own survival. The cold. The waves. The helicopter. What month is it? February, he told the rescuers. "But if they had asked me the day, I could not have answered."

Then he was quiet.

In the audience, there were sniffles and coughs, then some quiet sobbing. The *Poet* mothers were moved to tears, and then they followed the Cusicks out into the hallway on the break.

"Mr. Cusick," Lotte called out. "We're the mothers from the SS *Poet*. You told the truth up there, Mr. Cusick! You told the truth! It won't bring our boys back, but you told the truth, and it makes us feel better now. Like we know a little bit on what happened to our boys."

Hughes would not cross-examine this man now. He would be recalled. Cusick seemed like a very brave man. Hughes thought he was telling the absolute truth, too, and that Marine Transport Lines had done the unthinkable—sent the old tub out in the winter storm. Now he could only play out a weak hand.

But Hughes was an attorney. Cusick was a direct threat to his client. Hughes's job now was to destroy or discredit Cusick. No hard feelings. Nothing personal. He made no apologies for it. It is how the advocacy system works.

But even before the cross, Cusick was not out of the woods.

Toward the end of his testimony, he had reddened and become teary. Calicchio had spoken to Cusick and Bea at a break. You don't have to do this right now, you know. We can wait. Calicchio, the kind uncle. But Cusick wanted to forge on. Calicchio remained concerned, and not without reason.

Near the end of the testimony, Cusick's attorney received a call from Bob's doctor in Boston. The enzyme tests were all wrong. Cusick's heart wasn't up to snuff. The message was simple: Get him back to Boston or to a cardiologist, and get him there quick.

And that was where he was headed as he stepped down from the stand. Cusick was surrounded by the *Poet* mothers now, and a crowd of media people. It might have been dizzying in itself, but the strain of the last few days caught up with him.

Bob Cusick stumbled and seemed nearly to fall. People were holding his elbows to steady him. He was okay, but he was red in the face. He seemed bewildered and lost for a few seconds.

Then he smiled. Smiled at his clumsiness. Smiled at the whole damned thing as he and Bea left for the cardiologist Howell had found for them.

Chapter Seventeen

THE DIVE

Some say the world will end in fire
Some say in ice

Robert Frost

About noon / Wednesday, Feb. 16, 1983
Marine Electric marker buoy / 30 miles off Chincoteague

While Bob Cusick was testifying before the *Marine Board,* Michael Carr, the Coast Guard scuba diver who had wanted to go out on the rescue helicopters, cleared his regulator and surveyed the mild chop on the water thirty miles off the coast of Virginia.

Now he would get his chance at the rescue, however slim the odds. His main mission this day was to survey the wreckage of the *Marine Electric* and determine whether it was a hazard to navigation. The ship was 605 feet long, the water 130 feet deep. Any current or turbulence might set the ship on end and leave part of it sticking out of the water. The chances of the *Marine Electric* sinking a second ship were real.

The chances for a rescue were unreal, however, and Carr told himself that. Yet, no matter the odds, no matter how many times he repeated them, the thought stayed with him. The guys might still be down there. They might be alive.

It was four full days after the sinking. Two factors had slowed this dive. The *Marine Electric,* after capsizing, had bobbed for hours on the surface. When she finally sank, no one was in the vicinity to record the coordinates. They knew the general area, but the ocean was vast and the weather had been rotten. They had not found her.

But on this day, a ship equipped with sensitive sonar had picked up the bones of the ship on the bottom. A line tied to the deck of the sunken ship floated up from the bottom and moved in the sway of the ocean surface. This one last slim tendril of hope from the *Marine Electric* snagged the sonar ship.

So now all Carr had to do was go hand over hand down the line to the ship—the first bit of luck the old girl had had in days.

There's not much chance in this, Carr thought as he slipped into the Atlantic, adjusted to the shock of the cold, and then grabbed the line and worked his way down it. There were only a few scenarios for the engine room guys, and most of them involved death by fire or ice. Only one scenario could mean life this long after the sinking.

Most probably, the surviving officers thought, the tons of shifting engine room equipment had crushed them. A quick death. The superheated steam would have escaped and flooded the area as well. If any of the men had survived those fates, they would have been trapped in cold water down below and lived not much longer than the men on the surface.

It was not impossible that some or all of the men had run up from the engine room below, made it to the deck, and then were dumped into the water. There, without life jackets, they died and were lost. Those who knew the engine room guys thought this improbable. Price was still asking if the engines should be secured when Kelly yelled at him to get out. It was a long run up lots of stairs to the top.

Another scenario had by far the slimmest of possibilities. The men—some of them, one of them, all of them—had managed to make it part way up the stairs to the deck when the ship capsized. They were tossed when the ship capsized, but landed okay and then made their way to dry, warm quarters. There, they still rested, waiting for rescue, waiting for Carr's tap outside the hull. This scenario was highly, highly improbable. Still, it was not impossible.

Carr descended silently in the murky water, diving down the line. He could see only ten feet in front of him, and ten feet of the line looked like any other ten feet as he dove.

But then, the line turned to a dark ominous shadow in the murk, and a few feet later the bulk came into focus as he touched the hard steel hull with a thump. Through his face mask, the *Marine Electric* came into ghastly focus.

She was torn up badly. Immediately, he banged on the hull with a hammer, listening in the stillness of 130 feet below the surface, in between the rush of his breathing and the bubbles from his respirator. The silence was such that any answering tap would be heard. If anyone was down there, they could tell.

He would bang and listen, bang, listen. Then he would flipper to another spot on the hull and bang again.

There was nothing. No answering taps. No sign that Price and Browning or Wickboldt or the others were alive. The silence was final.

Other members of Carr's team reached the wreckage and began rapping and banging. They spread out and methodically covered all parts of the half of the ship they could see.

The echoes faded like "Taps" played at Arlington. The ship was silent as a tomb and, in fact, now had to be considered a tomb.

It would be months before the divers learned they had tapped on the bow section. They could not tell with ten-foot visibility, but thought they had reached the stern, where the engine room was located. The ship had been ripped apart on the bottom, and the old T-2 stern was 605 feet away from the bow. The two halves were still held together by a thin metal strip, but in between was a void. The divers came to the ripped end of the bow and could not see the stern through the murk. They had no way of knowing.

They determined that the ship was not going to shift and slowly began their ascent, decompressing on the way up.

When the news came that the divers had found no signs of life, the families, in their own minds, picked the best end for their loved ones.

Did they drown? Did they die of hypothermia like the men on the surface? Were they crushed by tons of shifting equipment and huge engine room gears and fixtures? Did the boiler give way and send out superhot steam? Were they alive in an air bubble for a while before the cold drifted them gently into apathy, stupor, death?

In their minds, the families picked an end. Or tried to.

Marsha Price now knew for sure that Mike was dead. She could no longer hold on to hope.

But in some part of her mind she did. Mike got picked up by a passing boat, she thought, that took him to Europe. He couldn't communicate all these weeks, but now he's in port. He got picked up by a boat, but he had amnesia. Just now, he remembered who he was.

If nothing else, you knew how stubborn he was, he just plain swam those thirty miles to shore. This is Mike we're talking about here!

She knew he was dead and knew those other thoughts were just denial and that he was never coming home.

Still, days, weeks, months after the tragedy, she would be doing some household task, washing the dishes or vacuuming, and the phone would ring or the doorbell would chime.

That could be Mike! she thought, and her heart would soar.

Chapter Eighteen

THE SERIAL SINKERS

*Recklessness, induced by the war, . . . extended its mischievous
tendencies into all branches of trade and is particularly observable
among those in or on board some classes of steamers. A large number of
boats have been used during the war as transports, tugs and freights,
these have been depreciated by long and continued use—purchased and
put on duty without proper examination and even without precaution
or regard to safety. This will doubtless be found among the most
prominent causes of the terrible calamities which seem to be beyond
the reach of official remedy.*

1865 official inquiry into the loss of Sultana

TUESDAY, MARCH 15, 1983 / *PHILADELPHIA INQUIRER* NEWSROOM

As Gene Roberts read the updates on the progress of the investigative piece on the *Marine Electric,* three things seemed true beyond question. That one reporter would never again question advice to drill down. No one would ever laugh at Roberts for insisting there be a maritime beat. And that the system Roberts was looking at was as insidious as it was tragic.

They had known these ships were serial sinkers. Yet, through the years, rationalization, denial, greed, and stubbornness had conspired to keep the ships at sea. The government, the shipowners, and even the unions knew at some level that the old World War II ships were an unreasonable risk. Despite loss after loss after loss, the ships were certified as safe and sent back into service.

There was nothing secret about it, if you drilled down and looked at the files. The problem was: The public eye had never seen. The public heart had never felt.

The question was: Could his team prove it?

The drafts of stories in front of him tried hard to make the case.

Some ships—like the *Schenectady* in 1943—simply broke in two at dockside. Hurried panels were called to inquire. At first, they suspected the fault was in the new welding methods used during the war. Welding was a weapon every bit as important as planes and guns. Welding and the new industrial techniques it allowed produced more ships than the German U-boats could sink. The technique had been employed with all the urgency brought by wartime pressures.

But the problem went beyond welding, to the steel itself. The steel was not the right blend of iron, oxygen, and alloy for ocean-going ships. Its temperature-transition properties were poor, and the metal was not ductile in cold water. When the water temperature fell below fifty degrees Fahrenheit, brittle fractures might occur. Even new, the hulls contained "dirty steel" or "tired iron" unfit to challenge high waves and cold water. When the conditions were right, some hulls burst like crystal.

Cracks in such steel were common in the past, but the cracks on old-style riveted ships stopped when the fractures hit the seam of a new riveted plate.

On the all-welded ships, the cracks shot around the ship at the speed of sound. The *Schenectady* had not even been at sea. She had not suffered the stress of any service at all. She simply broke in two like a glass ship.

This was wartime, though, and the ships could not simply be scrapped. The solution was "crack arrestors." These were riveted, higher-grade steel straps placed around the ships in great belts. The thought was that a crack starting in the welded part would shoot only as far as the crack arrestor, thus allowing the ship to stay afloat.

The ships with brittle steel thus were kept going. There was no choice. Risk management in wartime was more about how many men would die than if they would die. The ships and the seamen were part of the war effort.

It is uncertain even now how many "lost ships" were torpedoed out there and how many simply broke in two before or after the crack arrestors were installed. A 1952 study found a total of 148 ships that had suffered a known and confirmed "Group I" casualty—a splitting-in-two or major hull fracture. More than 700 had experienced some sort of fracture.

But they floated well enough to win the war. They did their job.

Certainly, there was no exposé here for Roberts. The war was the war.

But after the war, the old ships kept sailing. And kept sinking.

The American maritime establishment felt that the emergency ships constructed in wartime were suitable for the merchant trades. The men, their unions, and the government were all accustomed to the high risk of war. These risks were nothing by comparison.

Or so it seemed at first.

The *Southern Isles,* a converted wartime landing craft, sank and claimed seventeen lives in October 1951.

Then in December 1951, the *Flying Enterprise,* a wartime ship sailing from West Germany, suffered cracks in her deck and was disabled in a storm. Only one passenger died, and the captain chose to remain on board after he ordered all others off. His highly publicized heroism was so admired worldwide that he received a ticker-tape parade in New York City. The Coast Guard report on the matter concentrated on the heroism and said nothing of how the welded ship may have fractured to begin with.

The SS *Pennsylvania* set out to sea just one month after the *Southern Isles* men were lost. Her deck cracked. The owners "fixed it." The ship went back to sea into a winter storm, and she and forty-six men went down in the Pacific.

The Coast Guard reports suggested that the *Pennsylvania* tragedy may have been due to improper loading by the captain, even though the courts said the ship was structurally unsound and the owner negligent for sending it out in a clearly unseaworthy condition.

One month after the *Pennsylvania* was lost, two T-2 tankers, in the same place off Cape Cod, at the same time, went down, summoning forth one of the most heroic of American Coast Guard rescues. In this case, the Coast Guard investigators concluded that the crack arrestors weren't really doing the job. But the Coast Guard took little action against the owners or its inspectors.

What was clear was that the T-2s were staying at sea, along with the converted Liberty ships and Victory ships and the C-4 troopships and the old Great Lakes vessels, despite clear and ominous evidence that the very steel within the ships contained structural weaknesses.

Despite five sinkings in four months and the deaths of more than seventy men, despite two tankers sinking on the same day, the wartime vessels stayed in commerce as a mainstay of the American Merchant Marine.

A year after the Cape Cod disasters, the Coast Guard claimed victory. A study showed that in the one-year period after it took steps, no more T-2s had gone down.

The shine of that policy dulled quickly when more war-built ships started sinking.

The *Southern District,* a converted Navy LST landing craft made of brittle steel, was carrying a load of bulk cargo and twenty-three men off the eastern Florida coast. On December 5, 1954, ship, men, and cargo all disappeared and were never found.

Then the *Washington Mail,* a converted wartime cargo ship, went down off Alaska in a mild storm. There was a trail of the usual clues that this might happen. In 1954, a fracture developed at the corner of the deckhouse. In 1955, another fracture spread at another corner of the deckhouse. Then, in March 1956, the crew heard deep rumbling sounds within the core of the ship. Five seconds later, the SS *Washington Mail* split cleanly in two.

The fix for this problem was the same as before. Inspect more. Inspect harder.

But the Coast Guard inspectors who approved the faulty ships for service were never censured, even though the *Washington Mail,* for example, broke in two precisely where the ship had fractured earlier.

The policy chased its tail. Old ships could sail safely only if they were inspected carefully.

But how did an inspector gauge the soundness of steel plate

when the steel itself, at a molecular level, was the problem? When the ships sank from fractures, the marine boards or the Coast Guard commandant absolved the inspectors and the owners.

As to owner responsibility, the degree, as always, varied. The policy guideline was to withhold vessels from sailing into cold, rough water. The owners, many of them, were gaming the system. They continued to send the ships out into the North Atlantic. The steel cracked in cold water. Cracks let in water. Water destabilized the designed, acceptable stresses on a ship. The ships sank.

A dysfunctional and deadly circle of blame formed. Often, the owners of a ship that sank blamed the Coast Guard inspectors for certifying the ship safe. The Coast Guard in turn would blame the officers. Rarely, if ever, were the owners or inspectors brought to task in a Marine Board of Investigation. Rarely, if ever, were the old ships inspected so thoroughly that they were forbidden to go to sea.

The system Gene Roberts's reporters were reviewing existed even under men of good will and good intentions. In 1954, a young man named Clyde T. Lusk graduated into this system from the Coast Guard Academy and would watch those trends uneasily. He intended to make marine safety his life's work. Many, many years later, as an admiral, he would write a letter on behalf of Dominic Calicchio, defending his strict inspections of passenger ships in Miami. Lusk was, according to all who worked with him, a good man, one of the best in the Coast Guard, a man who worked within the system but was always aware of its flaws and the need to correct them. He was that way, his colleagues said, as a fresh Academy graduate and, thirty years later, as chief of staff to the commandant, and later still when he became the vice commandant, the second most powerful Coast Guard officer.

Never was Lusk bitterly disheartened by the system, as Calicchio sometimes was. He was proud of the work the Coast Guard did to elevate world shipping standards. The new ships, the modern ships, were subject to very tough standards. The Americans and the Coast

Guard were right alongside the British, the Norwegians, and the Swedes in ship safety standards.

But Lusk and other marine safety inspectors, however earnest, also knew there were things beyond their control. The economics of shipping, for example, was a force they could not form or fashion.

"You couldn't always get what you wanted," he said years later. "We all wanted double-hull tankers years ago, but the reality was if we required them, there would have been a lot of people cold during the winter. The Coast Guard could not simply order all the safety requirements we wanted. We would have shut down the oil industry."

And then there were the politics of the day. The unions, the shipowners and the shipbuilders had formed a powerful alliance. Together, they often topped all other political contributors. The unions in particular were politically aware. They had been battered during the war, branded as "Reds" by some, and then afterward saw their men of the Merchant Marine excluded from veteran status and benefits. So much for the thanks of a grateful nation. Postwar, the unions were cynical and single-minded in making certain they bought and kept political influence. The unions wanted jobs on ships, period.

The ship operators and the shipbuilders joined them in an iron triangle of political strength. Other nations were allowing ships to fly their flag even if the ships were built in foreign yards. Some allowed them to carry foreign seamen as well. But in America, the iron triangle controlled policy, and the policy was U.S.A., all the way. Ships flying American flags would be built in American yards and be crewed with Americans. Period. Not even the agricultural lobbies could break the iron triangle. The iron triangle policies meant higher rates for bulk grains shipped abroad, which meant fewer bushels sold. The farmers, the grain traders, even huge agribusinesses like Cargill, could not break the maritime alliance and its hold over Congress.

The problem with the American-all-the-way policy was that American yards were so expensive, owners could not afford to build many new ships. Even with generous government subsidies, the U.S.

fleet grew older every year—far, far past the age the Coast Guard considered optimal for safety.

And the policy laid down by Marine Boards of Investigations sounded good but, in reality, worked poorly. The American Merchant Marine was declining, and any close Coast Guard attention to defects was seen as unpatriotic and antibusiness.

"Whenever we found serious things wrong with a ship, there were tremendous, tremendous domestic pressures to keep the ship going," Lusk said. "The owners, the unions, and sometimes congressmen too, all would say we were putting them at a great competitive disadvantage. It was a very complex system in which we made our decisions.

"So we adopted a policy that economics would determine when a ship would be scrapped," he said. "We had a policy that a ship would keep on sailing until an owner said it was not economically viable anymore. We did not just say a ship could no longer sail; we hoped the owner had the good sense to stop sailing it when the economics were no longer there."

The problem with the policy was that some owners always saw value in even the oldest and rustiest ships. Samuel Plimsoll found the same situation in the nineteenth century when, in an age of steel ships powered by steam, wooden ships of sail continued to be used in the tramp trades. Always, some owners were willing to take a chance on marginal, cast-off vessels.

And in the United States, the government actually encouraged such actions by subsidizing rates for ships that were so old and inefficient they could not compete in the open trades. Then, too, laws required that only American-flag ships could sail from one American port to another. U.S. shipyards could not build ships for these trades cheaply enough to make them economically viable. So the policies combined to assure that the Great Lakes and coastal trade fleets were made up of very old U.S. vessels. And because they were not replaced by new ships, they sailed on and on.

Until they sank.

In 1958, the *Carl D. Bradley,* an old Great Lakes ship built before World War II, suffered structural failure and sank with thirty-three of her thirty-five men lost.

On December 21, 1960, the old T-2 tanker the SS *Pine Ridge* sank. It was by now an old story. The ship split in two in a storm. The bow section sank, killing all the officers and some crew—seven men in all. The vessel was equipped with twelve crack arrestors, half again as many as required by Coast Guard policy set after the Cape Cod debacle. The ship was seventeen years old, just short of retirement age for most vessels.

Some might have been encouraged that the old ships were nearing that magic twenty-year mark where most ships were scrapped. Soon, they all would be gone.

Then the same alliance that had pressured the Coast Guard to go easy on the old ships was insisting that their economic life could be extended. The plan was to split a ship in a foreign shipyard and then weld a large midsection between the old bow and the old stern. The new ship would be like a stretch limousine with a new Mercedes mid-body attached to a patched twenty-year-old Chevy front and rear.

There were dozens of T-2s out there, queuing up to be expanded under this program. The old ships now would have their life extended by another twenty years.

Some of them literally were sinking twice.

The tanker *San Jacinto* broke in two and exploded off Virginia in 1964. When Roberts's reporters ran the lineage of the *San Jacinto*, they found she was composed of a new bow welded onto the old stern section of the *Fort Mercer*—the T-2 that had split in two back in 1952 off Cape Cod.

This "jumbo-ization" intersected with Roberts's story in 1961. The T-2 tanker SS *Gulf Mills* was towed to a West German shipyard for enlargement by Marine Transport Lines. There a new midsection was fitted to the old stern and bow. The ship was old already at age sixteen. As the SS *Musgrove Mills,* she had dodged torpedoes during the war. In 1947, she was sold to Gulf Oil, and had been a workhorse for fourteen years.

She came out of the German yard with a new steel midsection strung between her old bow and old stern. The old bow had fresh steel reinforcements. And she also carried a new name—*Marine Electric.* She joined the fleet of the Marine Transport Lines in 1961—one of several jumbo-ized ships in the MTL fleet—not as a tanker but as a bulk carrier.

Amid the christenings of their "new" ships and the excitement of this scheme to revive the American Merchant Marine, Marine Transport saw that something was very wrong—about as wrong as could be in the shipping business.

In April 1961, the old Liberty ship SS *Marine Merchant,* a Marine Transport Lines ship, was steaming north off Nantucket carrying a load of sulphur. She had undergone a Coast Guard inspection one month and three days earlier. She had all the recommended "structural strengthening" modifications, including hatch reinforcements, a deck crack arrestor, a gunwale crack arrestor, and alterations to her bilge keel.

But she hit heavy weather, with winds of more than fifty miles per hour and twenty-foot waves, on April 13. About 10:30 that night, the officers and crew heard a distinct "loud report." It was the all-too-familiar crack of brittle steel. The ship had snapped in two, crack arrestors be damned, and quickly began settling in the water toward midship, with the bow and stern gradually rising higher. The men abandoned ship and lost four dead.

In 1963, Marine Transport suffered another sinking of an old ship, and not even the benumbed U.S. Coast Guard could ignore it. Media types hovered about for weeks. This time, congressmen pressed their case for lost constituents.

The *Marine Sulphur Queen* had been outfitted to carry molten sulphur and, like the *Marine Electric,* had been "jumbo-ized," with old T-2 tired iron in her bow and stern. The *Marine Sulphur Queen* sailed one stormy day in 1963 and simply disappeared with all thirty-nine hands near Florida. Only the most ghastly remains were found—a life jacket with a bit of a crewman's shirt tied to it. A Coast Guard investigation noted simply:

"Numerous tears on the life jackets indicated attack by predatory fish."

Ten buckets of dull gray euphemisms could not paint over this tragedy, and the Marine Board of the time issued a hard-hitting, tough report. No definite reason for the sinking was ever determined, and the ship was never found. But the officers investigating the loss of the *Marine Sulphur Queen* were faced not with one or two or three or four or even five T-2 failures. Their report in 1964 stated: "The Board has extensively considered the possibility that the casualty to this vessel was caused by a complete longitudinal failure of the vessel's hull girder causing it to break in two. There are many factors bearing on this issue. Basically, insofar as this type vessel is concerned, the evidence indicates that there have been *ten known* cases of complete fractures of T-2 type tank vessels.

"That this type of casualty has persisted after the problem has been thoroughly studied and measures taken to prevent the same, tends to support the view held by some that *this type of vessel has basic design imperfections which cannot be feasibly corrected.*" [italics added]

The board's recommendations were simple:

"In the future the same conversion of another T-2 type tanker should not be approved. Further, it is recommended that no other conversion of this type vessel should be approved which deviates from the originally designed features for the carriage of normal petroleum products."

If adopted, the action would at least put an end to the "jumboization" of T-2s for anything other than oil. Ships like the *Marine Electric,* for example, could not be enlarged if they were to carry sulphur or grain or coal.

As had become terribly routine, however, the board recommendations never made it past the commandant. The conversion ban will not be implemented, he declared. One cannot make such broad-brush generalizations. Conversions should be considered on an individual ship-by-ship basis.

Yet a federal district court judge determined that the *Marine Sulphur Queen* was unseaworthy and that the T-2s as a class were structurally "unreliable, to say the least." And by that time, the judge had not just ten cases of structural failure to cite in T-2s used as merchant ships, he had fifteen.

The Coast Guard, he noted, had been the last line of protection for the officers and crew on board the ship, and the government agency had served as merely a "rubber stamp" for the American Bureau of Shipping—a surveyor of hulls and structure. The Coast Guard had hardly inspected the ships at all, the judge stated.

And so the casualties sailed on.

The Coast Guard search-and-rescue people had developed their informal motto all by themselves. You have to go out. You do not have to come back.

After decades of old ship failures and sinkings, it seemed as if the Coast Guard marine inspectors had at some level developed their own unstated motto as well. It was a bitter one and, free of political and economic constraints, one no Coast Guardsman would have set as his own.

The old ships have to go out. They do not have to come back.

Each of the cases Gene Roberts read through could have stopped the next tragedy. Each was a link in the chain that carried down the *Marine Electric.* Yet nothing was going to keep the T-2s and the other old ships from going to sea. Nothing would save the *Marine Electric.*

The *Daniel Morrell* was next. It sank in the Great Lakes in 1964. Dennis Hale—the man who suffered so from survivor's guilt—was the sole survivor.

Here, though, a substantive policy action was taken. It did not, however, originate with the Coast Guard. The National Transportation Safety Board, in a rare break with its Coast Guard colleagues, questioned the Coast Guard's inaction on the *Daniel Morrell* sinking. The full, high-level board, composed of men and women selected by presidents and cabinet members, could take on the economic and political pressures. Shocked by the *Morrell,* the board spoke out.

The NTSB report was phrased in language that skirted just this side of disdain for the Coast Guard. Twenty-eight men were dead. Count the sinking on the Lakes of the *Carl Bradley* back in 1958, and you add in thirty-three more dead. Isn't it time, the NTSB asked the Coast Guard, to take some action here? We're dealing with ships that are very, very old. And sixty-one dead men.

"While we fully appreciate the economic aspects involved in methods that would help prevent failure of hull girders, from a safety standpoint, we recommend that you consider further action. . . ."

With that sort of juice urging it on, the Coast Guard did follow through with special inspections of Great Lakes ships. Most of the very old lakers were forced out of service after extensive inspections.

The scope of the Great Lakes "crackdown" never reached the *oceangoing* vessels. Perhaps it was because the Lakes fleet was truly decrepit. Ships were still sailing into storms after age sixty. The bluewater fleet was young by comparison.

The old World War II ships sailed on and on and on in the saltwater merchant fleet.

Then an old ship run by Henry Bonnabel, a tramp ship operator, suffered a fractured hull in 1973 in quiet seas. A crack in the *Silver Dove* had been hastily patched with cement just a few days earlier, and the ship was given the go-ahead by the Coast Guard. She soon went down with no casualties other than the Coast Guard's tarnished credibility.

But the *Silver Dove* sinking and operators like Bonnabel added a new dimension to the problem. As the merchant fleet approached the 1980s, the old ships were not just in danger of "material failure" in their hulls. All their systems were wearing out. Like old cars, even restored classics, old ships had many parts one could not tell were gone until they went.

Operators like Bonnabel kept the worst of the old girls running. Even if reputable companies were gradually rotating the vessels out of service, tramp ship operators were snapping them up to run in the government cargo trades.

In the twentieth century, Bonnabel was heir to the trade described in Plimsoll's day a hundred years earlier. David Masters, in his biography of Plimsoll, wrote of Dickensian conditions that held true a century later. First-rate shipowners would run a ship safely.

"But the time came when repair and replacements swallowed too big a proportion of profits and she was sold at the best price she would fetch to a new owner who did not worry if she had dropped down the scale in register so long as she could carry freight and earn a profit. By spending as little as possible on her and practising cheese-paring economies he may have made ends meet for years, by which time she had probably dropped out of the register entirely. . . .

"So she passed from hand to hand, if she remained afloat, until she was indeed a sea tramp owned perhaps by a needy man who still made the semblance of a living out of her . . ."

Unchanged, the practice was alive and well in 1983. A shipping executive who once worked for Bonnabel explained the curious economics of the ancient ships. Take a vessel managed by Bonnabel called the *California*. The *California*'s heritage is unclear, but it is believed that she incorporated the old stern of the SS *Sacketts Harbor*—a T-2 that broke apart in 1947.

"Matson Shipping ran this ship *into the ground* in the sugar trade between the U.S. West Coast and Hawaii," recalled the executive. "There was an informal agreement, an unstated agreement between the inspectors and Matson: Keep the ship running for a little while longer, okay, but then it goes to the scrap pile.

"Then, when all economic utility long had been exhausted, Matson turns around and sells it to Bonnabel's company, which takes it from the Seattle Coast Guard to the Tampa Coast Guard and gets it certified there.

"It takes $1,500 a day in repairs to run one of these ships, and $200,000 for your dry-dock at the end of the year.

"Bonnabel doesn't budget anything. He just loads these old tubs up with government grain and takes it as it comes. Finally, I couldn't take it any more and quit."

By 1974, Coast Guard statistics showed that 22 percent of all ship casualties were structural in nature. One of every three sinkings in the Atlantic and the Gulf of Mexico were the result of material failure, one of every two in the Pacific.

A full fifth of the U.S. fleet was more than thirty years old. Nearly 40 percent of the fleet was more than twenty years old—the normal scrapping age. A 1976 survey of merchant mariners showed that 99 percent said they had sailed on a ship they considered clearly unsafe.

As if to emphasize the fact, the *Chester A. Poling* went down in January 1977 off Massachusetts after fracturing in two at its pilothouse. She was more than forty years old.

Then there was the SS *Poet,* an old troop carrier. She carried Lotte Fredette's son to his death along with thirty-three others in

October 1980. There was abundant reason to believe the old ship was poorly kept by Henry J. Bonnabel. Her sister ship, also owned by Bonnabel, was a certifiable rust bucket called the SS *Penny*.

Coast Guard investigators did little to find out the real reasons the ship might have sunk. In fact, they seemed not to want to know. Even one of their own, a captain in the Coast Guard, had lost a boy on the ship, and yet the board was ever so timid in looking into Bonnabel's actions.

The system seemed to be eating its young. The Coast Guard had lost a son. Yet Bonnabel seemed almost protected by the Marine Board.

The board tentatively suggested that the Coast Guard inspectors could have looked harder and *could* have had more training. The Coast Guard *might* consider examining and auditing owner-operator track records to make sure they lived up to their responsibilities. There was evidence to show that the Coast Guard inspectors did not have sufficient experience and that the federal agencies responsible for the ship's safety were poorly coordinated.

But the commandant's report reversed even that weak critique. There is no evidence that the Coast Guard inspectors did not have adequate experience, he wrote. There was no evidence that the agencies were poorly coordinated.

It was the end of the story, except that thirty-four men undeniably had died on the ship of an owner with a very checkered history. The inspectors again and again had cut Bonnabel and his rickety old ships break after break.

It had been a clear chance for the Coast Guard to check the problems of the old ships. It had been an excellent time to draw a line in the sand.

And the case of the *Poet* was the last chance to change the system before the system sent the *Marine Electric* on her last voyage.

But nothing would be done.

Seamen drowned, froze, burned, were scalded, were bashed to death in lifeboats, and, it would seem, eaten by sharks.

Nothing slowed the use of the old ships. And nothing moved the government to crack down. The eye did not see. The heart did not feel. The system did not change.

In fact, the momentum was moving the other way.

In 1983, after the sinking of the *Marine Electric,* the U.S. Military Sealift Command sought out Bonnabel and one of his old rusty ships for a lucrative contract. The U.S. Maritime Administration and Marine Transport Lines were also collaborating on a project to extend the life of the old T-2s even further. The electric turbines would be replaced by diesel engines, a report concluded. This would give at least another ten to twenty years of life to the ships, and it was a lot cheaper than building new ones.

The institutional denial was so complete, the government policies did more than assure that the old ships continued to sail for the rest of their natural economic lives. They were *extending* the lives of the old tubs again. First, there were the wartime ships—good for twenty years. Then the "jumbo-ized" ships—good for another twenty years. Now, they were saying they could stick new engines in the ships—and go for another twenty. The government subsidized the study that concluded this and would guarantee the ships' revenue. They were moving toward implementation.

In fact, the government was now pushing the old ships into new services hazardous not just to their crews.

Gene Roberts read the early drafts of the story. It contained the sort of news that made a reader gasp and an editor smile.

The reporters had come across a company named Chemical Waste Management, which was in the final stages of creating incinerator ships for toxic wastes. PCBs would be loaded onto ships and burned a considerable distance offshore. This would be a big plus over dumping them in rural swamps and forests and was hailed as an enlightened, environmentally conscious breakthrough.

On a hunch, the reporters checked out the ships that would be used in the project. The toxic waste incinerators were to be constructed on the hulls of forty-year-old T-2 tankers.

This was a system beyond denial.

Powerful people were attacking Cusick now to show that the company had no "privity of knowledge" about the condition of the old T-2. That Cusick knew, but suppressed it.

They *all* had privity of knowledge.

The government. The surveyors. The inspectors. The companies. The shipyards. The unions. The shippers. This was far beyond the Coast Guard turning a blind eye and succumbing to political and economic pressure. The inspectors never had a chance.

Everyone in the system wanted the old ships at sea. They all knew, yet, somehow suppressed or ignored it.

And now they were going to ship toxic wastes on old, unstable T-2 hulls? Navigating ships through the ports of U.S. cities like Philadelphia and New York?

This was a system that went beyond Perrow's "error-inducing" theory. Beyond denial, Gene Roberts thought. Beyond absurdity, too.

This was madness.

He was still very quiet in the story meetings, and his silence had the effect of drawing all available information from his journalists, like a bilge pump draws water. He made one or two suggestions, and he added people to the team.

He read the drafts of stories but never micromanaged them. On the ones he liked, he would nod affirmatively. The ones he did not like, he remained quiet about. The team took the hint and rewrote them until he nodded.

Sometimes a series never got into print. They all knew that. Roberts would commit dozens of journalists to an investigation, and they would bang away at it for weeks, months. In the end, if the point was tentative or muddled, the case unclear, the stories would never see the light of day. It was what made the *Philadelphia Inquirer* the brilliant regional paper of its era. Roberts would never serve up a half-baked story.

This one seemed to be rolling along smoothly and with a sense of purpose. Larry Williams, the project editor, proposed a massive package of articles, charts, and pictures to Roberts. The series would cover page after page of the *Inquirer* for three days. Count all the words, and the *Inquirer* would be printing more maritime news in one week than other newspapers had printed in the past half-century.

Roberts read it through on paper—he did not much use computers and he nodded the whole way. It all seemed to be there. It was all fascinating and horrifying.

What it wasn't yet was a story.

"Nail it all down," he told Williams. "Keep working it."

Chapter Nineteen

MEMORIAL

The seas washed over them, and they were gone.
We shall not forget them.

Maine Maritime Academy monument

2 P.M. / SUNDAY, MARCH 13, 1983
ST. MARY OF THE NATIVITY CHURCH / SCITUATE, MASSACHUSETTS

Always a chief mate, never a master. It was only after that first hearing in Portsmouth, Virginia, that Bob Cusick became a captain, the master of a crew of grieving friends and families. He became the leader, however reluctantly, of a growing crowd angered at the loss of the *Marine Electric.*

After his initial testimony, Bea and Bob had felt exuberant. The doctor watched his heart and the enzymes closely, and soon all was as it should be.

The "why-you's" were gone. The hearing had been cathartic, cleansing Cusick of the guilty feelings.

Captain Farnham wasn't organizing a service to honor his ship's dead. Few of the survivors wanted to see Farnham anyway. That left it up to the chief mate, and the Cusicks searched for churches in the area and sent out letters and made phone calls.

The response was overwhelming. More than 300 said they would be there. They needed a big church or hall now, one that would accept eulogies from six denominations and religions.

In Scituate, that meant St. Mary of the Nativity Church, and on March 21, the mourners began filing in. Mary Babineau, the wife of Second Mate Clayton Babineau, thought she would find comfort among the others. She did, but gave comfort as good as she got.

Paul Dewey sought her out. Dewey, the able-bodied seaman who was brand new to the ship, was feeling overwhelming guilt, blaming himself, particularly for Babineau's death. They had worked so hard together, Dewey told Mary Babineau, they were so close, eye-to-eye. I lost my guys, Dewey said, I lost your husband. I should have saved him. I could have. I should have saved him. He looked at Babineau's teenage kids, and his cloud darkened further.

Mary Babineau smiled wryly. She was a devout Catholic. "All of my problems, she would say, they were so great, so much greater than I was, I just had to give them to God. It was all I could do."

But she also had that deep streak of black humor. She and Clayt had joked about his death at sea. "Don't worry," he had said. "If I die, that would leave you a rich widow, and I couldn't bear the thought of you clinking champagne glasses with your new husband."

She told Paul Dewey that story and added, "Paul, if the thought of me being a rich widow with a new husband and buying him champagne did not *propel* Clayt into that raft, nothing in this world would have. There is nothing more that you could have done, son. Nothing more in this world."

Her words made Dewey laugh.

"The things I *hated* about him—his lists, his *complete* orderliness— those are the things that are saving me now," Mary told Bob Cusick. "He had *everything* down. How to bury him. Insurance. How the settlement money should be used.

"He gave me six months with his lists, Bob. Six months on automatic pilot. After that, I don't know what I'll do."

"But you," she told Bob Cusick. *"You* know what to do. You're doing it. Like I said, Bob, you were the only one who knew every nook and cranny of the ship, who could show what the company did wrong. Clayt tried. They didn't do anything. *You* can."

Slowly, powerfully, the memorial service, without many more words being said about Cusick, took on that theme. And Cusick, without any guilt or concern about becoming Crusader Rabbit, quietly took up the mantle of leader and wore it as if he always had.

Clergy from six faiths conducted the service, and all of them tried to comfort those in attendance with a common theme: The men have gone on to a higher life.

"So this watery grave holds no grip on these men," said Clifford Olsen, the chaplain for the port of Norfolk who had helped Bob. "Their watery graves are only a temporary receptacle until the time they will be restored to their true life."

That message was echoed by others, including the Rt. Rev. Daniel A. Hart, auxiliary bishop of the Roman Catholic Arch-diocese of Boston, who read a letter from Cardinal Humberto Medeiros:

"Keep the bonds of love which tie you one to another in family and friendship sealed and unbroken."

And then he added:

"Make every effort to assure that other mariners who go down to the sea in ships do so in vessels which are safe."

Eyes turned automatically toward Cusick at that line, but the most emotional portion of the ceremony for Bob and most others came as he left his seat and crossed in front of the white altar and a glass vase holding thirty-one red roses, on his way to the lectern.

He began with a story about the ship's chief engineer, Richard Powers, who had perished on the life ring. He said Powers's father had served on the ship during World War II, when it was called the *Musgrove Mills*. The elder Powers had survived a torpedo attack on the ship. The father survived those wartime perils on the ship, fought the good fight for his offspring, only to have his son die in peacetime on the same ship so many, many years later. It was a strange world and hard to understand, Bob Cusick said.

Then Cusick praised his shipmates as professionals and said the *Marine Electric* had "one of the finest crews ever put to sea on a ship."

Then he read the names, one by one. The church was silent, except for muffled sobs. He read the list slowly, with tears in his eyes. He paused and held onto his anchor-shaped belt buckle for a moment before continuing.

Charles Johnson. George Wickboldt. Michael Price. Long, long pauses as he struggled. Some of the names strangled his throat, it seemed, as he said good-bye to them once more. He shifted his feet and choked on the names.

Friends all, added to the long list of Bob Cusick's lost friends. The names tolled from Cusick as if from a sad church's bell, tolled in mournful peals amid the sobs and shattered dreams of grief-stricken sons, daughters, brothers, lovers, wives, mothers, and fathers.

Later, as Cusick was comforting those same stricken people, he heard a jubilant voice and felt a big hand slap him on the arm.

"Chief, hey, Bob Cusick, I can't thank you enough," said the Gashounder, the seaman Cusick had fired for drinking. "You saved my life! And this sobered me up. I haven't had a drink since you fired me, and I never will."

Cusick laughed, and the tension in that small corner of the church fell away. The chief mate greeted him exuberantly and said, "You know, you're *absolutely* right. I *did* save your life. The fella who replaced you is over there, and his name is Paul Dewey. But he was young and fit as a fiddle. He made it. *You* wouldn't have!"

And the truth was, Cusick and Bea left the church with a spring in their step. They were mourning for the lost friends, yes, but the service had helped the families come to terms with their losses.

There were other memorial services, up and down the Eastern Seaboard, services as diverse as the crew. At the one for Jose O. Quinones, the cook, Bea and Bob were the only white people there. The crowd was nearly all white in the small Massachusetts town of Newburyport at the service for Michael Price. Coach Stehlin told the crowd of Price's special quality. Finally he said, slowly, mournfully, "Good-bye . . . Number . . . 62 . . . Good-bye. . . ." Again, Cusick read the names of his lost men and fellow officers.

And there did not have to be high winds and cold seas to create the moaning in the quiet air. It was there, mournful and tangible, almost as Kelly had heard it in the sea off the wreck weeks earlier.

The tears, the sobs, the silences as the names were read had no color, distinguished race not at all, built no barrier between the proud new head cook and the football star, in the same manner that the waves, the distilled cold, were ever so blind to color, creed, status, and race.

In the crowd, Heather Price was still confused about this strange adult behavior. Even some of her friends at school had acted odd. After the news of the capsizing—that meant sunk, she had learned—her schoolmates, never meaning to be mean, gathered in small knots and talked quietly with their hands to their mouths, looking at her.

They would be talking normally in the days that followed, and one of the girls would mention her father, and another would tell a story about her dad, and then they all would look at each other, wide-eyed, some placing their hands over their mouths, and change the subject, others saying, "Shhhhhhh!"

Heather knew all this had something to do with her and her dad. They had told her he was dead, but she did not understand that. Her father was often gone for days, weeks, months. She knew he would be home someday soon, if not this month, then the next.

Now, at this gathering, they said nice things about her dad again, and Mom cried some more. Afterward, a kind-looking man came up to her—that was Mr. Cusick, her mom said—and gave her a pretty locket.

"Honey," he said. "Your father was like a son to me. I know he would do this for my daughter, so I want you to have this."

The man had tears in his eyes and spoke very slowly.

"I wish it had been me," the man said. "It is not fair, and I do not know why some things happen the way they do. Why did God take him and not me? I want you to know, honey, that if I could trade places with your father, I would do that. I wish it was me."

Several days later, at the Massachusetts Maritime Academy, a bronze plaque was laid. The name of each member of the fallen crew was called out one by one. A single ship's bell answered back. At each bell, a young woman cadet in uniform stepped forward with a single rose. A single flower was placed on the plaque, and by the end of the ceremony, the plaque was covered with thirty-one single roses, as the families, healing now, struggled to find themselves in this new life of theirs.

Cusick had been freed somehow. The wreck, the guilt, the self-inquiry, the testimony. All of it cleansed. He felt a new freedom now, and he would use it.

He was swinging out there. He was going to meet Stan Rogers, the Canadian folk singer, and explain to the man face-to-face how his song had saved his life. He had contacted Rogers's office and written a letter to that effect, and Rogers had sent word back. Would Cusick do him the favor of attending a Rogers concert? There was one coming up in May in the Boston area, on Harvard

Square. Bring five of your close friends, and there will be seats, front row center. Rogers had heard the story of the *Marine Electric* and said he was writing a song about it.

It would have been nice if it had just stopped there. But there were men with a lot of resources who had not given up on *their* version of the truth.

Rohrer, the chief counsel for MTL, particularly, seemed to see Bob Cusick as the Great Satan of the *Marine Electric,* a man who not only didn't do all he should have done, but actually had *caused* the wreck somehow.

The second day on the stand for Cusick was just around the corner now, and this time it would not be a cruise on the Love Boat.

Robert Hughes's job was clear: Break him on the stand.

Rohrer was the true believer here. He seemed sincerely sold on Cusick's complicity.

Hughes believed none of it. Privately thought his client, Marine Transport Lines, in the wrong.

Professionally?

He was going to destroy Cusick if he could. It's how the justice system worked.

Though more and more, Hughes thought in another private part of his mind that it would be nice to get away from all this. Spend years doing anything that had nothing to do with the law. Maybe a few years down the road. . . .

Chapter Twenty

THE BANG AND HANG

"She's your command, skipper," the company says to me,
"For better or worse, you're the boss of this hearse
As soon as she's put to sea. . . ."

JAMES A. QUINBY
The Street and the Sea

10 A.M. / MONDAY, MARCH 21, 1983 / MARINE BOARD OF
INVESTIGATION / PORTSMOUTH, VIRGINIA

Attorney Robert Hughes III was waiting patiently for the hearing to
begin. Almost certainly, his job would be to riddle the testimony of
the chief mate, Robert Manning Cusick. There really seemed no
option.

Cusick had not played by the informal rules at the first hearing.
He had not chosen the safe path posed by the Officer's Dilemma. He
had had his chance. Instead, he had told how bad the hatches were,
how poor a condition the ship was in, how he had made sketches of
all these holes and given them to the captain, and how he had patched
a hole in the hull with a coffee can lid and informed Farnham.

And how he had survived.

Still, Cusick had a chance to confirm the Marine Transport
Lines story about the grounding, and some in the company hoped
he would take it. All he had to do was say it could have happened.
All he really had to do was remain silent. Or say he wasn't sure. Sluff
it off. These Marine Boards weren't aggressive. If they saw an easy
way out, they'd take it. It was a great story. Ship, in trying to rescue
fishing boat, grounds and sinks. Tragic heroism. Everyone is satis-

fied. The company would be off the hook for the worst part of liability.

Hughes had to be prepared for that *not* to happen, of course. And if it did not? Captain Farnham, Cusick's boss, was prepared to testify that Cusick did not tell him about some of the ship's serious problems, did not tell him, for example, that those dogs on the hatches were inadequate. Hughes could weave that into a defense. The captain is the company's agent on board. If the chief deck officer did not tell him about serious deficiencies, well, it was not the company's fault. The company, the law said, then had no "privity" of knowledge.

Still, Cusick seemed fearless up there. The normal rules of legal gravity did not seem to apply.

Worse, there was this Coast Guard captain. Calicchio was not your average board member, sitting in his chair nodding at the arcane Merchant Marine words of art. He seemed to know every part of a merchant ship, and he was comfortable in this courtroom-like atmosphere. He was leaning forward, eyes darting, part prosecutor at times. In fact, increasingly, Calicchio was leading the board. The other two members, professionally, cautiously, more and more were following this odd character, who seemed half lawyer and half sea dog.

Calicchio's ascendancy on the board had occurred earlier in March. He was pushing a Coast Guard inspector—the last man to have a shot at flagging the *Marine Electric*—and he was bearing in relentlessly.

Suddenly, a piece of paper was thrust at him by Paul Johnson, the chair of the NTSB panel. Johnson was red-faced and seemed angry.

Calicchio looked at the paper. It said simply: "Enough!"

Calicchio did not care for the man. Johnson had led the NTSB inquiry on the *Poet,* which concluded that the ship sank because of "synchronous rolling"—a highly theoretical phenomenon where seas and ship attitude meant the roll of the ship increased with each wave. Later, the conclusion was withdrawn.

Now Johnson—ex-Coast Guard but never a merchant mariner—was trying to tell *Calicchio* how to run an investigation?

Calicchio crumpled the paper and flipped it back at Johnson. He continued to question the Coast Guard inspector, but noticed that Johnson was now talking to Lauridsen, chairman of the board. The two chairmen had their heads together as Calicchio drilled the man in the witness stand.

"I think we've established our points," Lauridsen said. "Captain Calicchio, can you move on?"

Calicchio was dumbstruck. It was a crucial moment. His fellow captain was reining him in.

"No, no, I can't move on, Captain Lauridsen," Calicchio said. "There are unanswered questions here."

Lauridsen finessed it, allowing a few more questions.

But Calicchio was not about to let it go. After the board meeting, he caught up with Lauridsen, captain to captain.

"Hey, Pete, I don't like what happened back there," Calicchio said.

"Oh, I thought we had pretty much covered it," Lauridsen said. "No big deal."

"Well, no, no, we hadn't covered it all," Calicchio said. "And it's a very big deal."

Now we both have some choices to make, Calicchio continued. You and the NTSB guy can impose gag rules on me, but if you do that, you can remove me from the board right now or I can resign from the board right now. Right now, this very minute.

Or you can let me ask my questions professionally and methodically until we get to the bottom of this.

Make up your mind. This is not going to be another whitewash.

Lauridsen caved. "This is no big deal, Dom," he said. "I just thought it went a little long, is all. Do what you have to do. Keep it short when you can."

Calicchio purposely kept it long. No one interrupted this time. And it was Calicchio who was now beginning the examination of Cusick. Almost instantly, Calicchio was cutting to the core of the "grounding" theory.

As the *Marine Electric* turned to reach the *Theodora*, did Cusick have occasion to check the charts for position?

Yes, he did.

And was Bob Cusick familiar with the route and course in general? This was make or break time for the company's case. All Cusick had to do was finesse it.

"Yes. I'm quite familiar with that area. I spent many years on that run. . . ." Cusick said. And then he added:

"Incidentally, I have a chart here that I brought and I put down these courses on it, and I put down my judgment of where the vessel was during certain periods of time. If you'd like to see it, I have it here."

Did Cusick look at the charts on board the *Marine Electric* at the time of the *Theodora* incident? And if so, could he estimate the depth of the water then?

". . . Somewhere in the area of sixteen fathoms when we turned around to go back," Cusick said.

Hughes saw the grounding case begin to disintegrate. Sixteen fathoms was ninety-six feet. One helluva wave and one helluva trough for anyone to believe that a ship drawing thirty-four feet had grounded. Even with a monster wave and trough, there would be plenty of water under the ship.

And Calicchio, the prosecutor now, was underlining the point, again and again.

"At *any* time, while the vessel was—from the time it turned about to the aid of the *Theodora* to the time that it turned about to head back, on its original track, did you feel, hear, or get the sensation of the vessel at any time going aground? Bouncing off the bottom?"

"No, definitely not."

"Hitting a submerged object?"

"No sign whatsoever of it."

And later, Cusick volunteered:

"Well, I know there have been reports of Captain Corl bounding the ship off sandbanks, hither and yon, but according to the way I see it, the shoal areas would have been very, very far inshore, much farther inshore from wherever we were . . ."

Then he volunteered drawings of how drainage holes were covered up. Of the hole that he patched with the coffee can lid. Of the holes in the hatch covers that he submitted to Captain Farnham. Of how the Coast Guard could not have inspected the hatch covers when the ship was in dry dock, as the inspector said he had, because the hatches weren't even *on* the ship then. They had been taken off for repairs.

As Mary Babineau had said, he could tell of every ding and dimple in the old rust bucket. Now he was.

It all came out. He told how the support struts that really gave the hatches their strength did not fit right—so they were just carried loose on board the ship.

He told how the gasket material put on the hatches wasn't the right kind and how the gaskets would not let the knife-edge of the hatch close. The gasket material was different from the specified gaskets.

Actually, he said, he had something that allowed him to show the board how these gaskets did not work, were the wrong kind. A few months back, one of the ABs had asked if he could take some of the spare gasket material home to use as a bumper on his old truck, and Cusick had thought, *Might want a piece for my own van.*

Cusick reached into his briefcase and brought out a piece of the gasket that did not fit the hatches—a piece he had thought to use on his van bumper.

"So that's why I have this," Cusick said, brandishing the rubbery gasket. The board could see, right here? Where the flange was? This part here was far too narrow for the wide knife-edges of the hatch covers to fit. They would leave big gaps like this. Tons of water probably came through those gaps. The board was welcome to the gasket. They could place it in evidence so far as he was concerned, because he really wasn't going to use it on the van.

Hughes saw the company's case move even further from fact to posturing. The guy was destroying MTL's case, and doing it with a helpfulness, an earnestness, a good-naturedness that was nearly irresistible. Half out of frustration, half out of appreciation, Hughes remarked sotto voce in an informal aside, "What *else* do you have in your garage, Mr. Cusick? . . ."

But he also had to go after him.

"*Objection* to the chart of the positions," Hughes said. "Cusick wasn't on the bridge." The chief mate did not stand a watch. Cusick has discussed this with other witnesses—which he was not supposed to do, and is basing it on those discussions. He had no real knowledge of the ship's position.

It was the time for the union attorneys to leap into action and defend putting the chart into evidence.

Cusick beat them to it.

"This is not quite as learned counsel has said," Bob Cusick said, nodding toward Hughes politely. "This chart also has a lot of input on it from my position being up and down on the bridge from time to time and seeing where the vessel was close to this course track that was inked in on the chart and so on . . ."

The board admitted it. The board admitted it all, everything Cusick had in his garage except his wheelbarrow and leaf rake.

Then Calicchio was driving the session forward, hammering Cusick, yes, but hammering the condition of the ship more.

"Did anyone perform any tests on the hatch covers?"

"No," Cusick said, "not during my tenure there. No proper tests with a pressurized hose, that is."

"Were there any epoxy patches on the hatch covers?"

"There were epoxy patches, Red Hand we called it, because you mix two kinds of putty together and it hardens up. We had been putting them on from time to time during the period I was there and during this last three-month period. . . .

"It wouldn't stay on because it was to be a temporary thing until they could put [steel] doublers on . . .

"But this is not a repair that stays very good. To cover the holes we had to take some of this gray tape they call duct tape. It's about the consistency of a Band-Aid, you might say. The duct tape would bridge over the holes, and then we'd lay this putty on top of it. But when they opened the hatches and they'd bank together, it would come off a lot of times. . . ."

"Did you supervise these so-called Red Hand patches?"

"Yes."

"Who told you to put them on?"

"The master."

"The master was aware of these?"

"Yes, that's correct."

"On the fatal voyage . . . how many of these Red Hand, so-called Red Hand, patches were on the hatch covers?"

"Well, for all the holes that were on the hatch covers, there were not too many of them covered with this duct tape and Red Hand epoxy putty . . .

"I'd say there was probably no more than—I doubt if there was more than seventy or eighty on the covers . . .

"But there was a myriad of holes in these wasted areas that I described on the sketches. . . .

"And if we had attempted to put duct tape over *all* this area and put Red Hand over *all* this area, you'd probably have to buy the factory out, because you'd have to put maybe *thirty-seven feet* across the hatch areas of maybe a foot or two [wide] if you want to try and cover all this area where all these holes were wasted through. . . ."

"In your opinion," Captain Calicchio asked, "were these patches, do you feel that they were *adding* to the strength of the hatch cover?"

Band-Aids covered with glue? *Adding* strength?

"Definitely not, no, sir, I do not."

"Do you recall Mr. Andreopoulos [the maintenance manager] being on board the vessel making a survey of the hatch covers?"

"He told me, *'I received your sketches, Mr. Cusick. And I saw the holes in the hatch covers'* and he said, *'we're going to make a new hatch cover for that bad one that's the first lid on number four.'* "

"Who was the master at the time that Mr. Andreopoulos came on board the vessel and made the survey?"

"Captain James Farnham."

"Now, referring to your sketch, in which I believe there are ninety-two areas in question? . . ."

"Yes, sir."

"On the last voyage that the vessel made, were any of your requests for repairs for hatch covers completed?"

"No, sir. They were not."

"In other words, the vessel went out with these outstanding, in your opinion, these outstanding ninety-two areas, or ninety-four areas, in addition to what you just told me about hatch covers having epoxy patches or Red Hand patches and some having just holes in them?"

"That is correct, sir."

It was as if Calicchio were the prosecutor of MTL now. Who was this guy? So the master knew the hatches were a wreck and, from previous testimony, that the hatches were never fixed in dry dock, that the gaskets did not work, that the support rods were never installed. Farnham knew that the hatches were literally held together by tape and glue. The captain was the company agent; ergo, the company had to know. Farnham knew, and Andreopolous knew, and Thelgie, the Fleet Director knew, and therefore the formal corporate management of MTL knew and had privity. They sent the old tub out into a gale anyway.

Hughes was left with little now. There is an old saying in law school that every lawyer has heard, *"If the facts are on your side, hammer on the facts; if the law is on your side, hammer on the law; if neither the law nor the facts are on your side, hammer on the table."*

Hughes was not the table-hammering type. It wasn't his style.

But he thought there might be one fact he could still hammer. The "dogs." The hatch fasteners. Farnham had told him earlier that the chief mate, technically, never had told Farnham that the dogs were not in proper working order.

And Cusick had never really informed any Coast Guard inspector or hull surveyor about what was wrong with the ship. As an officer, he was required to. Hughes could point that out on cross.

Then Calicchio guided Cusick through the same routine.

Had he shown the poor repairs to the American Bureau of Shipping? Yes. The surveyor had just shrugged.

Had he pointed out the deficiencies to Coast Guard inspectors? Good Lord, Cusick said, they were obvious deficiencies. At one time, they spray-painted a hole in the deck white so no one would trip on it! They took chalk and outlined it, like detectives sketching a fallen body at a crime scene. If you were on the ship five minutes, you knew where that hole was.

"Look back at February, and all things being equal, if that vessel was going on a North Atlantic voyage [trans-Mediterranean to Israel], would you have made the voyage having in mind the condition of the vessel as you described it?"

"No, sir. I definitely would not. There's quite a few people who heard me make that statement."

"Why, sir?"

"Well, the old story. It didn't turn out to be a very good one, but we have in the back of our minds that if we could sail on a ship that isn't up to snuff, if it's along the coast that the Coast Guard is always going to be there to save us. Whereas, if we go out and make a trip across the ocean and anything happens, well, we bought the package.

"As it turned out, it wasn't a very valid thought. But I wouldn't have—I would *never* have gone across the ocean again on her until they renewed the hatches."

Captain Calicchio paused. No one saw him morph from uncle to prosecutor.

"Tell me, what's the difference between a Force 10 storm in the *middle* of the North Atlantic or Force 10 storm off the *coast* of the United States?"

"Well, sir, there is *no* difference whatsoever, and as it turns out most of us were under a delusion at the time."

"In other words, what you're telling me is that you felt safe in the vessel when the weather was good. So the safety of that vessel, in your opinion, was contingent on the weather?"

"We never thought that whatever happened up forward to get it to pull the bow down would happen . . . we knew that the hatches were not watertight, and we knew that they had ruined the watertight integrity of the hatches when they changed the size of the gasket on the forward end on the sealing bars. But still . . . we thought that unless green water was going to get up onto the hatches, that it was okay . . ."

"Was Captain *Farnham* aware of these conditions and how you felt?"

"Yes, sir, and he was equally as concerned as I was in any conversation I had with him about it. The old bow that we had. He was very, very careful with it. Any trip I ever made with him."

"Did you report [your findings] to the Coast Guard?"

"No, sir, I did not."

"Why?"

". . . The only way I can say it, Captain Calicchio, is this way. When you're on a ship and we're trained a certain way, there's a chain of command we're going through. We report all these findings; anybody will report it to the mate. The mate will report it to the captain, chief engineer. Then we figure it goes to the higher authorities, the company officials, and they take care of having the Coast Guard and the American Bureau of Shipping brought down . . .

"As I say, if I had bypassed the whole procedure, then maybe things would be different. But I didn't do it. I wasn't trained to do it.

"That's the only answer I can give you."

From the audience, you could see Calicchio subtly nodding his head yes, nodding slightly in agreement. Calicchio knew how it worked in the real world on a real ship. The body language, the expressions of the other board members, seemed accepting as well, almost sympathetic.

What did Hughes have left to hammer?

The dogs. Yes. The case was going to the dogs quickly.

"Mr. Cusick," Calicchio was saying. "Do you think Captain Farnham or anyone else above or below him told the Coast Guard about the poor conditions on the *Marine Electric?*"

"No. I don't believe so. . . . They did extensive repairs that were the *wrong* repairs to them in Jacksonville. When they came back, there was a complete change on the size of the sealing gasket and bar, which obviated any water tightness of that.

"I know that the company certainly *didn't* want to correct it. If they did, they'd have to take all these hatch covers off. They'd have to cut off these angle bars. They'd have to put on a new angle bar and proper gasket.

"So this is, you're looking at what, hundreds of thousands of dollars maybe. So we were going along with it and, as I say, we were figuring that we were running along the coast and we knew this condition. Most of us all knew it. Nobody was forcing us to sail on the ship."

"In other words, it was a tradeoff between safety and cost?"

"Yes, sir, that's exactly what it was."

So now it was Hughes's turn, and the turn of events really left him no choice. He would have to show that Cusick did not tell Corl or Farnham or Marine Transport Lines the full story about the *Marine Electric,* that Cusick knew it was an unsafe ship, knew about the hatches, the holes, the leaks. But liked the job so much, liked just sailing up and down the coast as permanent crew, like it was a day job, that he had sacrificed his good judgment and good sense and his own crew. That he was deluded, okay, but not in the innocent way he portrayed it. That he deceived Farnham and the company into thinking an unsafe ship was seaworthy.

The fencing began easily enough. Polite but metallic, edged thrusts by Hughes. Was Cusick *aware* that he was not supposed to talk to other witnesses? Read testimony? Look at the evidence and exhibits before his own testimony? How many other witnesses had Cusick talked to before he went on the stand?

The survivors, Cusick said, and he also had read the diving reports, which were technical and boring to him. Oh, and he had talked to Bill Long, his friend, the night engineer in Norfolk.

Hughes nodded knowingly and continued.

"Now, you were the chief officer on the *Marine Electric.* Did you have any responsibilities in connection with securing the vessel for sea?"

"Yes, I did. . . . Close up the hatches and put the dogs on. Put the lines away forward after we left the dock. . . . Have the devil claws put on the anchor chains and tighten up the turnbuckles, and finally, before we left, put the dogs on the companionway that leads down below to the forecastle head area."

"How about down in the forward part of the ship? Did you have any responsibility to see that areas in that part of the vessel were secure?"

"Yes. That is my responsibility at all times. I go down there and check around, as I did that day. . . ."

"When you were satisfied that the vessel was ready for sea as far as your area of responsibility was concerned, did you make any reports?"

"Yes. I made a report to the master as I always did. . . . I called him up over the walkie-talkie and said that the vessel was all secured forward. They had all the dogs on that we were able to put on and that I would send everybody back aft ready to rig out the pilot ladder and to let the pilot off. . . ."

". . . You had a responsibility to see that the cargo hatches were secured for sea, did you not?"

"That is correct."

"All right. What did you do to carry out this responsibility?"

"Didn't I just explain that? Do you want me to say exactly what procedures I went through?"

"Yes," Hughes said, and Cusick ran through the lengthy procedure he'd told Calicchio earlier.

"Did you personally check the number-one hatch to see if it was secured for sea?"

"Yes, I did."

"Did you personally check to see how many dogs were secured?"

"I didn't go around and count them. . . . I saw as many of them as we could put on were on. . . ."

"Were you satisfied with the securing of number-one hatch?"

"Yes. I was."

"Were you satisfied that the hatch was watertight?"

"No."

"Were you concerned about this?"

"No more than I had been for the last two years. As I have just explained."

"Did you . . . do . . . anything about the fact that you were . . . concerned . . . about the fact that the hatch was not watertight?"

"No," Cusick said. "As I told Captain Calicchio, we did not because we all were deluded. Thought we were okay in the coastal trades."

"Did you tell [the captain] that in your opinion the hatches were secured for sea?"

"You mean you want me to say whether I thought they were waterproof, is that what you mean?"

"I'm asking you to tell us what you told Captain Corl on February 10, when you reported the hatches secured for sea."

". . . I can't remember the specific words I used."

"Was the gist of your report that the hatches were secured for sea or were not secured for sea."

"The gist . . . was definitely that they were secured as far as we would secure them for sea, yes. Notwithstanding the condition of the hatches, now. I didn't purport to tell him that I believed that the hatches were in good condition, or that they were waterproof. No. . . ."

"Did you report that they were secured for sea, or did you give him a qualified report that they would be secured . . . but . . . ?"

Cusick's attorney, Henry Howell, objected.

"I would ask the board to consider the fact that Mr. Hughes represents the shipowner. They filed a petition to limit liability, and he's a very good lawyer, but I think that he's exercising an ability in an attempt to introduce testimony here that's not directly related to the cause of this vessel sinking in order to undercurrent his proceeding on the civil side in New York. . . .

"Mr. Chairman . . . He's trying to get this witness to say that he made an equivocal representation that the hatches were properly secured. And then, of course, it wouldn't be any knowledge on the part of the master or any knowledge of the owner concerning the casualties that later ensued if they involved the hatch covers.

"He's gotten an answer at least twice, and I just say that he's badgering . . ."

"Mr. Hughes," Captain Lauridsen asked. "Do you feel that you've gotten the answer to your question?"

"No, sir. This is a witness who said he had a responsibility for securing the hatches for sea. I'm trying to find out if he made an unqualified report to the master that they were secured or if he qualified it in any way . . ."

Lauridsen cautioned Cusick to answer clearly in short, responsive answers, in yes or no replies if possible. Which is exactly what Hughes wanted. He could back him into a corner that way.

"Ask the question again, Mr. Hughes," Lauridsen said.

"Mr. Cusick. Did you make an unqualified report to Captain Corl that the five cargo hatches were secure for sea, or did you qualify that report in any way?"

"I told him the hatches were secure for sea and said we put on a lot more extra dogs than we usually do. I did not elaborate or go over and over again that a lot of the dogs we couldn't get on because we could not get the hatches pulled together that tight over the sealing bars. . . .

"I did not tell him, I did not say that yes, unqualifiedly, this vessel is in perfect condition and these hatches are in perfect condition to go to sea."

"Mr. Cusick," Captain Lauridsen said. "You did answer the question by saying they were secured for sea and they used more dogs. You prolonged it by saying what you did not say."

But the long answers were working beautifully for Cusick. Hughes could not force him into an either-or trap. Either you told Captain Farnham the ship was secure or you did not. *Yes or no.* Hughes was driving toward that point. Farnham could be portrayed as having no knowledge of the hatch conditions. But Cusick ignored his own attorney's advice—say, "I don't recall, I don't remember"— and kept providing detailed context and nuance.

"Did you qualify for the master in any way your report that the hatches were secured for sea?" Hughes asked, with some heat in his voice now.

"No, I did not at the time bring out any of the deficiencies in the hatch covers, except to tell him that we had the hatches secured with all the dogs that could be gotten on them, more so, many more dogs were put on than what we usually put on. That's what I told him."

"But you had personal reservations at the time that you made this report?"

"Only in that the condition of the hatch covers and the . . . as I've explained, the fact that we could not put on every dog that we had on the ship."

Hughes paused to give the next question emphasis.

"Did you feel you had any duty to the rest of the crew to take any action in regard to your . . . personal . . . reservations?"

Make or break now. Nail the witness on the dogs or not.

Cusick paused. He reddened. He took a breath and fixed Hughes with his eyes. The redness left his face. His voice was calm and steady. Other things bothered him. This one did not.

"That's a pretty lousy question to ask me. After all, this ship has gone down and thirty-one of my shipmates are gone on it. . . .

"I don't see how I can answer that question," Bob Cusick said. Then he spat out the next sentence, as a challenge, a dare:

"Try it again . . . some other way."

Then both witness and attorney were at each other in rapid-fire sequence. Hughes could still nail him if he rattled him.

"Was the dry cargo hatch secured for sea?"

"The dry cargo hatch on the upper deck was as secure for sea as we were able to do it on this ship. . . . I can go through it again, if you want to . . . the dry cargo hatch underneath on the deck below—"

Hughes tried to stop him. To the board: "This is going beyond the question—" Bob Cusick did not care and just kept talking.

"—on the deck below the second deck. You didn't say which deck you want. Tell me which deck you want to know about the dry cargo hatch. I'll tell you about the hatch."

"I'm dealing with the main deck."

"The main deck. I just explained about it! The main deck. Upper deck. The dry cargo hatch was secured in place with every dog . . ."

"In your opinion, was that hatch watertight?"

"Yes, it was watertight."

"And did you so report that to the bridge?"

"I told them that everything up forward was all . . . I said everything up forward is secured. . . ."

"You mentioned in your direct examination that the dry cargo hatch on the main deck was below standards. . . . Was that ever the subject of a repair request issued by you?"

"Yes. We had some holes come on when we scraped it in the

cover. And we made a request that the holes be repaired and some small doublers."

"Objection to this," Howell said. "This is all repetitive and badgering. And Mr. Hughes is reading from company documents now that haven't been made available to us all."

That's where it stopped, where the legal wranglers tangled their lariats. Other attorneys on the union side piled in, asking for records that Hughes had. Hughes agreed to stop the questions for now. It was over. He had done what he could. Hughes thought he may have done some good for the company.

Hughes would tell them what he thought. They could blame Cusick all they wanted. Hughes had done his best and was done with it. He would not do his worst.

Over the next few days, Cusick's version held up. The hatch cover manufacturer's representative testified that he had warned the company the hatch covers were in horrible condition and outlined dozens of problems with the covers, all of which added up to two big facts: They weren't waterproof, and the company knew it.

The Marine Transport Lines witnesses did not fare well. Thelgie seemed smug when he said the hatch cover representative was just a salesman trying to peddle his wares. The fleet director offered no substantive rebuttal to Cusick's detailed testimony.

Then it was Farnham's turn. If the permanent master had struck some sort of deal with the company, he certainly did not deliver the company from its legal peril. He testified that the ship was sound and had a strong hull. He believed the hatches were watertight. He believed that had he been on the ship, he would have brought her through.

Then he made a weak effort to imply that he did not know of the hatch cover problems and had never been formally advised by Cusick of the problems. But Farnham's heart seemed not to be in the story, and he conceded that Cusick was a competent chief mate.

At first, Calicchio drilled Farnham mercilessly, noting all the problems with the ship, the ninety-plus holes, the patches, the chalk lines and spray paint on the deck, the hole in the hull patched with a coffee-can lid.

"Could you not see these things as you walked around the ship?" Calicchio asked.

"It was not my practice to walk around the ship," Farnham replied.

Then Calicchio's manner changed, and his voice dropped to a whisper. He was almost gentle with the master. He could afford to be. The ship's faults were so many and so clearly visible, Farnham's testimony was weak. Calicchio checked off his list, confirming that Farnham had not seen the terrible deficiencies—deficiencies a half-dozen others had said they noticed after five minutes on the ship.

Quietly, as if to an old friend, master-to-master, not really as a prosecutor, Calicchio finally asked Farnham the question they both knew was coming. Calicchio seemed almost sad as he said it.

"Captain Farnham, as the master, you have the ultimate responsibility . . . is that correct?"

There was a moment, a pause, but not a long one.

"That is correct," Farnham said.

"No more questions," Calicchio said, a short time later and Farnham was through.

And so Cusick seemed in good shape legally, despite ignoring his attorney's advice to say as little as possible.

Cusick was a man with a mission. "No, I have to say this because it is very important . . ." Cusick told his attorney at one point. "The board has to know this. *Has* to.

"The Coast Guard rescuers," he said, "are the best people in the world." He could never thank them enough for their heroism, and they had his eternal thanks and admiration.

"But on the inspections?"

"These vessels should be examined very, very closely, very thoroughly," Cusick was saying now. The board had actually asked him if he could help them with any other thoughts. Sort of an open-ended invitation to state his opinion. Willing pupils at his feet.

"I think that would do it," Cusick continued. "Most of them are reaching the end of their service now. I guess there's not too many of these old rebuilt vessels left. But when the vessel does get this old and you have these retained bow and sterns on them, the life does go out of the metal, and it comes a situation which it should be checked very much more thoroughly than in the newer vessels. . . .

"I think the other things, you don't need to flog a dead horse about survival suits. I mean, one of the reasons why I'm here is I had a kind of a halfway homemade survival suit. I think that and the fact I had this quilted padded underwear with the elastic around the waist. . . .

"The last thing in the world I ever thought that at a quarter past four in the morning, I'd be overboard from a ship that capsized, but she did. And if the men did have the survival suits, it would have been an easy matter for them to be saved. The Coast Guard almost did get a lot of them, and if they had survival suits they would have been out there plucking them out alive all morning long. . . .

"I'm sure there's other things. After thinking that I'll be able to come up with and maybe I could write them to you or communicate them to you. . . ."

And it was over and it was done. Or so everyone thought at the time.

Out there in the legal thickets, tigers still waited in the tall grass. Legal tigers backed by serious resources.

They could spend tens of thousands of dollars if they saved millions. And bringing down Cusick was the only way they could do that.

Chapter Twenty-one

DEATH SHIPS

*What aroused public opinion and moved legislative bodies was less the
cold calculation of total losses and relative risks than the shock of
individual disasters of a novel and terrible kind. . . .*

COAST GUARD COMMANDER P. E. SAVONIS
lecture on nineteenth-century maritime reforms

5:30 P.M. / SATURDAY, APRIL 30, 1983
NEWSROOM, *PHILADELPHIA INQUIRER*

Ron Patel, Sunday editor of the *Philadelphia Inquirer,* made the last
checks of the wire services and the police reporters' log before he
gave the word to roll press.

In the evening, as deadline approaches, the news desk of a big
newspaper is much like the bridge of a ship. No one doubted that
Patel was the master on this watch. Autocratic and possessed of a
finely honed news sense, Patel thought little of ordering a front page
torn to bits at the last possible moment if it was the right thing to do.

But this was a front page he would touch not at all. Nor did he
want to. Filling the upper left of Page 1-A of the May 1 Sunday *Inquirer* was a story graphically identified simply as "Death Ships."

It left little room for change, and it bore the imprimatur of Gene
Roberts—and of Patel. It was locked in the way Patel wanted it, and
only a nearby earthquake would move it from that spot.

Patel made a call to the pressroom and told the supervisor to go.
The big presses, the size of a ship themselves, began humming and
spewing out the front section of the Sunday newspaper.

Soon a million newspapers would drop onto the front porches

of subscribers, and bundles would land with a plop in front of newsstands.

The heartbreaking story of the *Marine Electric* was laid out in story after story, page after page. The headline read, "How the U.S. Sends Rustbuckets to Sea, Sailors to Their Graves." The conclusions were sweeping.

"The system that sent her to sea and sent most of her crew to their deaths sails on—guaranteed, propped up and subsidized by the U.S. government.

"Billions of dollars in government maritime subsidies, intended to promote the construction of a modern American merchant fleet, have perversely done the opposite—created a fleet of ancient and dangerous U.S. ships that have been taking American seamen to their deaths with alarming regularity.

"Government policies—fought for and won by both industry and labor and passed into law by Congress—have ensured the perpetuation of what has become, literally, a death fleet."

The reaction was instant and overwhelming. Legislators stepped forward. Union heads denounced the system. Bureaucrats buckled. For all the thousands of words written, not one letter to the editor or phone call challenged the facts and the conclusions.

For a short time, it looked as if the series itself would bring great reform.

Plimsoll, the nineteenth-century reformer, might have smiled at the innocence of that thought.

With one article, you could make the eyes see. With a series, you could make the heart feel.

But to make the head act? To bring true reform?

Plimsoll had published his own books. He was a member of Parliament. Yet even he spent decades and much of his personal fortune before they put his single simple load line on ships.

The *Inquirer* was just at square one.

Chapter Twenty-two

REVERSAL

He could smell the flowers of Bermuda in the gale but he died on that rockbound shore.

Stan Rogers song

SATURDAY, MAY 14, 1983 / PAINE HALL, HARVARD UNIVERSITY
CAMBRIDGE, MASSACHUSETTS

Bob Cusick had left the second hearing with a spring in his step and a song in his heart. The song, of course, was "The *Mary Ellen Carter*" by Stan Rogers, and part of the spring in his step came from the knowledge that he had done what he had set out to do—tell the truth. It appeared as if he had done it well. His attorney told him he seemed unscathed or, at the very least, defensible. Hughes had pursued him, as attorneys will and must, but there seemed no case—no solid case—against Cusick and his license. Now, if Cusick could show damages? If his neck were sore, for goodness sakes, could he just wear a neck brace at least?

Cusick's mind was on other things. The *Inquirer* series had buoyed him, said so many things he and the other officers knew. He had the support of a major newspaper now. He felt, if not invulnerable, then very strong. Almost giddy.

But a part of the spring in his step came from the song in his heart. From Stan Rogers himself. Cusick had written to Rogers's record company and told them the story of the *Marine Electric* and how, in his mind, the Rogers song with its chorus of "rise again" had saved his life. He had sent his heartfelt thanks.

Rogers, his family, and his band were exuberant. The *Marine*

Electric was precisely the sort of situation he wrote songs about, and he told Cusick he would write one about Bob and the old ship. Furthermore, Rogers would be performing at Harvard on May 29. Could Bob and five friends be there?

On May 29, Bob Cusick and his friends were right out there, lighting the place up, beaming from the front row. The old chief mate smiled as if he had seen God's Green Pastures and knew God's Great Cosmic Joke. There were tears in his eyes and in Rogers's too, as he belted out the Rogers standards. Rogers's songs always seemed to come deep from within him, from way down.

When he paused near the end of his program to introduce Bob Cusick and have him stand, when he said he was writing a song about the *Marine Electric,* the crowd cheered as few Rogers crowds had, hooted and crazily shouted them on.

And when he played the song that saved Bob Cusick's life, the energy filled the room. Cusick and his crowd joined in on the part that seemed to apply to the survivors of the *Marine Electric* crew.

> *To those of you adversity*
> *Has dealt the final blow*
> *Smiling bastards*
> *Lying to you*
> *Every where you go.*
> *Turn to*
> *And put out every strength*
> *Of heart and heart and arm and brain*
> *And like the* Mary Ellen Carter *Rise Again!!!!*

On twelve-string, Rogers strummed and picked so hard, urging volume and feeling from the guitar, that the strings popped, one by one. He turned it into an eleven-string. A ten. He did not care. Just smiled, laughed, and played harder.

> *"Like the* Mary Ellen Carter. . . .
> *Riiiiise Agaiiiiiinnnnnn!!!!"*

And it was over. The *Boston Globe* critic saw the crowd surge to its feet. Clapping, cheering, yelling. The applause from the audience shook the light fixtures. The band had never heard anything like this. It was the best.

Both Cusick and Rogers left the concert thinking themselves blessed. Cusick was recharged and reinvigorated with a warm glow that forever banished, it seemed, the cold North Atlantic.

He dreamed less and less of the lifeboat at night, and at the dawn of each day he looked forward to what was to come. He was going to hang in there and press a civil case in the courts—not for the money, but for the point of pride and justice. He wanted to see *them* on the stand—and to go back on the stand himself—in a real court of law. This should *never* happen again, he vowed. Bob Cusick was a leader now, no mere company man. He was chief mate and master of the surviving crew members. This was good stuff, heady stuff. He was a leader now.

There was that. And in the quiet parts of his mind and heart, the parts healed from the ordeal, he had other thoughts.

The sea slapped the beach near his Scituate home. It was saying something to him now that was different from the time in the water. Its rhythms were his rhythms. Its song, his song, somewhere in his heart, next to the Stan Rogers song.

He could hear that old song more every night, sung to him by the little waves that lapped up on the nearby shore. He would hear it and smile to himself.

Then he would remember the night in the water and shudder. It was a sweet song, the sound those little waves made, but the sound and the waves were out of his life forever.

Stan Rogers heard other songs as well, songs he would write and sing. He hummed the variations on tunes that could lead to the *Marine Electric* song and also an epic series of songs he planned about Canada. He and the band went to Texas for a concert a week later, and when it was over, Rogers stayed around, soaking up the other performers, telling the rest of his band to go home, he would join them soon.

The flight back was a time of looking forward to what was to be. Perhaps a reverie on what he might write. Wheels up at 4:25 P.M. Dallas time. Thursday, June 3. A few hours and home. Air Canada Flight 797. One stop in Toronto and then to Montreal on the McDonnell Douglas DC-9-3. He carried Bob Cusick's letter in his briefcase on the plane.

He settled in with the other passengers, none of them knowing that little things meant everything now. That on a plane, as on a ship, modern systems are complex and interdependent. Little failures, tiny failures in a system. As they failed, so did the bigger system. A man turned left. A woman turned right. A child stayed put. They lived. They died.

A little before 6 P.M. Dallas time in the cockpit of the plane, Captain Don Cameron, the pilot, saw three circuit breakers trip. Hardly critical-path stuff here. They controlled the aft lavatory's flush motor. Cameron reset them. They popped right back. Motor must have seized, he thought. At 6 P.M., he tried again.

"Pops as I push it," he said, but thought little of it.

A few minutes later, a passenger toward the rear of the plane summoned a flight attendant. *There's a strange odor,* the passenger said. The attendant sniffed and could smell it, too. She thought it was coming from the aft lavatory. Carefully, she took a fire extinguisher and opened the door to peer in. There was a light gray smoke, floor to ceiling. No flames, though. She inhaled some smoke, coughed, and quickly closed the door. She told another attendant.

Then Stan Rogers saw the attendant moving passengers forward quietly, with no panic. Everyone move forward, please? Move in front of Row 13 everyone. Just a little problem. We have some stuff burning in the lavatory.

About four minutes after six, the copilot had an edge to his voice when he said, "We'd better go down"—had better make an emergency landing. "I don't like what's happening," he said. "I think we better go down, *okay.* "

Rogers and the passengers only understood they were in trouble of some sort. They did not understand what kind of trouble. No one really did.

But the passengers quickly understood the thick clouds of smoke that began flowing from the bathroom. They understood that first officers did not normally run back and forth in the aisles with smoke goggles. Then, as a lot of the smoke cleared, the passenger cabin seemed normal enough again. So maybe it was a little thing. Then smoke reentered the cabin area.

At a little past eight past the hour, the captain called the Indianapolis control center again.

"*Mayday, Mayday, Mayday,*" he said.

"We have a fire. We are coming down. Need to land."

Almost immediately, the smoke increased and rolled forward. Thick, billowing, oily clouds of it. There was an acrid smell. Of burning plastic. Of burning electrical circuits.

Rogers could see the smoke growing thicker and thicker in the passenger compartment now, bunching up in the rear at first, now rolling forward. It was nasty-looking oily stuff. The flight attendants weren't talking about small problems anymore.

They gave the passengers wet napkins. They took some passengers and placed them next to the exit doors, giving them quick talks—briefings on what to do. How to open the door. Then they told the passengers how to evacuate. Don't rush. When we land, leave in an orderly fashion.

In the pilot's cabin, both pilots wore smoke goggles and oxygen masks. Perspiration steamed the goggles. That and the smoke made them lean forward to see the instruments. The first officer opened his sliding window briefly. Tremendous noise! Back it went.

No flames were visible to the passengers. But the old saw was grimly true: as surely as there was smoke, there was fire, a very hot, stubborn, ambitious fire, burning not far from the passengers.

Fumes, smoke, hot gases crawled forward unseen in the ceiling and then down the sides of the cabin, between the passenger compartment and the outer skin. The smoldering fire lacked only one element—oxygen—to burst into flames.

Rogers and the others could see the smoke roll down from the ceiling and in from the sides of the planes. Then they could see little of anything. The smoke was too thick.

Only along the floor was there a slight clear space. They were all coughing, gagging, strangling from the smoke. They were surrounded by fumes, some of them toxic. Carbon monoxide. Cyanide. Fluoride. All were in the smoke. All were inhaled by the passengers.

And they could feel the heat. From the sides. From the ceiling. Although it did not look like a fire yet, fire surrounded the passengers. On the sides. On the top. In the wall. In the ceiling. Hot, flammable gases were forming there.

Specialists in airplane cabin combustion say there are two deadly possibilities in such cases, both pyro-cousins.

A *flashover* occurs when the heat in the ceiling of the cabin becomes so hot that any combustible materials below catch on fire from the radiant flux of the ceiling fire.

A *flash fire* is really a mild explosion. Unburned combustible gases accumulate. When oxygen and open flame become available together, there is a sudden swoosh of intense heat.

Either could happen, the conditions were close at hand.

In the pilots' cabin, sweat was pouring from Captain Cameron's forehead into his eyes. Indianapolis had passed them on to Cincinnati and they were looking for the airstrip below. His copilot kept opening the sliding window periodically to air out, to cool off. They came in and out of clouds. They had visual contact. Then did not. Did. Then did not.

They were coming in, coming in . . . faces pressed to the controls, sliding the window, peering out, trying for visuals. Like drivers whose defroster is shot on a rainy night. Pressing close to the dials in the pilots' cabin.

"Crash-fire rescue vehicles are ready for you," the people on the ground said. "We are ready for you," Control said. "State number of persons and amount of fuel on board!"

"We don't have time," Cameron replied at seventeen minutes past six o'clock—seven local time. Just seventeen minutes had passed since the passenger had sniffed the air, smelled smoke, wrinkled her nose, and summoned a flight attendant.

Runway lights went up to full intensity at seventeen minutes, twenty-four seconds past seven. *"We see you,"* the captain said at thirty-five seconds. As he lowered the landing gear, the passengers could hear the familiar whine, the slowing, the noise of the slipstream. A solid *thunk* as the landing gear slid into place. Thank God!

Then that sudden slowing as the wheels extended, the slight shudder in the craft that made one start in alarm briefly, then smile and relax, knowing it was the landing gear.

"You are cleared to land. Wind from 230 degrees. Four knots."

It was almost twenty minutes after seven now.

Cameron palmed the flaps and rudder controls gently. The horizontal stabilizer was inoperative. He was bringing it in without systems. Seat-of-your-pants stuff.

In the cabin, the attendants were shouting out their "brace" instructions. "Stay calm. Don't panic." An attendant, amid the smoke, walked and crawled up and down the aisles checking seatbelts. "Stay calm," she said. "Don't panic."

Captain Cameron thought the airspeed was right and let the plane drop onto the landing strip.

"Now! Extend spoilers! Full brakes!"

There was no antiskid system, not since they had switched to DC current. The plane pitched and steadied. Rogers and the others were thrown back and forth wildly. A chirp sounded from the tires, and then a long, heartbreaking squeal and screech of rubber. All four main sets of tires blew out, and the screech changed more ominously to the grinding of steel against the tarmac.

And then they were done. Down! A remarkable, textbook emergency landing. They came to a rest, right side up, just short of the intersection with Taxiway J. They were safe. Stories to tell, but the worst was behind them.

In the front passenger cabin, the lead flight attendant threw open the left forward cabin door and began yelling, *"Come this way, come this way."*

The smoke was so thick; passengers could not see hands in front of their faces. They moved deliberately but without panic toward the sounds of voices or the dim visions of light and life, holding onto one seatback after another to trace their progress. They were down now. All they had to do was get off.

Another flight attendant crept forward through the smoke and found the right side forward exit. She opened it and deployed the inflatable slide. *"Come this way, come this way,"* she yelled out.

Elsewhere, the "designated doormen" were opening the wing

exits. Four made it out the right forward wing exit. One made it through the right aft overwing emergency exit. Six went through the left forward overwing exits. Some were standing. Others were bent over. Still others simply crawled, nose and mouth as low as they could go, seeking cool, cool air.

One woman could see nothing and hear no one. But she felt a cool draft. She followed the path of the air wafting through the plane now, and she made it out, thanks to the cool draft.

The cool draft. The cool, cool air. It was not a blessing. It was death. Only ninety seconds had elapsed since the doors were opened. Cross-currents of air entered and played in the cabin. There was fire with no air. There was air with no fire. Inevitably, they would meet. Cross-ventilated now, the tube of the plane was a kiln. The cool air and oxygen found the flammable gases, and it was as if someone had thrown jet fuel on a very hot grill fire.

There was a pause and then a whoosh. The flash fire exploded the length of the plane's interior. What had been a smoldering fire in the sides and ceilings of the plane erupted now into plumes and roaring blossoms of orange, red, and blue energy. Now the fire had air and needed combustibles. It leapt from the walls and the ceiling and sought everything. The seats. The luggage. The carpets. Clothes. The people under the clothes.

The lead attendant waited at the door. No one was coming. There was a flash, and the heat was overwhelmingly intense. He leapt from the plane. Seven passengers and one attendant made it out the left-hand side ahead of him. Another attendant went down the right forward side. The pilots tried to come back to help but were met by a wall of fire and heat. They opened their cabin exits and bailed.

It is not known where Rogers was exactly. Informal reports, told to his mother by the investigators, included a story of a big bear of a man who was clear of the fire and then went back to help people. He went back and guided them, yelling, *"This way, this way,"* in a big booming baritone. He himself had all but been out and safe when he turned and went back to help, they told her.

Perhaps that is how it was. No formal mention of Rogers is made in the government report, but it is how the legend is told now, and probably there is truth to it. Rogers stood six foot four, and no man or woman would have prevented him from going anywhere he wanted on that plane.

Then what? At the door? Did he hear the words of his own music? Feel the deep source of his songs? Hear the twelve-string playing the chords? Rise again?

Did he turn back, as his mother said she was told? Rise to his own standards? Stand tall at the last and yell out, as she was told, *"Come this way! Come this way!"*

There are computer models for flash fires. The lower you are, the better your chances. If you are five feet six inches tall and are standing, you may live for 159 seconds. Kneel down to around three and one-half feet? Add forty-four seconds to your life. Duck down to eighteen inches off the ground? You can expect to live 202 seconds.

There are no predictions in the model for the seconds of life for a man standing six feet four inches.

In all, eighteen passengers and five crew members made it out alive.

No one else did.

Twenty-three people lay dead inside the plane. Stan Rogers was among them, his baritone voice forever still. The letter from Bob Cusick was in a badly burned briefcase a few feet away.

Bob Cusick heard the news the next day, and he tossed his head back as if poleaxed. *Oh, no. Oh, no.* The wrong men were dying. Why Rogers? Why him and not Bob Cusick? Was Cusick cursed?

The wrong men were dying. The young men were dying.

It threw him back into the low place again, and Bea saw the light die in his eyes once more.

He had been out of that place for weeks now. To see him go back, lost, as dead as Farnham's voice, bore Bea down as well.

And just as that happened, more bad news hit them, the worst possible, according to his lawyer, Henry Howell.

MTL was not done with Bob Cusick. They were out there now, floating over the wreck in a world-class research vessel, sending down divers and robots on sleds with video gear, spending thousands of dollars a day.

In June 1983, they issued a press release saying they had found substantial anchor damage to the vessel's hull. Almost certainly, the release said, the anchor slipped loose as the ship was buffeted by waves, slipped loose and swung again and again, all eight tons of it, like a mad mace, holing the ship and sinking her.

There was one man responsible for that accident. Not Thelgie. Not Farnham. Not even poor Phil Corl. None of them had privity, and neither did MTL.

Only one officer was responsible for storing the anchor so negligently. This man obviously acted in haste, as the blizzard began to blow, and did not do his job professionally. The man who had not done his job, of course, was Bob Cusick.

Bob Cusick was no longer the hero. Bob Cusick was the bad guy.

They were asking the Marine Board to reopen for new evidence and to name Bob Cusick a formal "party of interest"—legal shorthand for "major suspect." Rohrer was coming after him now, throwing everything the big company had at the chief mate.

The press release and the plane crash together changed everything. Calicchio had felt comfortable that he had properly steered the investigation toward the condition of the ship. He had hoped to take on the whole awful system that kept these old ships at sea. Howell had felt confident as well, after the first two appearances by Cusick. Now the attorney saw the Marine Transport Lines tactic as—he had to admit it—a beautiful legal maneuver by Rohrer, outflanking the case Howell had built against the company. Howell was deeply worried now.

All they had built would come crashing down if the company could put the blame on Cusick.

Cusick, once so far along on the road to recovery, was back in play. They were coming after him, and now, when he seemed so weak, beaten, lost, there was no song he could bellow into the wind to save him. Stan Rogers and his song were dead, and with them something of Cusick had died as well.

He was down, and no part of him felt like rising again, ever.

Part Three

TOWARD HOME

*[The seamen's] home is always with them—
the ship; and so is their country—the sea.
One ship is very much like another . . . there
is nothing mysterious to a seaman unless it be
the sea itself, which is the mistress of his
existence and as inscrutable as Destiny.*

JOSEPH CONRAD
Heart of Darkness

Chapter Twenty-three

TIGERS IN THE
TALL GRASS

What are you doing out here?

CAPTAIN HENRY DOWNING
to Diver Jeremy Shastid

SATURDAY, JUNE 5, 1983 / *MARINE ELECTRIC* MARKER BUOY
ATLANTIC OCEAN

When he heard the news of Stan Rogers's death, Robert Cusick went into a deep funk. All during the spring of 1983, there were still forces working for Cusick. The *Inquirer* series published in May had told the story of a system in which everyone from the maritime administration to the seamen's unions assured that the old ships went to sea.

But at the same time, with massive resources, Cusick's enemies went into hyperdrive in a furious attempt to show that the chief mate, not the company, had sent the *Marine Electric* to the bottom.

The tiger in the tall grass stalking Cusick was Thomas L. Rohrer, the attorney from Marine Transport Lines, and he was not crouching in some legal thicket.

He was crouched over a video screen aboard a vessel that was among the world's most sophisticated diving and underwater discovery craft, the *G. W. Pierce.*

With him in the viewing room of the ship on a fine June day in 1983 were a marine architect and experts from Steadfast Marine, a world-class operation that had done high-profile dives on the famous shipwreck of the *Edmund Fitzgerald*. Their attention was riveted on a grainy black-and-white video of the wreck of the *Marine Electric,* 130 feet below on the ocean floor. A robot-controlled camera on an underwater power sled transmitted live video, and they were gliding the sled back and forth over the sunken ship.

The robot, unlike human divers, did not have to decompress as it surfaced. More video scans of the wreckage could be made this way as Rohrer and Captain Henry A. Downing, the head of Marine Transport Lines operations, ordered pass after pass.

The viewing room was wonderfully modern. It gave the marine architect and MTL's legal Big Gun unprecedented flexibility, and they were leaving no potential exculpatory evidence unexamined. The results were worth the $150,000 and change that MTL was paying to Steadfast Marine for a few intense days of reviewing the wreckage.

Below, what happened to the old ship at the very end seemed clear. She had twisted as she floated after capsizing and was torqued by the seas into two sections. The midsection—the part added to the old T-2 in 1961—came loose, most of it, and took its own path to the ocean floor.

Nearly a mile away—connected over some of that distance by a trail of 24,000 tons of coal—were the original bow and stern of the T-2 tanker. The two halves were connected by one, last stubborn crack arrestor and torn remnants of the midsection.

The old bow and stern rested upside down. There was massive damage to the old T-2 bow, and damage, too, at the number-two cargo hatch. Most significant to Rohrer, there were marks and sharp punctures stretching up and down the hull of the ship. These were marks that could only have been made by a loose anchor pounding hard against the hull.

These components—the anchor, the anchor chain and apparatus, the sharp holes—seemed to attract the attention of the robot, directed from above, and the human divers, as chum attracts schools of feeding fish.

Up top, the smell of warm blueberry muffins drifted from the galley of the *G. W. Pierce* and only made a good day better for Rohrer. The news had made his day and his case. They had found the turnbuckle on the anchor restraining system. It was loose. Robert Cusick had not made it tight.

Captain Downing was there, too, and for the first time in weeks both men had reason to smile. They had in their hands rock-solid bona fide proof that their company was not at fault in the wreck of the *Marine Electric.*

Cusick's testimony had seemed so compellingly forthright and honest. Now they could show that it wasn't true. Or at least not complete.

The turnbuckle was a screw-type device that held the anchor and chain tight against the ship. About the size of a large man's arm, it "took up," or made taut, the slack in the chain clasping the big anchor against the ship's side. Loosen the turnbuckle, and the anchor could flop and bang. Tighten it, and the anchor snugged up against the ship, tight as a tick.

Now they had proof that Cusick did not tighten the turnbuckle. The chief mate had been sloppy. There had been a storm coming and he hurried to make the anchor tight, but he did not make it right. The starboard anchor turnbuckle was way too loose. This caused the anchor to slack from the side of the ship and then to come free and swing like an eight-ton mace again and again against the side of the old ship. The anchor holed the ship and breached her hull. It was enough to make the ship settle lower and lower in the water, until finally she capsized and sank.

And there was more than enough evidence for Rohrer to take to the Marine Board. Now, finally, it was time for the MTL legal tigers to spring from the tall grass.

Those who talked to him in these days said Rohrer was fervent on the matter, not at all like Robert Hughes, the attorney in Norfolk who represented MTL but quickly concluded on a personal level that his own client had been at fault for sending the old and battered *Marine Electric* to sea.

Rohrer was a true believer. Those who knew him said that, all through the spring and summer, he talked of little but Bob Cusick and how the chief mate was in reality the source of the old ship's problems. Grab lunch with Rohrer, and he wouldn't shoot the breeze about golf or baseball or anything but Cusick. He was a true believer in his client's innocence and in Cusick's complicity.

And if you were a maritime attorney representing a company like MTL, it was not hard to understand how that could happen. Maritime law might work against seamen when their ship sank, but another part of it worked *for* the seaman who was willing to fake a fall or a back injury during the routine operations of the ship while it was still afloat.

This was so because the U.S. system excluded seamen from workmen's compensation in the event of injury but gave them legal redress in the courts. Because the redress really acted as a sort of worker's compensation, the courts had come to conclude that plaintiffs' proof of injury need be only "featherweight." Seamen and, particularly, longshoremen were given such huge legal edges in personal-injury cases that many times the only question was damages, not proof of negligence.

Stories were legion of how longshoremen and their crane operators would count down *five-four-three-two-one-zero.* The crane operator would then let a huge container fall from one foot as four longshoremen fell gently to the ground, yelling in mock pain, "Owww, my back, my back." Many of the stories were true. It was hard to exaggerate the fraud. "Lenient" was how some termed the system. "Racketeering" was another description and, in some cases, very close to the truth.

So claims of "pain and suffering" had hardened admiralty attorneys representing shipping companies. Much of the pain and suffering was a sophistry that had become a legal industry. There was as much pain and suffering among the companies who paid fraudulent claims.

Specialized law firms *would* fly engineers and attorneys halfway around the world at the drop of a hat to a shipwreck if there were serious injuries. Literally, the law firms, some of them, chased ships, not ambulances, and they really *did* issue their waterproof business cards to seamen.

This part of the U.S. system had driven up insurance rates to an unconscionable degree. U.S. mariners accounted for only 5 percent of oceangoing ships insured by the syndicates of Lloyds, but 60 percent of the injury claim values.

So Rohrer was accustomed to having questionable claims worth millions in damages filed against the company, and he intensely fought these claims, as he now was fighting the *Marine Electric* claims. He really *had* spent a lot of his career listening to lies from unprincipled claimants seeking large damages for small or nonexistent damages.

No doubt Cusick would show up in a neck brace any day now, talking about pain and suffering. Already the families of crew members had filed more than $100 million in suits.

So he was going after Cusick formally now. He had already asked the Marine Board of Investigation to reconvene, to hear this new evidence, and to make Bob Cusick a "party of interest." This would mean that Cusick had the right to be represented formally at the board hearing and to cross-examine witnesses brought against him.

But the simple way of saying it was that Cusick, like Captain Farnham, like the late Captain Corl, like Marine Transport Lines itself, would be considered a prime suspect in the cause of the tragedy. In fact, he would be the main suspect, if the board granted the motion.

The survivors, the families, and the unions all got wind of this. It would have been hard not to. MTL had issued a press release in June stating it had new evidence that a badly stowed anchor had come loose.

They were queuing up for Cusick, of course, but what could the union do? For MTL, the cost of the *G. W. Pierce* and the experts was large, but nothing compared to losing millions if the company could not prove the seaworthiness of the *Marine Electric*. For the survivors, such an expense would be purely on spec. No single one among them could rationally put up such money even if they had it.

Well, they would do what they could. They needed *some* check on this technological juggernaut. Family members kicked in nickels and dimes, and the unions chucked in some petty cash to hire a diver.

All told, they came up with $4,200.

So in the arms race to explore the wreckage of the *Marine*

Electric, Marine Transport Lines had the equivalent of a modern combat tank. The survivors and family members and unions? Maybe a snowball.

On the bridge of the *G. W. Pierce,* they first saw the little boat as a blip on the screen and assumed it was one of the dozens of recreational fishermen out for the day. But then the blip headed unerringly toward them and the marker buoy, and as it got closer, they could see three men and a lot of diving tanks.

Captain Downing hailed the men in the boat. "What are you *doing* out here?" he yelled.

"Diving," Jeremy Shastid said from the little boat.

"Not today you're not," someone next to Downing said. "We got four, four-thousand-pound anchors to drop, and we wouldn't want you to get hit on the head with one."

Just what Shastid needed. More trouble. More threats. The $4,200 wasn't much to start with, but the last few days had made it seem even less.

At six-foot-three and 210 pounds, Shastid was a ruggedly handsome man who was trying to find his niche now that he was no longer a diver for the U.S. Marines. Things had been simpler in the service. A long scar on his forearm was a souvenir of nondive duty in Vietnam. When asked about the scar, Shastid would say simply, "He cut me, I shot him."

Civilian life was not so simple, and he had wandered into some gray areas. Once he had posed in the buff as a centerfold for *Playgirl* magazine. But it wasn't really a field he wanted to pursue. He wanted to be a commercial diver. The way to break in was to take what was offered. And the unions and the family members of the *Marine Electric* crew were offering.

So he had steered his twenty-four-foot open boat toward the wreck, thirty miles out. He had no warm blueberry muffins, just a deli tub of chicken salad and a couple of Cokes. He pumped his own gas at the dock, letting the nozzle drain for a long time in hopes that he could squeeze out a few drops to help cover costs.

Until a few days ago, he'd had a regular "assistant," but the man had been scared off a few days earlier, so all he had on board was a seventeen-year-old helper and a reporter named Tim Dwyer from the *Philadelphia Inquirer.*

The assistant had resigned the day Shastid came upon a clam boat out of Maryland sitting squarely over the *Marine Electric* buoy. They were salvaging the wreck and had run a Jolly Roger flag up their mast. Worse, the men brandished rifles at Shastid and the assistant, making it clear they wanted them to leave.

The rifles themselves had not bothered Shastid. His military training left him wondering where exactly he might place the underwater charges to sink the clam boat. What bothered him was not the rifles but the disrespect. The guns had just been so unnecessary that he could not let it go. He wanted, somehow, to get these guys.

The incident rattled his assistant badly. Thirty miles of pounding out to sea in a small boat. Then the skull and crossbones. Guys with rifles pointed at him. The assistant quit on the spot and demanded that the spot be moved immediately back to shore.

But on this day the ship at the buoy was not a pirate vessel but the *G. W. Pierce,* the sleek ship chartered by MTL. They had beaten him to the buoy that day. And now, a small flotilla of boats, an inflatable dinghy, and a seagoing tugboat were aiding the company divers and robots. They were intent on bringing up that important anchor apparatus, though Shastid did not know it.

On the bridge of the *G. W. Pierce,* some smiles faded, too. What was this? They had heard of freelance salvage divers on the wreck. This boat looked about that type. Only any self-respecting pirate would have had more sense. This far out in an open boat? It violated every law of good sense.

They warned the men in the small boat against diving, and then Lieutenant Commander E. F. Murphy, on board the company ship to observe, squinted at the small boat.

"Where are your life jackets?"

Shastid scrambled around the small boat and finally pulled out two life jackets from his gear. He was one short of Coast Guard regulations.

"You are in violation of basic Coast Guard requirements for small boats," Murphy said.

Murphy squinted again at the boat. Was that *Dwyer?* Timothy Dwyer? The reporter from the *Philadelphia Inquirer* who had been covering the Marine Board?

It was. The *Inquirer* team was everywhere, it seemed. In the "stacks" of research records. At the hearings. And now—somewhat foolishly, Murphy thought—this far out in a twenty-four-foot boat.

"Tim?" Murphy said. "Is that *you?*"

It was, Dwyer confirmed.

"Tim," Murphy said. "What would it look like if a reporter from the *Philadelphia Inquirer* who was investigating the Coast Guard for sending unsafe ships out to sea was arrested for being out at sea in an unsafe boat without a life jacket?"

Dwyer paused for just a moment, thought it over, and replied.

"How *would* that look if you did that?" Dwyer replied. Dwyer *knew* how it would look. He would become a media hero and the Coast Guard a villain. And maybe that wasn't far off now. He and Murphy had developed a good relationship at the hearing, and Dwyer thought Murphy was one of the good guys. Now what was happening?

But both Murphy and Marine Transport Lines backed off. They saw the same headlines Dwyer saw. "Reporter Barred, Arrested at Site of Tragedy." Quickly they switched gears and graciously welcomed Dwyer and Shastid on board the *G. W. Pierce* for a tour.

Murphy took Dwyer aside. Murphy had had several informal conversations with Dwyer at the Marine Board, but this recent confrontation was uncomfortable. "Tim, you should not be out here," Murphy said. *"People have a right to know,"* Dwyer said, beginning to bridle. "No, no, no, not *that!*" Murphy didn't care about Dwyer coming on the company ship. It was the *safety* concern. Ever the Coast Guardsman. "Tim, *never* go out this far in a boat like that," he told Dwyer. "And particularly not with someone like *that.*"

Murphy nodded toward Shastid. The freelance diver was sniffing at the blueberry muffins. Sniffing around the bridge. Sniffing around the screen that showed the robotic divers. Sniffing where he shouldn't, by MTL's standards anyway. Just wandering around.

Shastid was indeed impressed. He saw modern robotic marine-survey equipment and television viewing rooms. The ship was fully air conditioned and equipped with two-, four-, and six-berth state-rooms. She carried a crew of seven officers and seamen.

The company operating the diving ship was legendary. Steadfast Marine of Falls Church, Virginia. They had surveyed the wreck of the *Edmund Fitzgerald* just a little while ago, and even the union attorneys conceded that Steadfast and its president, Robert E. Kutzleb, were some of the best in the world. As for the Coast Guard? The Coast Guard *itself* had hired these guys when the Coast Guard's own, the cutter *Blackthorn,* went down in Tampa.

The professional complement was complete. There was even a marine architect on board overseeing the whole business, gliding the robotic diver past the ship in endless passes. It seemed like an automatic scanner reading a bar code, picking up any minute evidence that might exonerate the owners.

Now most of the other men were inside watching the robotic diver crisscross the hull on its power sled. Shastid wandered into the viewing room and popped his head in next to Dwyer's, soaking in everything he saw on the video screens from the robot below.

Then Rohrer saw what was happening and bellowed, What is going *on* here. He quickly escorted Shastid out of the room. You could hear the two men shouting at each other in the hallway.

Rohrer returned to the viewing room a few minutes later without Shastid. "He can stay aboard and have lunch, but I don't want him to participate. I don't want to share information with them; they haven't shared it with us."

Outside the video room, Shastid looked more hurt than angry. Hell, he'd offered to take the Coast Guard along on his boat. They had told him his chances of success were "minimal."

There were nods in the viewing room. Both the Coast Guard and MTL officials agreed on some things. Shastid was bizarre.

A *Playgirl* centerfold? And this was his first commercial diving job? And on such a shoestring budget. A guy who bought his boat stripped down from the factory for $14,000. "The engine goes for $6,600, but I got it for $4,300," he had told them. A guy who—look at his stuff—had written the ship's location on a piece of scrap paper and then put it in a zip-lock plastic bag?

With the reporter there, though, the MTL people wanted to do the right thing. They decided to halt operations and let Shastid dive. If nothing else, it might be good entertainment.

The ex-Marine's congenial smile came back, and he began putting on the layers of his diving suit—heavy lined union suit, then a dry suit, insulated socks, and rubber gloves. Billy Young, his young assistant, tried three times to anchor the boat near some homemade buoys. The professionals on the big ship chortled, stifling outright laughs.

Finally, Shastid fell into the water off the side of his boat and began his descent. Down below, the shadow of the *Marine Electric* came into view, and Shastid flippered over the hull and hatch covers, taking flash pictures with a waterproof camera primitive by the standards of the robot. There was only about ten feet of visibility. His job was to check out the hatch covers and keep the company honest on the anchor damage. He had only about ten minutes down below during each dive, because of the lengthy decompression time. Ten minutes wasn't much time to cover anything at 130 feet, but he began methodically documenting the damage to the ship.

Then, near the stern, he smiled broadly through his face mask. Sweet revenge. The pirates had been working on the ship's propeller, and there, attached to the ship, were two huge "lift bags" they had left behind for their return. Big mistake. The inflated, balloon-like objects were used to give heavy items flotation. Then they could be floated up to the surface.

Now Shastid was about to salvage from the salvagers. He drew his dive knife and began sawing through the securing lines.

A few minutes later, on the surface, there was still no sign of Shastid, but up popped a large inflated lift bag. Another of the bags popped up. Many minutes later, so did Shastid.

Shastid wrestled with the bags. They were bigger than his boat, so he could not get them into it. Still, he was determined to get them to Chincoteague, partly to salvage the salvagers' equipment, partly for vengeance against the pirate divers who had brandished rifles.

He tried towing the bags. This did not work. Then he tried lifting them again into the boat. They were too heavy and large. Then he tried towing them again. His boat would not move. One bag filled with water and sank.

On board the *G. W. Pierce,* the professionals watched Shastid and thought, What a lunatic! The guy comes out to dive on the ship and gets sidetracked by a few bucks worth of balloons.

Then they watched in concern. The fool might actually sink himself and kill Dwyer. The former was fine. The latter not so hot. Dead reporters were bad press. So the *Pierce* hauled anchor and began following the little boat.

Shastid tried towing the last bag again, this time with a longer line. It still did not work. Finally, he flashed a devilish grin to Dwyer, took out his diving knife, and slit the bag, sending it to the bottom in one swipe.

"If I can't have it, *nobody* can," he said.

"I wouldn't have taken them if they hadn't taken the guns out," Shastid explained. The rifles were just so unnecessary.

A while later, Shastid looked genuinely hurt again. He knew the *G. W. Pierce* people were laughing at him. As they bucked back toward shore, he told Dwyer he didn't understand why Rohrer was so angry with him for not sharing information. He *said* they were welcome to come along on his dives, but no one took him up on it. Why were these guys laughing at him, anyway? He really did not like that at all, and his smile disappeared again, just as it had at the pirate ship.

On the *G. W. Pierce,* of course, they had had more than one good laugh at Shastid. That boat. The map in the zip-lock. And him concentrating on those lift bags and all.

But somewhere they had all missed the point. Had not seen the pattern forming.

The pirates had threatened Shastid. They had disrespected him. And now the pirates had no lift bags and were out of business. He had punctured their big balloons and sunk their big plans.

The point the *G. W. Pierce* guys missed was: They had just done the same thing. They had threatened him. No diving today, we wouldn't want those anchors to fall on you. They had laughed at him. Disrespected him. Not stuff you normally wanted to do to an ex-Marine, especially not an ex-Marine diver. So unnecessary.

Shastid set out to puncture their plans as well.

• • •

He came back to the site the next day and the next. And the next. He could not blow up the *G. W. Pierce,* of course—not in peacetime—but he could sure outwork them. Or try to. He was no robot, but he dived and he dived and he dived and then he dived again. Each time, he shot roll after roll of film showing the old ship's condition.

He dived far beyond any chance of the $4,200 covering his costs. He would dive until they told him to stop. And until the *G. W. Pierce* guys stopped laughing. All told, he would make thirty-eight dives to the *Marine Electric* and spend more than six hours on the bottom.

Even after all Shastid's work, Cusick and his friends were not sure. They could not be optimistic about this.

For Rohrer and his crew of experts were coming for them now, coming at Bob Cusick long and hard, with yards of videotape, hours and hours of surveillance on the bottom, to tell their story.

MTL now had powerful ammunition. Even the union attorneys acknowledged that Steadfast Marine was a legend in the industry. If MTL could show that Cusick or his crew had botched the handling of the anchor and that the anchor broke loose and punched holes in the ship? No damage awards. The $100 million in filed claims would be chasing only about $1 million, because the court would grant · MTL its motion to limit liability.

The Big Gun from New York would be in Portsmouth soon to guide the divers and the marine architects through their testimony on the anchor theory. Rohrer and MTL were preparing a second assault on Bob Cusick, and the only thing the attorneys for the families and the unions could throw back were the photographs from Shastid's dives.

That was all they had, and that is what they would throw.

Even if that was like throwing a snowball at a tank.

Chapter Twenty-four

THE HIRING HALL

. . . ships are but boards, sailors but men . . .

WILLIAM SHAKESPEARE

1:00 P.M. / MONDAY, JUNE 28, 1983 / NORFOLK, VIRGINIA

At home in Scituate, Bob Cusick knew little of the dueling divers and seemed at times to care even less what happened to him. There were rumblings again about him being recalled to testify. Henry Howell had warned him that Marine Transport Lines was trying to nail him, spending over $100,000 just on the dives. Cusick seemed elsewhere, somewhere even beyond his funk, as if he were preoccupied with an important but elusive thought.

The Cusicks had filed a civil case. Howell briefed him on how that was going and how, if Bob ever developed any pains, he shouldn't be afraid to admit them. Wear a brace. It would help the case. The doctor said your lungs will never be the same. That one ear. Your heart. You know you're never going back to sea. They've deprived you of your livelihood. There really *is* pain and suffering. A little physical manifestation of that, you know, a brace or something. It's not a lie.

"Start thinking about the anchor case these guys are building," Howell said. "I can use all the help I can get."

The fact was, Bob Cusick was in another world now. Cusick did not care about the anchor. Let MTL do its worst. He just did not care. He had no fears, just this lingering guilt, reborn by Rogers's death, the nagging furies that muttered a chorus of "why you?"

"Press our suit," Cusick told Howell. "Let's give 'em hell."

But that was not the answer to the voices that asked "why?" in the early-morning hours.

The answer was elsewhere, and he knew it, heard the song more clearly every night in the little waves at Scituate. He had done what he had done at the hearings. Hell, he was no Crusader Rabbit. There had to be something else, closer to his core, with some real meaning.

"Meaning" was evermore an elusive concept. The man whose song saved Bob Cusick from a maritime disaster was dead at age thirty-one in an aviation disaster. It had been less than one week since the concert at Harvard.

Where was the meaning in that? People asked how something like this could happen to such a young man. It seemed to Cusick that the wrong men—the young men—were dying. He could not fathom how this could happen.

Rogers's mother pondered the same question and told the *Boston Globe,* "Maybe that's the one last thing he was put on earth to do, to save Bob Cusick so Bob could live to tell his story. Maybe that's why God put him and his songs here."

When Bob Cusick talked to her on the phone, she said it again. Maybe that's the reason Stan lived, Rogers's mother said. So he could save you. His song could. So you could testify. Do what you did.

Cusick did not know if that was true. He did not believe in a God who worked that way. He believed in a God who created tides and winds and ships and fire and songs and airplanes, then let all of those things work out the rest. He believed in a God who moved from within, taught you to choose what was right and true, and let all of those other things fall where they may.

Even if it were true, even if he had been "chosen" somehow, he had held up his part. He had testified. He had told the truth.

But that wasn't a career. That wasn't a calling. Ralph Nader of the Seven Seas? That wasn't Bob Cusick.

The dead feeling stayed with him for days, but he hung in there. Life went on, just as surely as death claimed his friends, and sometimes you had to swim down to swim up. If he listened, he thought, if he listened and did not fear, he would hear from within himself what he was supposed to do.

In late June, before the Marine Board reconvened, Bob Cusick and Bea went to a friend's wedding in Norfolk. They had time on their hands. The wedding spoke of new beginnings, new chances, new songs, but Cusick heard instead an old song, low and sweet, deep within him, the one he had heard sung to him so many years ago. He heard the song again in the steady rhythms of the waves lapping in the great waters around Norfolk.

"Think I'll stop by the Norfolk union hall, see if there's anyone I know there," Cusick said. Bea looked at him. "Just stopping by," he said. The old smile.

Bea knew something was happening, even if he did not.

Chapter Twenty-five

ANCHOR MEN

Mr. Howell may fall out of his chair.

THOMAS L. ROHRER
chief counsel of MTL,
on the expected outcome of expert testimony

It would be the first time.

RESPONSE OF HENRY HOWELL
the officers' union attorney

10:00 A.M. / JULY 28, 1983 / MARINE BOARD OF INVESTIGATION
PORTSMOUTH, VIRGINIA

Henry E. Howell, Jr., could see Rohrer spread out his papers on the desk and shoot his cuffs like the big-league New York attorney he was.

Howell was past his sixtieth birthday, but he still loved trial work. Normally, there was nothing he liked more, particularly, as was now happening, when a big-city boy came south to Tidewater, Virginia. *Loved* to barbecue those boys. Show them his Colombo meets Colonel Sanders act.

But in this contest, Howell knew he was on the spit. In the pit.

This was a mismatch. Rohrer *was* big league and did know what he was talking about. He had decades of experience in the maritime field and was an expert in admiralty law. Worse, he had Steadfast Marine executives keyed up to testify that Bob Cusick, Howell's client, was the man who caused the wreck.

And Howell? He was a good politician—in fact, legendary in Virginia—with a disarming Virginia-gentleman air to him. He could dial up the drawl as if by rheostat. You expected a bottle of fine bourbon at his table in front of the board and a Tennessee walking horse in his parking spot. Indeed, at times, he wore a light seersucker suit and a fine straw hat.

And all of that hid the killer instinct and fine mind of a first-rate trial attorney.

What he did not have was current maritime experience. He had served as lieutenant governor of Virginia, and then spent a decade crusading as a populist. After political office, there were political plums for him and his law firm. One of them was representing the International Organization of Masters, Mates & Pilots in Norfolk—the deck officers' union. Touched by the plight of the survivors and the dead men's families, Howell decided to handle the case personally.

In some ways, that was a favor. He was very good in the courtroom. But some of his clients wondered if he had the background for this one. Did he know an anchor fluke from a flounder?

Moreover, even Howell conceded that he seemed to be slowing down and was a little rusty. It was difficult to tell whether he really was stumbling verbally and did not understand an answer, or whether he was playing that Southern version of Colombo—the brilliant detective who pretended to be dumb. Sometimes, he would turn from a "dumb" question with a sly smile on his face as the witness tripped himself up. At other times—more times, actually—he seemed genuinely befuddled. Often, he asked that the microphone be moved closer to the speaker, or that the stenographer read back words he seemed really not to hear. He did nod off at his table at times, as technical testimony droned on and on.

Howell looked about him, awaiting a legal miracle that did not seem present in the courtroom. Even his client was not there, only Bea. Bea had told him what Bob had done, and that was not good for their case. Howell needed Cusick here, if for no other reason than to pick his brain and to tell Howell what really had happened.

Now Rohrer was about to drive his battle tank full of evidence right through this befuddled spot in the defense. MTL was tired of the way the board had bumbled about with Howell, and now the Big Gun was here.

Neither Rohrer nor Howell wasted time letting everyone know how aggressive their battle would be, that of the hundreds of hours of testimony, the next few would be the ones that counted most.

The fifteenth day of testimony began at 8:58 A.M. on July 28, 1983. Multiple exhibits from the MTL dive were introduced and labeled, as were a few from Shastid, consisting of photographs and logs. Ominously, the petition to make Cusick a formal "party of interest"—in essence, a suspect—sat squarely before the board. It was up to the board to determine whether MTL had evidence that implicated the chief mate.

Howell went on the attack. There is that old legal saw: "When the law is on your side, hammer on the law. . . ."

Howell hammered on the table. It *was* his style, and he hammered well. Besides, at the moment, he had no facts.

"Captain Lauridsen," he said to the Marine Board chairman, "we have an inquiry to make which we think is relevant. At the time of the last hearing, Captain Downing, on behalf of Marine Transport Lines, sent a letter to the widows of the men who were lost at sea expressing regrets for the loss but stating that it was due to a grounding of the *Marine Electric* while offering assistance to a fishing trawler.

"We later read in the paper where Captain Downing . . . felt that an anchor . . . *flogging* . . . incident had caused the—was the primary cause of the accident, and we feel that we're entitled to know if the grounding theory has been abandoned or whether or not Marine Transport is attributing it to the ground and the new theory of the anchor flogging. . . ."

Howell was up against it with no new facts, only Shastid's little underwater clicks. So he hit the buzzwords. He brought in the widows. He talked about a "flogging anchor." He pointed out the conflict in the theories. Which is it? We should know. If they are still sticking with the grounding, this dancing anchor act has no relevance. Go one way or the other, boys.

And Rohrer jumped on it. Letting them all know the Big Gun was in town. That things had changed in Portsmouth.

"I am here for the first time. Does the board allow this to go on all the time? I mean, Mr. Howell just *carries on* any way he wishes?"

Chairman Lauridsen sighed and moved them back to the business at hand: taking testimony. Later, he would say to a colleague, it seemed as if these two attorneys presented more testimony in their skirmishes and editorial asides than the actual witnesses did.

In fact, it would take a full day for the board to make its way to the key testimony of Robert E. Kutzleb, the world-renowned salvager and president of Steadfast Marine. And it was here that Rohrer began hammering on the facts. Relentlessly, he laid his chain of evidence.

Fact, said Kutzleb. They had retrieved an anchor and its chain and holding mechanisms. And it seemed to Kutzleb, who was ex-Navy and had mastered many ships, that a key part of the anchor mechanism had not been properly engaged by the ship's crew and officers.

The turnbuckle was a mechanism that helped secure the anchor when a ship was at sea. It was a screw device, much like the ones that kept guy wires of telephone poles taut.

The whole of the anchor restraining system was complex enough, but it rested on one simple principle. Screw in the threaded bolt of the turnbuckle, and a restraining chain snugged up the huge anchor and anchor chain tight against the hull. Screw the bolt out? There would be more slack, and the tons-heavy anchor apparatus could swing and bang the hull.

Kutzleb said the turnbuckle he recovered was "fully extended." It was nearly unscrewed.

"It's fully open. A couple more turns and the threaded rods would probably fall out. . . . Normally . . . it's tightened up and the threaded portions are well into the barrel or body of the turnbuckle."

In other words, the turnbuckle was loose, and that made the anchor chain floppy. Could Kutzleb even say for sure that the turnbuckle *was* secured when the *Marine Electric* set sail on its last voyage, Rohrer asked.

Two events happened then, and the least obvious—the one Rohrer never saw coming—was the most important.

Howell rose from his seat and objected loudly. Kutzleb has no credentials and qualifications to make this sort of assessment, the attorney said.

That was the obvious event. What Rohrer didn't see was Dominic Calicchio's reaction. The former Merchant Marine master twisted in his seat and grimaced ever so slightly at Kutzleb's testimony, as if a problem student had run her long, long fingernails down Calicchio's inner chalkboard. The expert had made a mistake. An understandable mistake. But a mistake that pained Calicchio.

Rohrer could not have known that, of course, and was self-confidently closing in for his first kill with Howell.

"You have *problems* with Kutzleb's credentials to make the assessment of whether the anchor was properly stored?" Rohrer seemed to be saying. "Oh, please, please, pretty please. Make my day."

He walked Kutzleb through his background. Newport News Shipyard, design section, two years. U.S. Navy, commander of two ships, one search and rescue, one salvage. They used four 3,000-pound anchors.

"I probably laid, oh, well into, say, eighty, ninety, or a hundred moors. Maybe more. . . ."

Okay, Henry? Rohrer seemed to nod at the gentleman from Virginia, and he asked the question of Kutzleb again. ". . . are you able to say whether or not that turnbuckle had ever secured that chain on the *Marine Electric?*"

"My personal opinion is that it probably wasn't made up tight. . . ."

Rohrer, the maritime and admiralty law expert, was establishing his point beyond doubt.

"When that turnbuckle would secure the claw to the anchor chain, what would be the *normal* position of the two thread ends with the barrel of the turnbuckle bell?"

In other words, World Renowned Expert, if this thing were done right, would it be on the final two threads like this? If it had been in place, would it not have been tightened much, much farther up, screwed in farther to hold the anchor securely? If we did not have a sloppy and negligent chief mate? All unsaid, but clearly where it was all going.

"The threaded stock would probably be well into the turnbuckle body itself."

The expert confirmed what Rohrer wanted. If the anchor had been properly secured, the turnbuckle would not be on its last two threads, but well, well into the body of the screw mechanism, many turns in. This was the equivalent of a screw just threaded into its hole, not secured or driven home. The holding chain never had the slack taken out.

And that was all Rohrer needed. No way Henry Howell was going to crack Kutzleb's testimony.

Suddenly, the balance had shifted from old hatch covers to the chief mate's negligence. For if the anchor was not secured, then a storm of this nature might send it dancing along the side of the ship, holing it, letting the storm waters in, dropping the bow. And MTL had pictures to show that *had* happened. Even new hatch covers would give way under those circumstances.

And just that fast, MTL was out of the soup. And Cusick was back in it.

The board was throwing cream-puff questions at Kutzleb. This guy Dominic Calicchio was asking about how the dive robots worked with a sort of puppy dog look on his face. No problem. Steadfast was a legend. They would probably want Kutzleb's autograph afterward.

But then Calicchio's manner changed abruptly. The open expressiveness of his face morphed. Now he was looking at Kutzleb with a furrowed brow and those hooded eyes.

"All right, sir, on the turnbuckle . . ." Calicchio began. "What is the holding . . . where is the holding power of a turnbuckle?"

"Where is the *holding* power?"

"Yes. As you screw in your ends, once they go through—the part that has passed—has that got any holding power? . . ."

In other words, Calicchio was in effect saying, once you screw in the tightening bolt, does the length of the part that has been screwed in really matter in the strength of the turnbuckle? Two threads in or thirty threads in? Does it really make a difference? The part that has passed beyond the threads? In such a large apparatus, as large as a big man's arm, with such hard steel, such big threads, did you need more than just the two turns? Did that really help the holding power?

The expert: "Not to my knowledge, no."

"So no matter how many screw threads were in and out of the turnbuckle, the turnbuckle itself was sound so long as some threads were holding it in one piece?"

"Yes," Kutzleb replied. "That was true."

"Now whether the anchor clasp was secure or not depended on one thing and one thing only," Calicchio continued. A securing chain ran from the turnbuckle to a pad eye on the deck and then to the big anchor apparatus. "How taut was the securing chain from the turnbuckle to the anchor mechanism? Was *that chain* tight, with no slack, holding the devil's claw clasp securely?" Whether there were two threads through the screw or thirty made no difference. It could be tight with two or loose with thirty. It all depended on the length of the securing chain.

"The length of the securing chain? Turnbuckle to the anchor? Do you know that distance? Loose or taut? Do you know?"

"No, sir, I do not."

"Isn't it a fact that when you're using the turnbuckle that the purpose of the turnbuckle is that it can be lengthened or shortened to make up the distance. Is that correct?"

"Correct." Kutzleb said hesitantly. Wondering where this was going. Not used to this sort of questioning.

"All right. Isn't it possible for a turnbuckle to be tight—to be screwed as tight as you can and yet the threads not go all the way through the barrel?"

In other words, like this one?

"Certainly it's possible, yes, sir." Kutzleb on the defensive now. "I wouldn't do it, but it's possible."

"I agree with you"—Calicchio, the master with twenty-three years at sea, far more than Kutzleb, just clearing his throat for a lecture—"that most turnbuckles that you will see will have a *lot* of the threaded part into the barrel, which is a *useless* piece, really, once it's gone through the thread. . . ."

"Uh-huh." Kutzleb, accepting a lecture now from his elder.

"But also a turnbuckle, depending on the length and the use of it and *where* it hooked onto the chain and the distance from that point to the turnbuckle to the pad eye . . . you may not have enough threads to go through the barrel but still it will be as tight as you can possibly get it on."

In other words, Cusick may have screwed in the turnbuckle just two threads deep, and that was as tight as he could get it. The holding power was there. The line was taut.

"Naturally." Kutzleb, the professional expert, acknowledging that he accepted the point of the lecture and agreed.

But the word must have landed with an echoing clang in Rohrer's head. In just a few short moments, this Coast Guard captain who looked like a puppy dog had changed into something else entirely and established that the turnbuckle certainly *could* have held the anchor just fine and dandy. In fact, probably did. Kutzleb may prefer a fully screwed-in turnbuckle, but the expert himself just admitted that two threads, three threads, thirty threads—it made no difference.

What Howell could never have done, Calicchio just had. He had turned the turnbuckle gambit.

The first of the company's star witnesses was neutralized at best. At worst, *turned*. Kutzleb began by saying he thought the anchor was stored improperly but ended by agreeing with Calicchio that it probably was okay.

Howell, the landlubbing trial lawyer, circled the wreckage of the testimony. He may have been rusty on admiralty law, but he knew how to strafe witnesses forced from cover and on the run.

"Did the company ever talk about maybe bringing up the *hatch covers,* take a look at *them?*" "No," said the witness. "Hmm," said Howell, "brought up the eight-ton anchor but no one-ton hatch covers. Correct?" "Yes," said the expert.

Then Howell dialed down the drawl to a very slow pace and added a puzzled, quizzical tone.

"And you had the robot . . . to do everything it could to . . . ascertain whether or not there had been a grounding?"

"Yes, sir."

"And there was no evidence . . . of any grounding . . . that was picked up by the robot?"

"Not that. . . . No, sir."

"All right, sir. Now what was the first time that you *ever* heard . . . of a theory whereby the anchor *flogged* a hole in the bow and . . . caused it to take on water and turn over and go to the bottom? . . . And who first mentioned . . . that *remote* possibility?"

"I object to that!" Rohrer out of his seat.

"I *thought* he would," Howell said, flashing an approving smile, almost as if he were proud of Rohrer. "I just wanted to see if Mr. Rohrer was *following* me."

And a few minutes later, Howell was at it again. He had asked the witness whether there was a log or file that showed when they first noted the holes supposedly made by the anchors.

"Do you have the logs, sir?"

There was a long pause while Kutzleb rustled through his files. Howell let the pause linger, linger, linger, then added in a helpful-sounding tone:

"We are looking for the entry *'At last, Eureka!, we have found what caused the vessel to go down'* and it says *'damage caused by anchor flukes stoving in side of vessel.'* "

"Come *on*, Mr. Howell!" Rohrer said. "Captain, do we have to waste time on this?"

And Howell was back at him with a hurt Southern drawl: "That took exactly . . . three and a half seconds. If the chairman please. I'm just trying to *stimulate* the witness."

And a few minutes later, Howell had thoroughly confused the expert while taking another swipe at the Big Gun from New York.

"Did you ever discuss with Mr. Rohrer your thoughts about what had caused the hole, that you thought probably the anchor had caused the hole?"

"Might have at supper or something. I don't know, sir."

"You made no notes at all concerning your observations . . ."

"No, sir."

". . . of the robot videotape and your conclusion."

"No, sir."

"Do you feel qualified to reach that conclusion, in view of the fact that you are not a naval architect or a metallurgist and—"

"That's why I *didn't* come to that conclusion, sir."

"Sir?"

"That is why I *didn't* make a conclusion."

"So you reached *no* conclusion as to what had caused that hole?"

"No."

Rohrer, on his feet:

"Wait a minute now!"

"Mr. Chairman," said the gallant, silver-haired gentleman from Virginia. He was Robert E. Lee now, dignified and rising to a point of Confederate officer's honor. "If he has an *objection,* he should address them to the chair. If he wants to *coach* his witness, he can't do it."

Rohrer told Howell that wouldn't be necessary. The board and Howell would receive all the proof and conclusions from their next witness.

"Mr. Howell may fall out of his chair," Rohrer said.

"It would be the first time," Howell drawled back, in a voice that was all lawyer to lawyer but said in its street-smart undercurrent, no country bumpkin around at all, *Pal, the odds have turned.*

Calicchio had made his point, but his anger had not subsided. He knew where this was going and now Rohrer was bringing on his next expert—the marine architect who had been on board the *G. W. Pierce* survey.

Funny they would hire one of the best-known experts in the world to run the robot divers. And one of the least-well-known in the world to interpret the results. Howell fall out of his chair? Calicchio was figuratively falling from his, but not the way Rohrer wanted.

Calicchio listened carefully as Rohrer walked the expert through his paces. The man, Jan D. Van Rynbach, had a master's degree in naval architecture and marine engineering and had been working in the field since 1951. He ran J. D. Van Rynbach & Associates, Inc., in New Jersey. It was a two-man shop. He had chaired a few marine boards himself—for the Liberian government, which was famous for its discreet understanding and nonpublic inquiries into sinkings.

What did he find on the *Marine Electric?* Rohrer asked.

"The starboard anchor was missing. The hawsepipe was empty. Several sharp cuts were found in the starboard side shell plating aft and above the level of the hawespipe opening in the side shell, looking like they were made by the sharp points of the flukes of the starboard anchor."

And there were heavily grooved areas, "such as you would expect to be caused by an anchor chain chafing around the stem. . . ."

"And what caused the damage?" Rohrer asked. Running his expert through his paces.

"The shell damages and the grooves are caused by the anchor and by the anchor chain, starboard side."

Did he discover hatch covers in the course of the robot's sweeps of the wreck? What were they like?

"Yes. . . . They were not damaged. There were one or two that showed some signs of damage. . . . They had suffered during the casualty. During the [sinking of the ship], as they came off the hatch coamings."

None seemed damaged or collapsed, he added. The plating was intact.

And then he was done, and Rohrer turned to Howell as if to say, "let's see you, with your Southern charm, sink this guy."

But Howell would not be the man on attack. Calicchio had given another inner groan as the first round of expert testimony ended. He knew what was coming. The expert was going to say that all of the hatch cover damage was inflicted *after* the sinking and all of the anchor-caused damage to the hull happened while the ship was afloat, in the storm. And the latter was all caused by Bob Cusick's negligence and bumbling.

It just didn't happen that way. When a ship hit the bottom, it was all over. It was anyone's guess as to what caused damage where. If the unions came in and showed him caved-in hatch covers, he would say the same. "When she hits the bottom, all bets are off," Calicchio was fond of saying.

Of course there was damage to the hull. The ship, he suspected, bounced along the bottom, bow first. The torque was so powerful that the entire midsection of the ship was wrenched loose. Of course the ship looked different on the bottom. On the way to the bottom, the anchor probably flogged everything, when up was down and the ship was twisting and turning.

"Tell me, oh, tell me," Calicchio said to himself, "this guy is not going to take it where I think he is. He is *not* going to tell me the anchor caused this damage *before* it sank. A *flying* anchor that at the height of the storm flogged the ship while it was still on the surface?"

And then Calicchio began. His eyes were hooded again, and he tapped a pencil rapidly. It was not hard to tell he was agitated.

"Good afternoon, Mr. Van Rynbach. All of the damage that you have testified is all damage that you found on the *Marine Electric* while she was laying on the bottom. Is that correct?"

And Von Rynbach said, "Yes, it was."

"When do you feel this was done? When the vessel was afloat and in the upright position, or after she sank?"

"I think it was done between 1 A.M. and 4 A.M. on the 12th of February."

Calicchio winced. Not *just* while the ship was afloat. The expert even gave a precise time. Like Quincy, the television coroner, fixing a time of death. Save us all, Calicchio thought, and plunged on.

"How do you feel that the anchor let go? We do know from prior testimonies that they had the brake on tight and the windlass was out of gear and that the pole was down in the wildcat."

That all systems were in place to secure the anchor as all anchors are secured.

"How do you feel the anchor let go?"

"Because of the excessive forces in the seaway."

"The what?"

"Acceleration forces. The bow going up and down at a very rapid rate and pounding."

Funny, Calicchio thought. The officers said the bow *didn't* pound. Ships in ballast might pound, rarely those fully loaded. And not a twit of evidence from the divers to show pounding.

"Well, what happened?"

"It slipped through the ring." The anchor gave way.

Calicchio pursed his lips and leaned back. This was not going to be pretty.

"What is the purpose of the chain stopper?"

"To hold the anchor. To take the load off the brake when you are anchored."

"Mr. Van Rynbach, I'm sure you have heard of the Society of Naval Architects and Marine Engineers. You are probably a member of it, the same as I am?"

"Yes, sir."

Calicchio marked a paragraph about anchor systems in the society's book *Ship Design and Construction*. He asked Van Rynbach to read it, and he did.

"Am I correct that the statement says that the stopper will hold the chain when the brake is released? Is that correct?"

"When everything is static, yes. When the chain is jumping up and down, that may not be the case."

Calicchio asked slowly:

"The chain is jumping up and down?"

Yes.

"Wasn't it jumping up and down on the port anchor?"

No. "The port anchor was snug."

"At one time they were both snug," Calicchio said.

"That remains to be seen, sir," Van Rynbach said. Taking him on. Big mistake.

"Yes, sir," Calicchio replied in mock formality, not feigning his incredulity now. "In your experience as a naval architect, aren't anchors designed and windlasses designed and the brake in the windlass designed and the stopper designed to hold the chain in a seaway?"

In other words, aren't all anchor systems designed to commonly withstand these sorts of stresses? Aren't there three back-up systems—the windlass, the devil's claw anchor clasp, and the stopper?

"Now, let's just, hypothetically, take what you just said, that the anchor slipped, somehow it got by the brake, somehow it got by the stopper, and somehow it got by the devil's claw. That in essence what you have is the vessel *anchoring* itself at sea. Is that correct?"

In other words, if all three back-ups somehow failed, wouldn't the eight-ton anchor just play out and hit bottom?

"Maybe the anchor was not snug to begin with . . . the anchor chain can slip through a brake a bit at a time," said Van Rynbach. "That has happened before on other ships."

Calicchio's eyes riveted on Van Rynbach now as he said, "Would you mind telling me . . . what ships? And in what conditions it happened in?"

"I couldn't come up with the name of a ship now. But I have heard of such things in the past."

"Have you heard the term 'walking out an anchor chain'?" Calicchio asked. When the brake is released and the anchor windlass is put in reverse to check the anchor?

Van Rynbach had.

"Do you know why that is done?" The old salt, Calicchio, treating the expert like a kid. "Isn't it done because you can't control the anchor chain with the brake alone, to just let a few links out? Once it starts running, it keeps going?

"Isn't that correct?"

"Yes, sir. I have personal experience with that."

"And it makes a lot of noise when it's going down, doesn't it?"

"More than that."

"So what we have now under this scenario is the anchor letting go, the starboard anchor, and it's leading across the bow. Now as it leads across the bow and puts force out, there would be more chain that would be coming out, would it not? It would take the route of least resistance and you would get more chain out?"

"Gradually."

"And you would come to the bitter end of the chain, isn't that correct? Let me present this to you. If it did go to the bitter end of the chain, the bitter end of the chain is made fast by a weak pin, is it not?"

In other words, the very end of the anchor chain is held by a weak link designed to have less strength than the part of the ship where it is attached. So in extreme emergencies, the anchor would not just hit and hold and rip up the ship's bulkhead where it was attached. The weak link would break and let the anchor come loose.

"It is not so weak."

"But it is weaker than the bulkhead, isn't it?"

"I don't know."

Calicchio grimaced again and threw up his hands. He emphasized "weak" in his next statement.

"That is the purpose of putting a *weak end* in the chain, so you won't disturb the bulkhead. The *weak* link will let go first."

"I've seen the exact opposite happen."

"Would you say that the *weak* link has less strength than the chain itself?"

"No."

Calicchio shook his head and mumbled under his breath.

"Have you calculated how much energy would be required for the chain or for anything to break the stem of the *Marine Electric?*"

"No."

"Have you calibrated the strength that would be required?"

"No."

"Have you calculated the strength of the link of a chain?"

"I don't know offhand."

"Well, as a naval architect, would you think that the strength of the stem would be stronger than the chain?"

He was convinced, Van Rynbach said, that the chain could have caused the damage.

Calicchio moved on. His contempt for the witness increased.

"I *think* you said yes to this: Once an anchor starts falling, it *keeps* falling. Is that right?"

"Correct," he said. "Though some fall fast, some fall slowly."

Calicchio moved on. "How far back was damage done to the ship? Am I right in understanding that it was sixty feet from the bow?"

"Yes. Sixty feet."

"How?"

"The anchor was flailing around."

Howell interrupted. He had complained before of poor hearing. But he had an acute ear for a misstep by a hostile witness.

"The anchor was *what?* I didn't get that."

There was a pause.

"Flailing around."

It sounded sillier the second time. Howell rolled the word slowly in his mouth, as if he were sipping bourbon. "Oh . . . *flailing."* Howell smiled. He liked that as much as his word, flogging.

Calicchio was merciless now.

"I just made a little diagram. I had nothing else to do. I dropped the anchor down to where the first divers had found a big fracture, which was thirty-eight feet from the stem and twenty-eight feet from the keel. . . . In order for the anchor to hit that position . . . the anchor would have to swing sixty-five degrees. . . . *An eight-ton anchor would have to swing sixty-five degrees to reach that position. To sixty feet, it would have to go more."*

"Is that . . . *common* . . . for an *eight . . . ton . . . anchor* to swing . . ." Calicchio was speechless for a brief second and then continued.

"You said the anchor was—I would have to get the word you used, but *floating* around."

"Flailing."

Van Rynbach seemed to be shrinking each time he used the word now.

"It did in fact swing *more,"* Van Rynbach said. "I believe, because we found those cuts by the flukes in way of the ship's name."

"Yes. The name. I think you said the cuts were above the name . . . the name on the *Marine Electric,* I believe, is above the anchors. . . ."

This was becoming a farce. Now he was telling Calicchio that the anchor hadn't merely swung sixty-five degrees, which Calicchio considered an analysis beneath contempt. The expert was telling him the anchor had swung 180 degrees. Straightened its chain out completely. Swung up in defiance of gravity, not down with gravity.

The uneven fencing continued. Calicchio said flatly that the damage was much, much more likely to have been caused by torque as the ship broke up underwater. That the anchor would give way when the ship capsized, of course, and on the way to the bottom might bang it around. That the ship, bow heavy as it was with tons of coal and water, would have danced, nose first, on the bottom, perhaps for hours before breaking up. This would explain the anchor marks, but without doubt they were postsinking, not during the voyage.

Van Rynbach said no. The ship settled gently and evenly to the bottom in its current position, the anchor damage already sustained on the surface.

Calicchio went at him one last time. He was treating Van Rynbach as if he were a child now. "Picture the ship capsizing to starboard. What do the anchor restraints on the starboard side *want* to do? Stay closed and hold the anchor? Or open up and let the anchor go?"

"Open."

"And in what direction would the anchor fall?" Calicchio asked. Would it fall into the sea, with all the men of the ship, in the direction of the capsizing? Or would it fall up? Into the chain locker of the upside-down ship. "Would you like a little diagram? Maybe it might help."

"Yes."

"Now, what does it appear that the starboard anchor *wants* to do?"

Like a teacher to a first grader. A slow first grader. Fall up? Fall down and out?

"It would come out possibly. If it was not restrained."

Calicchio gave him a mocking look of approval and then moved on to another basic.

"Mr. Van Rynbach, we all know that vessels are designed to float."

Van Rynbach did not say otherwise.

"I think we also realize that when a vessel hits the bottom, it is going to experience some stresses that can't even be calculated. . . . Now, a vessel such as the *Marine Electric* . . . a piece of the midship body found a mile away . . . wouldn't you expect to find a whole lot of damage on that vessel on your survey?"

"We did."

"Yes, sir," Calicchio said sharply. "But this is all *after it sank*. Is that correct?"

"Yes," said the expert witness.

Calicchio pushed back ever so slightly from his desk. With that little motion, he signaled that $150,000 of ocean bottom research had just turned turtle. The MTL case lay at the bottom next to its old collier. Calicchio had rammed, holed, torpedoed, burned, bent, and broken the Marine Transport case. The expert who started out saying the damage was done while the ship was afloat now said the damage occurred when the ship was on its way to the bottom.

Now Howell moved in for some fun with Rohrer. Perhaps he could make the New Yorker turn different shades of red.

"You said the anchor came loose and started, uh, *flailing about?* At what point? What was your conclusion?"

"I have not come to any *definite* conclusions, sir," Van Rynbach said. "It is far too premature, I think, for me to pretend that I have any conclusions."

"All right, sir," Howell drawled on, reveling in it. Relishing it. This was the part of the Colonel Sanders-meets-Colombo act where the bumbling fool turns out to be the genius.

"Mr. Van Rynbach, I have reached the age where I am subject to correction, and my memory used to be photographic and I could remember the transcript well. I could remember it like *that,*" he said, snapping his fingers.

"I can't do that anymore, but I distinctly recall Mr. Rohrer asking you for a conclusion as to what put the hole in the vessel. And . . . you said it was a *flailing* anchor. Wasn't that your conclusion? A . . . *flailing* . . . anchor?"

"That is *one* of the theories. There are many conclusions that we have to arrive at in this investigation. . . . I am convinced . . . now . . . that the damage on the starboard side . . . was caused by the anchor and the chain. . . .

"But, let's make this very clear. Is it your conclusion that the damage occurred while the ship was still afloat, on its rescue mission to the *Theodora?*"

"I am *not* prepared to state that at this time. Too early. We have to do a lot more thinking and checking."

"So you don't know *when* the anchor broke loose?"

"I cannot give you a definite answer, no, sir."

"Could it have broken loose as Captain Calicchio said? As she sank? And the damage done afterward?"

"I can't tell you."

"Cannot give me your opinion at this time?"

"Right."

"You could not deny or affirm that?"

"I *have* no opinion."

The expert was in full retreat, scrambling to preserve credibility and professional decorum. The opinions he had stated were now fully retracted.

But Howell was not done yet. When Van Rynbach thought he was, Howell tacked suddenly.

"Did you give any consideration to the number-one *hatch panels* giving way? Did you look at the sketch that Mr. Cusick made of the various holes and openings that existed in the panels of number-one hatch?"

Or a report by the hatch cover manufacturer that said the covers were pitifully rusted.

"No, sir."

"Were you asked to by Marine Transport Lines? Or just the anchor theory?"

"Just the anchors."

"Did you look at the hatch covers at *all?*"

"They seemed okay. I've not been asked to look at them. What I've seen, they have been okay."

"So," Howell said, "you were aware that Captain Calicchio was concerned about the hatch covers, which weigh one ton, but you cruised your robots away from the hatch covers and decided to bring up an eight-ton anchor? Very curious. Did you not have some professional obligation to examine the hatch covers?"

"This is an important case here, Mr. Van Rynbach," Howell said sternly. "You are an *expert* hired by Marine Transport Lines to determine the cause of the sinking. You read that . . ."

Rohrer was on his feet, objecting angrily:

"He is testifying here as to *his* observations on . . ."

"I haven't finished yet, Mr. Chairman," Howell said. "Again I seek your protection against this *gentleman* who will not let me complete my question before he notes his objection."

"Mr. Howell just goes on," Rohrer complained, almost to himself. "Trying to get opinion after opinion."

"Take *control* of the situation, Captain," Henry Howell said to chairman Lauridsen. Howell was a model of Southern composure, relaxed and gracious. He grinned slyly and said:

"I don't want to have a hand-wrasslin' with the . . . *gentleman.*"

When order came, Howell had one more trial lawyer's gift for Rohrer and Marine Transport Lines, a souvenir of their trip to the South. Van Rynbach had testified that hours and hours of underwater video review had shown nothing wrong with the hatch covers. Howell picked up several photographs taken earlier of hatch covers and gave them to Van Rynbach. In the stack were some of Shastid's hand-held shots.

"Did you see *this* portion of the hatch cover panels on your videotape?"

Van Rynbach allowed as he did not recall.

"Well, what's your opinion of the hatch cover from these photos?"

"Not that bad," Van Rynbach said. "The stiffeners looked okay."

"What is the condition of the gasket?"

The expert paused and then said it.

"Not good."

Bingo. The expert had been turned again.

Nice to have those photos, Howell thought.

Shastid's photos.

Shastid's little snowball, taking out a key piece of that big old tank. Making certain no one from the *G. W. Pierce* was laughing at him.

The board hearings ended formally that day. A final decision would not come for months. But one crucial point was obvious.

No way was Bob Cusick a party of interest. The flailing anchor was just that: a desperate, flailing legal theory.

And if Howell was happy, Calicchio was even more so. Not

because he had punctured the pretenses and conceits, the sophistries and the hopes, of Marine Transport Lines, but because he could feel the other two members of the board shift toward him.

There was Ed Murphy, the earnest lieutenant commander, trying to get his arms around what he had just heard. Asking questions of these experts.

I'm *trying* to understand, he seemed to say at one point to Van Rynbach. Not angry. Almost stuttering. Sir, I am trying to understand. You are saying the anchor swung thirty-eight feet back, then sixty feet back, then hit above the name of the ship and, I don't see, I don't see . . .

"That's your belief? That that crease which goes roughly directly athwartships was—would not an anchor chain make such a crease in the hull of the vessel that goes directly athwartships, doesn't it seem—Let me phrase it this way: Did you describe a *way* of leading the chain from the hawsepipe that it would go *across* the vessel in that perpendicular manner?"

But he *was* beginning to see. Welcome to the big city, kid, Calicchio thought, where anchors could fall upward if you let them. *This* is how it worked.

Lauridsen, too, was shaking his head at the MTL gambit. Lauridsen, the quiet, pipe-smoking captain with stars in his eyes, who wanted the flag rank so much, was agreeing with Calicchio on almost everything.

Calicchio thought he could pull it off now, make a real report that changed things.

He wasn't alone anymore.

Now if he could only hold it together for the final report.

Chapter Twenty-six

THE KILLER CARD

But now obey, thy cherish'd, secret wish,
Embrace thy friends-leave all in order;
To port, and hawser's tie, no more returning,
Depart upon thy endless cruise, old Sailor!

WALT WHITMAN

1:30 P.M. / MONDAY, JUNE 28, 1983
MASTERS, MATES & PILOTS HIRING HALL / NORFOLK, VIRGINIA

In Norfolk, when he and Bea were there for the wedding, Bob had announced he was just going down to the hiring hall. Just to check out old haunts.

In the hall, Cusick noticed there was a position open for a third mate on a ship sailing that day.

Just out of curiosity? Cusick said to the union hiring hall agent. How many people are stacked up for that job right now? How long has this slot been open?

Even if he wanted to, Cusick knew going back to sea would be a matter of weeks, months. You had to wait in line. Had to spend your time on the beach. You didn't just walk in off the street and catch a ship. Only two days before had he become eligible to ship out again. His "card" was far too "young." It would have to age. All officers carried a card stamped with the date last shipped. You needed at least 100 days on the beach to have a "killer card"—a card that would give you a good chance at a ship.

And that time would give him time to do some thinking. Even if he were to go, give his old life another try, could he really face it?

What kind of ship would it be? Another old tub? Where would she be going? Across the North Atlantic again?

Well, he had a lot of time to think about it. Just asking. No harm in just asking. It would be weeks or months before his name came up on the list. "How many names do you have?" Cusick asked the agent. "How old a card would you have to have for this ship? Just curious."

The union agent turned. Knowing who Cusick was.

This ship was a freak situation. The regular third mate got drunk in Baltimore, and they fired him just before sailing to Norfolk. So the ship had rolled in just a little while ago, and the union had just posted the slot. It was twenty minutes to two now, and the slot would be called promptly on the hour. This was the time the union official could call a buddy, bank some votes, reward his friends, get them off the beach and onto a ship.

"How many cards are in front of you?" the agent said to Cusick, repeating the question back to him.

"None, sir," the union man said.

"No one is ahead of you, if you are interested in this job."

Chapter Twenty-seven

SHIPS ON THE RIVER KWAI

Somewhere, anytime, someone is getting it.

John McPhee
Looking for a Ship

September 1984 / *Philadelphia Inquirer* Newsroom

To the *Marine Electric* team at the *Inquirer*, the "flailing anchors" triumph of Cusick's attorney seemed like the last battle. Surely the war was won. Surely the system would be reformed now. The government could not blame this one on "operational error." The next logical step was to start scrapping the old ships.

The *Philadelphia Inquirer* had published a series entitled "Death Ships" in May 1983, and the team had laid out the issues plainly and in great detail. The *Marine Electric* should never have been at sea, the series said, but in fact government subsidy and cargo reservations assured that she was. The government safety inspections were slipshod and negligent at best, and the old warhorse ships had been known to be unsafe for decades. Still, hundreds of men had died on the old ships, and dozens more would unless government policy was changed.

The articles caused a stir. Congress held hearings, politicians promised reform.

Then there was nothing. Worse than nothing. Weeks passed, then months, then a whole year, and it was February 1984. The Coast Guard Marine Board of Investigation report had not been issued. No one seemed to know when it would be forthcoming.

More months passed. It was September 1984—closing in on two years since the sinking. Still no Coast Guard report. No word from Calicchio and the others. The Reagan Administration took no steps to set age limits on the ships. Admiral James S. Gracey, the Coast Guard commandant, even testified to Congress that the Coast Guard system of inspections was working well.

"Increased age of a ship does not bring the inevitable conclusion of unseaworthiness," Gracey said. No one at the congressional hearing challenged that pronouncement.

And it was the same for the seamen. They saw the old ships as their last lifeline to a job, even if the ships sank and men died and the Merchant Marine suffered. The rank and file seamen were upset about the sinking but more concerned about catching a ship. An *Inquirer* reporter had hung about the hiring halls in Philadelphia and shot the breeze with seamen. You *bet* they were worried about the old ships. But what were you to do about it? Sit on the beach?

"If the *Marine Electric* pulled in here tomorrow, I'd get on board," a man named Gregory Brown told one of the reporters. "I've got a wife, two kids, and a mortgage, and I haven't worked in six months."

The unions had the same philosophy. Hate the old ships. Got to work them. The Seafarers International Union newspaper carried a scathing attack on safety aboard the old ships, lamented the loss of the *Poet* and the *Marine Electric,* and lambasted the Coast Guard for poor inspections.

But in the same newspaper, the union also boasted of clinching a contract aboard the *Amoco Trader,* "the first newcomer to the U.S.-European route in 15 years." The ship was owned by Henry Bonnabel, the tramp ship operator of the *Poet.* The *Amoco Trader* was another of the leftover World War II ships.

One of the reporters began whistling the theme from the 1950s movie *Bridge on the River Kwai* every time someone in the newsroom wondered why the unions did nothing. In that famous movie, proud and disciplined British POWs kept their morale and health by building a graceful bridge over the River Kwai. They were led by their commanding officer, Colonel Nicholson, who completely lost sight of the larger fact that the bridge completed a crucial

Japanese rail supply route. The supply route would mean the death of thousands of Allied soldiers. Only at the last possible moment did Colonel Nicholson come to his senses—and spectacularly blow the bridge.

The phrase *"Bridge on the River Kwai* syndrome" had crept into the language of pop sociology to broadly describe a situation in which the short-term positives disguised a much larger, long-term evil.

The movie seemed to fit this situation exactly. Only no one was coming along to blow the bridge.

As for Cusick, it was true that he was safe now. Wherever he was. No one seemed to know exactly. Wherever he was, Cusick was safe from prosecution.

But the system wasn't safe. Nothing had changed there. What the *Inquirer* said was going to happen almost certainly would happen. Another of the old ships would sink. More men would be killed.

But the *Inquirer* wasn't doing much, either. The team's effort had faded without impact. The fact was, heavy lobbying by the unions was *increasing* the use of old ships by increasing cargo preference programs. The U.S. House Merchant Marine and Fisheries Committee eliminated from its staff-written bill a provision to deny cargo to very old U.S. ships. Good maintenance and good inspections can assure the safety of the old ships, said Representative Mario Biaggi, chairman of the Merchant Marine subcommittee. The *Inquirer* editorialized against such actions, but Philadelphia was far, far outside the Beltway.

So it all was disappearing, dissolving into time. The eye had seen. The heart had felt. But the head had not acted. No one had come forward besides Calicchio, Bob Cusick, and the *Poet* mothers. And now Cusick wasn't around anymore.

Unless there was a Colonel Nicholson to blow the bridge, there never would be change. The unions, like the British POWs in the movie, were in dire times. No one in the unions would take a stand on the old ships. No union official would return reporters' calls more than once.

Where was Colonel Nicholson? Who would blow the bridge?

* * *

His name was Jesse Calhoun. He had a long memory and a longer history of doing what needed to be done, sometimes in a rough and direct way.

He was head of the Marine Engineers' Benevolent Association, or MEBA, one of the powerful maritime unions. MEBA raised more money per capita than any other union anywhere. Calhoun hired the best lawyers and lobbyists in Washington—young men in their thirties who knew how to wear suits and shoot their cuffs at the negotiating table. They could spin issues so fast Calhoun himself became dizzy. And they could order the right wine at the right time over power lunches in the fine restaurants inside the Beltway.

The legend of Jesse Calhoun is that he knew how to work a table as well. Work it in the old way, that is; serve up a power lunch of his own, though what he served would not be understood by the yuppies he employed now.

Years later, union officials would still tell the story. In the 1960s, as Calhoun was negotiating a master agreement with dry cargo carriers, he got into a shouting match with the Farrell Lines bargainer. Calhoun hollered above the din:

"Frank, if you lie to me again, I am going to get up on this table and kick you in the teeth."

The meeting calmed down—until Frank again began citing endless statistics and details.

At the other end of the conference table, Calhoun said nothing. He stood on his chair. Then he stood on the table. Then he calmly walked the length of the table, took a little running jump, and kicked the company man square in the teeth.

Well, the modern world was not that simple, Calhoun knew, but he could act in other ways that made the point. He had read the *Inquirer* series on the *Marine Electric*. MEBA had bought 100 copies of the series, and what he read was close enough to the truth that it made him want to stomp down the table and kick Marine Transport Lines in the teeth.

Jesus, what a mess! One of his union members had called him earlier in the year on behalf of Michael Price, one of the engineers and MEBA members trapped in the engine room. Send a diver down and cut those guys out, the man, George Dolak, had said. The family members think they are still alive.

"No way they are alive," Calhoun replied. "We both know that only happens in the movies. The boilers would have exploded when the ship capsized. Superheated steam would have flooded the engine space."

"Yeah, I know," Dolak yelled back at him. "I *know* what happened to my friend, you son of a bitch. But do something for the families. Cut the men out! Tell them you're going to try, at least."

With the swearing and yelling, Calhoun and Dolak were too much alike to carry on much of a conversation. Dolak called him at the office. At home. A half-dozen times a day. "Man, there is nothing I can do! Goddamn you, stop calling me or I'll sue you!"

But it pained Calhoun, too. He remembered his days in engine rooms. And he had gone back for men who were down.

He wanted to do something now. But there were jobs at stake. The MTL engineers were represented by MEBA—Calhoun's group—but the company deck officers like the chief mate and second mate were represented by the Masters, Mates & Pilots. Down the line, MEBA could get the deck officers, the captains and the mates, if Calhoun played his cards right. In the rough-and-tumble, cutthroat world of maritime union rivalries, that could change when the contract came up in '84. MEBA could flip Marine Transport Lines to choose MEBA as the deck officers' union.

And Calhoun had to stay in contention for that. MTL was the largest bulk carrier. If he could organize them, take them away from the MMP . . .

In one way, though, he hated to work with them. Marine Transport Lines had frosted him for years. Decades! They put on *airs* of running a class operation, but in his mind they were just a junk-ship operator. Always had been. Always would be.

Boy, did he know that from personal experience.

Calhoun was a kid of sixteen when he joined the Merchant Marine in 1942, less than a month after Pearl, on board the SS *Malay*. She was an old Marine Transport ship built between the wars. The god-damned company had forgotten to put in a proper galley, so after the shipyard was done with her, they had had to go back in and steal some space from the engine room to expand the galley. They took part of the ventilation system, and that turned the engine room into a steamy, 100-degree hell that Calhoun walked into.

A rotund, overweight assistant engineer greeted the young man and made him a deal. Jesse could work the regular four-hour shift. Or, he could perform a simple task. "Just crawl up above the main boiler and turn on the valves to blow some steam, to blow the tubes—and, well, you just have to do that, maybe forty-five minutes of work, and you're done for the watch."

"Great," said the young Jesse. "What a deal." Until he tried it. He'd thought the engine room was hot. In the crawl space, it was 140 degrees. He was flat on his stomach or his back, in odd positions, reaching for the valves. He was poached. Parboiled.

But he did it.

The old tub was in the Atlantic when her condenser pumps blew, and she headed for Philadelphia. The Navy turned her away. "You ain't coming in here," Calhoun recalled them saying. "We're full-up. You've got enough in you to get to Texas. Go there."

So they did. Or tried to. But on January 19, 1942, off North Carolina, a German submarine surfaced and shelled the *Malay*, then sent a torpedo into her just forward of the engine room. Jesse and a young friend were fit and nimble. They scrambled free, counted heads, and came up short. Then the kids went back. There, they found the fat assistant engineer, wounded and immobile. They struggled with him and made little headway at first. But eventually, they hauled him up the hatch and out onto the deck and into a lifeboat.

They were out there in 1942, watching the ship go down, they thought, and Calhoun was sad to hear four men had died.

But deep down he was damned *glad* the *Malay* was sinking. Deep down he said to himself, "Thank God, you're sinkin', you sonof-abitchin' junk ship, you. You ain't a-going to be around to torture nobody no more."

Then, somewhat to his horror, the ship stayed afloat. The master and engineers had stayed on board. The sub had fired its last torpedo and could not stay on the surface to shell her.

Calhoun and the crew rejoined the ship the next day from the lifeboat, and she was towed into port and salvaged.

Goddamn, you could never get rid of these old rust buckets! They just stayed around and tortured you!

So in 1983, Calhoun remembered what it was to go back for men. He did not leave downed men behind, trapped in the engine room.

Calhoun remembered, and Calhoun never forgot and he never forgave. The *Malay,* 1942. The *Marine Electric,* 1983. His man down in the engine room, 1942. His men, in the engine room, down there dead, 1983.

Junk-ship-operatin' sonsabitches, putting on airs. That was the attitude of MTL, so far as he was concerned, continuing to that day when the phone was ringing on his desk in the summer of 1983.

On the phone was a top officer of Marine Transport Lines, James Rand himself, the CEO. Could Jesse help them? They were having trouble locating parts of the *Marine Electric* on the ocean floor. The Navy could help, the company man said, and Jesse, being a man of influence, could get the Navy to help.

"Sure," Calhoun said. Would do what he could. "Remember us come contract time.

"And, oh," he said to the MTL man, "while you're diving down there? You may remember there are six men still down. The engineers and the cadet. Their bodies are down there in the engine room. Cut 'em out, will you? Take some torches down and cut 'em free. As a favor. Give the families some closure. Let them bury their dead men on land. It's rough when you lose your men, rougher still when they are just gone at sea. The families need to bury the men and their grief. They need to have them buried proper."

"Sure," the company man said. "I'll look into it."

Smiling bastards. "Liars," Calhoun said to himself. Cheap, junk-ship-operatin' liars. Nothing had changed since the *Malay.* This was all about damage control for MTL. They'd spent tens of thousands on their dives, not a nickel on cutting the men out. No way he'd ever hear back from them. This was just legal damage control.

Why, if he was at the table across from this slick son of a bitch Rand, he'd like nothing better than to stand up on that table, walk down it, and kick this smiling bastard in the teeth.

But he couldn't do that. If he could organize MTL later next year, he'd add dozens of men to the union roster. Can't piss them off now. Not like the old days. He had contracts to settle. He had money to raise. Ships to crew.

Besides, he had men in suits who could kick people in the teeth so smoothly they didn't even know their dentures were scuffed. His suit-and-tie guys were just down the hall, in Suite 800 at 44 North Capitol Street in Washington, D.C. Hell, he did not know if these guys had ever been on the water. But they knew how to get things done. Much more subtly.

Months later, Calhoun gave his suits a call. The gist of his message was classic Calhoun. I wantcha to buy 5,000 copies of that *Inquirer* article, Calhoun told them. Send it to every goddamned congressman and every goddamned union official and every goddamned shipping executive and anyone who has anything to do with maritime public policy.

Let's wake these people up. Let's kick 'em in the goddamned teeth.

Also? Cut the guys in at the *Inquirer.* Give them what they need. Tell our guys to talk. Give them a call.

Show them the goddamn junk that's out there.

A reporter from the team in Philadelphia picked up the phone the next day and knew immediately that he was talking to a Washington professional.

"Look, let me get right to the point. Can we go off the record here? I represent MEBA for Jesse Calhoun, and Jesse has had enough, okay? We're off the record, right? On background? I can't say it any simpler or more directly. He's read the articles, and he thinks it's time to end this stuff.

"So here it is: He wants to put you on some of these old tubs. Guided tour. Can you be in Tampa, day after tomorrow? Okay, we're flying over two guys to meet you there from New Orleans, and they'll put you in touch with the right people."

"Sure," said the reporter.

And in his mind, he saw the graceful bridge explode in orange plumes and blossoms of fire-drenched smoke and then begin to fall slowly into the River Kwai. They had their Colonel Nicholson. Maybe they could blow the bridge. The conversations would all be on the record this time. No statistics. No sources. The on-the-record statements of the old-ship sailors—the material they'd been trying to get for three long years. What Roberts had said months back was now coming true. People would go on the record eventually. Lay down the history, lay down the stats, the people would come around.

Maybe they *could* nail the old ships this time.

A day later, the reporter was in Tampa, legally but stealthily boarding the SS *Penny*, escorted by knowledgeable MEBA engineers. The vessel seemed made of rust. It was the twin sister of the lost ship SS *Poet*, owned by the tramp ship operator Henry Bonnabel.

William Francis, the chief engineer, was sixty-two, a wizened master engineer whom colleagues thought an expert at his profession—particularly in keeping the old ships running. Someone asked how things were going on the *Penny*, and he said things were going great, if you don't mind not sleeping. Some fellows had been knocking on his door at one o'clock this very morning.

"Chief, we got a big hole in the bottom, and I can't pump the water out," the night engineer shouted.

Francis ignored them. The night engineer must be drunk, he thought. We're at dockside. We can't be sinking.

The door-banger persisted.

"Chief, there is water pouring into the engine room, and we're going to sink before daylight if we don't stop it!" the night engineer called out again.

This time, Francis woke up. On these old ships, that *could* happen at dockside. When he got to the engine room, he found the night engineer sober—and fourteen tons of seawater an hour pouring into the number-six double-bottom ballast tank.

Forget heavy seas. Forget long voyages. The ship was literally sinking at the dock.

The cause of this calamity could not have been more mundane. A crew member had merely dropped a sounding pole into the number-six tank to measure the depth of ballast. This had been done almost every day for nearly forty years.

The pole struck bottom and punched right through the ship's hull.

That was Francis's first problem that day. The hull was patched. The strike plate reinforced. Then the *Penny* set off on Coast Guard sea trials. Drop the anchor, the Coast Guard told the officers. Drop anchor, the officers ordered. And the anchor dropped, and dropped. It did not stop. It broke loose from its aged chains and rested now somewhere on the bottom.

All this happened on a ship contracted by the government in the name of a strong U.S. Merchant Marine. A company controlled by Henry Bonnabel would receive $1.7 million courtesy of the federal government for hauling a cargo of phosphate fertilizer to Mombasa, Kenya.

Chief engineer Francis had worked five years for Bonnabel. A wiry, cussing, crotchety man, Francis preferred living on his small ranch in Wyoming. But the pay was too good to resist. He was the master engineer of these old ships, and they paid top dollar for his skill.

Now, with his union's blessing, he was talking about the conditions aboard the *Penny* and his experiences aboard the old ships. The union men, for the first time, were complaining publicly about conditions aboard the old ships, and the reporter from the *Inquirer* was scribbling notes furiously.

The deck of the *Penny* was not just rusted. It *was* rust. One of the jobs of crew members was to rake up those scales. Each night, they created a knee-high pile. Rust covered the hatches. Rust engulfed the winches and the doors. The pipes and portholes were rusted. The ceiling of the ship's forward chain locker was rusted through from the top. Rust discolored the white paint of the ship's name and dripped down the side of the ship in orange-red tears.

"Well, the circulator blew up yesterday, and the feed pump is giving us some problems, but mechanically the ship is fixed up better than on any other trip," Francis said in his Wyoming drawl.

He drew in on a nonfiltered Pall Mall cigarette as he paged slowly through four legal-size pages of Coast Guard repair requirements on his desk. In his super-cool, air-conditioned cabin, sweat still streaked down his face from the steamy 100-degree heat of the engine room. Oil smudged his hands, face, and the thin hair of his balding head. Salt from dried sweat edged his blue workman's jumpsuit.

"Course, that don't mean she won't break down a week from now when she's out at sea," Francis said. "You're always going to have problems on these old ships. And course, the work they're doing now, they should have done last time, and got away *without* doing."

Carleton Pirez, a former chief engineer of the *Penny* who often sailed for Bonnabel, interrupted, leaning forward, a vein throbbing in his forehead as he talked forcefully and rapidly.

"Look, I'll tell you what this man wants, and what we all want," he said. "For one thing, the wiring on these old ships is old, and it gets wet, and you can't rely on it.

"That's one of the chief problems. You never know what time of the day or night what's going to happen, what's going to go, when you're going to lose the plant [engine].

"You keep sweating that the son of a bitch will keep going till you get into port, and you start sweating the most when you get caught in a storm, and you lose the plant. Then is when you never know, you *never* know what's going to happen, and you really worry.

"This man here," Pirez said, looking at Francis, "wants his fall-back units working. That's all. You got two of most things in the engine room, two generators, say. He wants them all working when he starts out so when one of them goes wrong out there, which it will, he's got a fighting chance.

"All he wants is a fair chance out there."

Pirez finished and looked down at the floor. Francis looked straight ahead at no one, Pall Mall in hand, neither confirming nor denying what Pirez had said. A bemused smile spread over his face.

"Well," Francis said after a moment. He spoke slowly, pausing as if to search for the last word of his sentence. When he found it, his face looked as if he had tasted a tablespoon of vinegar.

"Let's just say that the *Penny* is a ship that's likely to make you sleep . . . *lightly.*"

Bonnabel, the owner of the ship, told the reporter that the newspaper was just flat wrong about how the owner operated his vessels.

"That is where we disagree," Bonnabel said. "The ships are safe. The Coast Guard has *certified* them safe. I have a responsibility to meet Coast Guard requirements. What else do you want?"

Where was the Coast Guard? Caught between Bonnabel and the officers, and nearly as frustrated as the engineers.

"We fully intend for the *Penny* to be completely up to standards," said Lieutenant Commander Wayne Ogle of the Tampa Marine Safety Office of the U.S. Coast Guard. "We have living seamen on board this ship, and there is a lot of tough water on this trip."

"The fact that he has the ship loaded and has got a contract doesn't change anything," Ogle said. "The requirements hold. He won't get anywhere with us arguing economics. He knows what he has to do."

But one thing Ogle could not do was say simply junk this old rusty bucket. He had to keep making inspection requirements until the owners decided to junk the ship. If Bonnabel fixed up the *Penny,* she would weigh anchor. And this was so even though Ogle and others could not tell what would go wrong in the next moment. Bonnabel in fact had agreed to pay for more than $200,000 in patchwork repairs to the *Penny,* and she was set to sail—until the sounding rod went through the bottom.

"You heard about the hole in the hull?" Ogle asked. Then he shook his head. "That has us more than a little bit upset."

"You lower it down, it hits the bottom plate," Ogle said. "Do that for forty years, and of course it wears away at the striking plate."

"We went over every inch of that hull," he said, shaking his head. "Then the sounding rod punches through the bottom."

The Coast Guard inspectors became frustrated by it all, because there seemed to be no one else out there who cared, least of all this owner.

"You saw the condition of that ship, pretty indicative of the company's attitude toward things," Ogle said. "It is unfortunate that we have to deal with that kind of attitude toward running a ship."

Recently, Coast Guard Captain T. L. Valenti had tried to shift responsibility back onto Bonnabel and apply some pressure. Valenti wrote, in a letter dated Oct. 14, 1983:

"I firmly believe the owner of the vessel, master and chief engineer share the ultimate responsibility for the safety of the vessel and crew."

But Bonnabel sidestepped the issue completely and laid it back on his officers.

And left the officers in the Officers' Dilemma. If they object to safety problems, Bonnabel can easily replace them.

And if they sail a ship they know is unseaworthy—and say so— the Coast Guard can pull their license to sail. The bang and hang.

The double bind produced strange scenes. Francis was suddenly silent in his cabin, while union officials fidgeted in their chairs. The plain-speaking chief engineer was asked a straightforward question. Was the *Penny* safe?

Francis did not reply. Barney Snow, the officers' union representative from New Orleans, spoke instead.

"Now you have to be careful how you phrase these questions, or you could get our boys in some real trouble," he said. "If he's going to sail this ship, he can't tell you this ship is unsafe. I can tell you that, and that the union is tired of sailing on these old rust buckets. But if that man there tells you that, well, the Coast Guard would be all over him in a minute."

So Francis skirted that issue. And Snow explained that a lesser engineer would not even dare speak to a reporter, for fear of being fired.

"Those young third assistant engineers you saw in the engine room don't have any choice but to be here," Snow said. "They've been waiting for fourteen months to get a ship.

"They don't like this one? Well, the only thing they can do is get back in line and wait another fourteen months."

So it was that the Coast Guard and the officers became both allies and adversaries. Ship officers cannot easily state that a ship is unseaworthy. Yet, they often root quietly for the Coast Guard inspectors.

Few officers speak up. Few crew members file safety complaints. Francis is the exception. "He don't care," Snow said. "He's always going to get jobs." But even crusty Bill Francis would not comment directly on the seaworthiness of the *Penny*.

"Well, the Coast Guard asked me to sign a letter on seaworthiness," Francis said. "I ain't a-gonna do it. . . . That's their job."

The danger aboard led to a black-humored jocularity among the ship's officers.

"I don't think I want to work anymore on that hole in number six tonight—how much water have we got under us right now, Cap'n?" Francis said. The whine of his drawl set small smiles on the faces of the other officers, who were sipping whiskey and swapping stories in the cozy cabin.

"I think I'll sleep *well* tonight," Francis said. His cabin was well above the engine room, but two decks below the other officers. "I don't think the water will get up *near* this far when she sinks."

"Oh, no, the water *will* come up this far," another officer replied. "It won't go up another deck where *I'll* be sleeping."

The smiles spread. The stories continued. Francis chuckled and sipped the whiskey.

Bonnabel talked to the *Inquirer* team again, and the shipowner again complained that the newspaper, not the *Penny's* condition, had scared the Coast Guard into thinking she was unsafe and singling him out.

It wasn't that the *Penny* was actually seaworthy. His complaint was that *none* of the ships out there was very seaworthy, and he was hurt that the newspaper had for years singled him out and not gone after the big brand names.

"We will compare records with any line," he said. "That is the state of the industry. You should have spread out the blame much earlier."

Roger Szoboda, an engineering consultant in New Orleans hired by the union to review the *Penny*, said the ship was no worse than many others he had seen run by major lines.

"As the business goes, the *Penny* isn't in bad shape," he said. "It's just like an old car. You can fix it up. Get it running pretty good. You can do your best on it.

"You look it over. Everything's fine. That doesn't mean a wheel won't fall off when you take it out of the driveway.

"There is a 'one-trip-more' mentality among the unions, the owners, and the inspectors," Szoboda added. " 'Let's fix her up so she can make one more trip. Well, it isn't fixed right, but let's let her go because she's only going to make one more trip.' "

Usually, there is one more trip. And a trip after that. And a trip after that. The officers were powerless to stop the sailing.

Two hours before sea trials, the master of the *Penny* resigned. He was replaced.

The third mate of the ship, telling union officials he wanted "a long and pleasant life," also resigned. His replacement, after coming on board the ship, resigned a few minutes later.

"He was replaced by a mate so dead broke he couldn't pay his union dues," a union official said.

A few days later, the story was back on page one of the *Inquirer.*

Today, the story said, while families of the thirty-four men killed on the *Poet* gather at Old Swede's Church in Philadelphia for a memorial service, the *Penny's* crew, led by her new master, is still working to repair and prepare the ship for another voyage. And then the article told of the officers who could not quit but were afraid to stay, of sounding rods that holed ships, of Coast Guard inspectors who could not do what they felt was their real job, of congressmen and commandants far, far from the field who were blind to the problem.

This will happen again, the newspaper warned. Another old ship will go down, and men will die. It is a certainty. This is urgent.

Still, the story said, one year and eight months after the sinking of the *Marine Electric,* the Coast Guard has not released its report on what should be done.

Jesse Calhoun distributed the articles to a thousand influentials in Washington and New York. He bought another 5,000 copies of the series and sent them out again as well.

The general sense of his message *seemed* straightforward. Guys, gals, he said, this has to change. This newspaper is thumping us too hard, making real trouble for us. I don't like what they are doing any more than you do, but we have to change. Besides, they have got some points. These old crappy ships. They have got to go.

Yet all the while, Calhoun was bargaining with Marine Transport Lines to become their officers' union and feeding the *Inquirer* even more information.

That's how it worked.

The team at the *Inquirer* started phase two of their project. The *Philadelphia Inquirer,* 102 miles from the sea, was not going away. The paper reached a million people and senators from three states. There were dozens more stories about the old tubs out there, and it looked as if the *Inquirer* would do every one of them. They just weren't stopping. Roberts gave them a blank check to keep going.

In nearly every story and editorial, the *Inquirer* said it again and again and again. Another ship is going to sink. You can't dodge this one.

In effect, they said, the train is coming. It's at the Bridge on the River Kwai.

Blow the bridge.

Chapter Twenty-eight

SCHOONER RIGGED

Hark to the song of the sailors on board . . .

Robert Louis Stevenson

2:10 P.M. / Monday, June 28, 1983 / Norfolk, Virginia

In Norfolk, after he left the hiring hall, Cusick rushed back to talk to Bea. He had gone to the hiring hall just to see old friends, he thought, but then there was this third mate's job. "How many in line for that one?" he had asked.

"None," the union agent said. "If you're interested, there's nobody ahead of you, sir."

And Cusick had thrown in his card. Put in for the job. Twenty minutes passed, and they called out the ship's name at 2 P.M. sharp. Cusick hollered back his number. No one else contested it. He had the slot.

Well, he had no clothes, no gear! Just wedding clothes. Nothing to go to sea in.

"Hey, Bea," Bob Cusick told his wife, "don't ask questions, and don't tell me I'm crazy. Come with me. We're going to Sears. I need some clothes. You can buy me a coat."

Bea burst into tears. She did not want him to go, asked him not to go. But she knew the sea's pull on him. Knew he had to get the whole thing out of his system completely. Knew this was the only way to do it.

She helped pick out the clothes. Khakis. That was the basic uniform for American Merchant Marine officers. They went to Sears, Roebuck together, bought him some khakis, then borrowed rain slickers and other gear from Bob's friend Bill Long. They were sending Bob to sea "schooner-rigged"—with only the bare essentials—and he was to catch the ship in Norfolk that very night as she set sail for Savannah, Georgia.

This felt right. Very right.

Still, he did not know what he would do when he was actually back on the bridge, when he actually had a ship beneath him again and saw the big waves again. A queasy feeling coiled up in his stomach and then spread.

What kind of ship would he draw? Could he face one of those old rust buckets again? What if there were heavy seas? Christ, what if it was a T-2? He could see the waves in his mind, feel them carry him up and down in the lifeboat. He'd sworn he'd never go back to sea, never go on water like that again.

Yet here he was.

Chapter Twenty-nine

BEAU GESTE

Always bring a gun to a knife fight.

Entrepreneur Michael Bloomberg

December 1984 / New Orleans, Louisiana

In a world of complex systems, little failures mean everything. One system depends on another. A gasket fails, a hatch floods, a ship sinks. A motor shorts, a fire is fanned, a plane burns, a song dies.

In the world of policy, deep in the bureaucracy, it is no different.

Little actions, done or not done, make a difference. Little people, little acts. A small lie, a little compromise, a chain is broken, change dies, crashes, burns. A man turns left and does one thing. Policy shifts. He turns right, policy shifts elsewhere. He accommodates, keeps his voice still, policy does nothing.

Little people. Little decisions. Little quiet acts of courage. They would be done. Or not. Drops of water, little ones, formed a path down a mountain, coursed to make rivers. Little acts, small ones, formed cultures, coursed one way to form great tradition. Took another and soaked unseen into the ground.

Little acts made all the difference, but by their nature—being little—rarely ever were they seen.

Now it was December 1984, closing in on two years since the wreck of the *Marine Electric,* and Dominic Calicchio was watching all his issues dissolve with time. They dispersed. Soaked unseen into the ground. Began to disappear. Time was a solvent, so very powerful. Dump thirty years of issues into a beaker filled with six months of time, and the fluid clouds only for a moment and then clears, the issues dissolved and invisible.

A thousand pages of testimony. Tears. Tales of men on a life ring, dying one by one. The anger of the widows. The faces of fatherless children. All forgotten.

The *Philadelphia Inquirer* was keeping the issues alive. But the newspaper reached a region, not the nation. The stories helped, Calicchio thought. But overall, the *Marine Electric* was fading, fading away, like a Polaroid picture running in reverse.

Captain Calicchio was back in New Orleans now, but the good times did not roll for him. He was just a little person in the Coast Guard, becoming smaller and smaller by Washington's measure. The transcripts and reports from the *Marine Electric* surrounded him and only made him feel even less powerful.

Now it was more than twenty months since the Marine Board hearings began, and the board's report was completed. They had transmitted it to the commandant and headquarters in July 1984.

But the commandant, who had to issue his comments and actions to implement the board findings, was ominously silent, and had been for months.

Somewhat to Calicchio's surprise, Captain Lauridsen, the quiet, pipe-smoking chairman of the board from Washington headquarters, agreed with the tough recommendations in the report. Lauridsen may have had stars in his eyes and ambition for flag, but Lauridsen was doing the right thing here, *knowing* it could not help him capture the flag of an admiral's rank.

The National Transportation Safety Board had issued its report in January 1984, less than a year after the wreck of the *Marine Electric*. And while there were tough parts, the NTSB report stopped far short of what Calicchio had hoped for. In fact, parts of it angered him just as much as that little note passed to him that said "Enough!"

The strong points demanded respect. The NTSB told the Coast Guard, in effect, We recommended five years ago, after the wreck of the *Chester A. Poling,* that the Coast Guard require survival suits be aboard all ships on winter North Atlantic runs.

You didn't do it. And many of the thirty-one men dead on the *Marine Electric* paid with their lives. Almost certainly, there would have been more survivors.

The NTSB also concluded that the cause of the sinking was a fracture, either in the old T-2 "tired iron" section of the bow, or near the number-two cargo hold. The fracture could have resulted from "local wastage" or deterioration, too—they could not tell. Probably, neither could the inspectors.

The part that made Calicchio seethe quietly was the NTSB conclusion that the deteriorated hatch covers played little role in the sinking. The seas weren't high enough to break the hatch covers, the NTSB said. Perhaps *after* the ship was lowered in the water by the fracture, the hatch covers *did* give way. The main cause of the wreck was still the fracture.

The conclusions angered Calicchio for a number of reasons. First, the testimony he heard indicated there *was* green water over the hatches all during the rescue attempt—up to six feet of it, and in quantities ample to flood the holds. The pressure on the hatch covers would be like flinging a municipal swimming pool full of water directly onto the chewing-gum-patched hatches, and then doing it again and again.

Moreover, he had run exhaustive technical tests with computer models, and the results showed that the capsizing simply could not have happened the way the NTSB said it did. There had to be water over the top of the hatches and on top of the coal to make the ship capsize. Water seeping in from below would not do it—it would lower the ship, but not sink or capsize it. At times, fishermen in trouble would take on water to give their boats weight and stability, in effect to serve as ballast.

In other words, even if there *was* a slight fracture in the hull, the ship would have remained buoyant and upright, floating a little bit lower in the water, the extra water inside no heavier than the water outside. If the hatches had been strong, the ship would have remained upright. Water seeping into the cargo holds would not displace the coal.

Only water and weight high on top of the coal would capsize the ship. Only if the water got above the coal would the ship be prone to capsize. In Calicchio's theory, the hatches did give way because they were weak and could not stand the pressures they had been designed to take. When the green seas boarded the bow of the *Marine Electric,* the covers gave way even though they would have held up if in good condition. This failure admitted tons of water on *top* of the coal and *did* impact the ship's center of gravity.

This is what caused the sudden capsizing. The computer models and Calicchio's twenty-three years of experience at sea told him this was the only way to explain how the ship capsized and sank. A crack in the old bow or elsewhere would aid the seas in pounding the hatches, but the only reason the ship sank was that it had badly maintained hatches, patched with spit and chewing gum, glue and Band-Aids. Had the hatches held, the ship would have been low in the water, but still afloat.

Above all, what enraged Calicchio was that the NTSB finding might very well get Marine Transport Lines off the hook in later civil cases and encourage owners everywhere to continue using the old ships. This was so because "fractures" sometimes are seen as beyond the scope of owner knowledge. Unless there was clear prior knowledge that the hull would fracture, how could the owners be held liable? The ship had passed both the Coast Guard and American Bureau of Shipping inspections, and the hull was said to be strong. The history of T-2 fractures did not necessarily count in a court of law, because the Coast Guard had ruled that this class of ship was safe if the crack arrestors were added. MTL was in compliance on that point.

In short, the report fell far, far short of the National Transportation Safety Board's tough report on the *Daniel Morrell*—the report back in the 1960s that criticized the Coast Guard and in fact flagged all the old lakers from winter service. Calicchio wanted to write a note to the NTSB investigators that said, simply, "NOT enough!" Their report might exonerate a company that had so foolishly kept the ship in service.

By contrast, the report Calicchio, Murphy, and Lauridsen had approved was far, far tougher on the Coast Guard and on all the other *Marine Electric* players. It was as tough as you could get on the owners without taking out a pistol and drilling them right through the heart on the steps of the Portsmouth hearing room.

The report ran for 137 single-spaced typed pages and documented in spare and precise prose the problems with the ship and the agencies that were supposed to make certain the *Marine Electric* was safe.

The report also documented what did *not* happen. There was no indication that the ship grounded, and the theory of a "flailing anchor" was preposterous. The anchor and its chain were securely fastened and came off as the ship capsized, as nearly any anchor would. The damage to the hull caused by the anchor—if any—came after the capsizing as the ship sank and bounced along the bottom.

In short, Robert Manning Cusick, the chief mate, was not at fault.

Who was at fault? What went wrong?

The deteriorated deck and forward dry cargo spaces were flooded by boarding seas, initially lowering the ship in the water. The dry cargo spaces forward flooded first and brought the bow down, allowing the six-foot boarding green seas to pound the number-one and number-two hatches to smithereens. The ship, now top-heavy, then capsized in the rough seas.

A fracture in the old steel, if it occurred, might have brought the ship lower in the water and helped the seas board and batter the hatches. But it was not the cause. And a major fracture was unlikely because of the way the ship settled slowly on an even keel. Computer programs clearly showed that only flooding of the cargo space resulted in slow settling and sudden capsizing.

As for why the dry cargo space flooded and then the hatches failed, the report was relentless. In clipped, professional language, it documented chapter and verse of the foul-ups.

The Coast Guard inspector "failed to insure that the requirements of the Load Line Regulations were met during the February 1981 overhaul . . . it was incumbent upon him to insure the repairs [to the hatch covers] were sufficient and proper. . . . Since the vessel did not meet the regulations, the inspector should have taken steps to revoke the Load Line Certificate [necessary for the ship to sail]. . . . The inspections made were incomplete and misleading. Inspectors cited certain examinations as being made and found to be satisfactory when in fact they were never made and indicated that the vessel was in full compliance with the applicable regulations. . . .

"The American Bureau of Shipping surveyor issued the Load Line Certificate in Jacksonville 1981, without inspecting the hatch covers—a major component of the Load Line Survey. . . . In spite of the surveyor's recollection of examining the hatch covers, the covers were not placed aboard until the day before the ship sailed. . . . The inspection made was incomplete and misleading in that the records show the vessel to meet all applicable load line regulations when in fact it did not."

Even though the ABS surveyor had thirty years' experience, "his inspection was incomplete and his report was inaccurate, in that the cargo holds were noted as satisfactory and they were never entered, and the hatch covers met the Load Line regulations and ABS Rules, when they were in a deteriorated, non-weather-tight state."

And the kicker:

"Basically, ABS surveys and visits are oriented toward protecting the best interest of marine insurance underwriters and not for the enforcement of Federal safety statutes and regulations. Since the cost of these surveys and visits is borne by the owners . . . the attending surveyor is subject to the influence of such persons."

The most skewering words were reserved for the owners, Marine Transport Lines:

"*The ship was poorly managed and horribly maintained with respect to repairs to the hatch covers, main deck and holes in the cargo hold area caused during off-loading. . . . The hatch covers were wasted, holed, deteriorated, epoxy patched, deflected, weakened and missing securing devices and crossjoint wedges. . . .*"

"Records show that in the last two years of her life, the *Marine Electric* had upward of 400 doublers or patches placed on the hatch covers, and over a dozen doublers on the main deck between the hatches. No tests were performed after the patch repairs were made to affected areas on the hatch covers. . . . Tests to prove the weathertightness or strength of the covers were never performed. . . .

"*At no time was the Coast Guard notified by the owners . . . of the hatch cover or hull repairs made after February 1981 as required (by law). . . . At no time did the owners . . . notify the regulatory bodies of the approximately 95 wasted areas on the hatch covers that were noted in the Chief Mate's sketches. . . ."*

Moreover, they almost certainly violated the law in covering up the cargo hold drain areas with solid plates.

The crucial part of the report, though, was not just its finding of facts, but its recommendations on policy.

In very clear terms, the Marine Board said that James Thelgie, the fleet director of Marine Transport Lines, should be investigated for violation of federal criminal law and that evidence should be turned over to the Justice Department for investigation and prosecution. It suggested that James Farnham, the captain, have his license reviewed and also be investigated for violating criminal law.

Then, in a sweeping policy recommendation, the report called on the Coast Guard to take back its authority for inspecting ships from the American Bureau of Shipping because the ABS had done such a poor, poor job on the *Marine Electric.*

"By virtue of its relationship to the vessel owners, the ABS cannot be considered impartial. . . ." Their total and complete negligence in this matter ". . . raises questions about the professional integrity of their surveys."

Clearly, some other objective agency must take charge of these vital inspections.

But not the Coast Guard. "The Coast Guard is an impartial agency, but the inexperience of the inspectors . . . raises doubts about the capabilities of the Coast Guard inspectors to enforce the laws and regulations in a satisfactory manner."

First, the ABS recommendation took the breath away from the Washington brass.

This wasn't so much change as revolution. Private ship surveyors worldwide were charged with assuring the fundamental structural integrity of a ship and had been for more than a century. To change this in the United States would be change of the first magnitude.

Unspoken, but nevertheless a major factor, was the fact that many Coast Guardsmen pulled the plug and retired early, knowing there would be full-time jobs and salaries for them at the ABS—in the private sector.

Moreover, the Reagan Administration cost-cutters were proposing more responsibility for the private ABS and less for government regulators.

Hardly had the brass recovered from the ABS jab than the Marine Board came around with a roundhouse right. There should be an objective agency, but the Coast Guard inspectors were incompetent to perform that task.

"Commission a panel," the Marine Board said, "and staff it with senior marine inspectors with real Merchant Marine backgrounds. Let them come up with a task force report on marine inspection policies and staffing."

This recommendation was far more inflammatory to the brass than the first. Where other marine boards had suggested to the board that, well, maybe one or two inspectors had made little-bitty mistakes, this board said the whole system did not work and should be worked over thoroughly.

There was no finessing this one. No sliding off it. The problem was placed squarely on the inspectors, and a remedy placed next to the problem.

Calicchio did not sulk so much as do a slow burn as the weeks turned into months and summer became fall and then winter. Where were the commandant's action and recommendations?

Calicchio began calling Lauridsen. "When are we going to get this report out?" Calicchio asked. "Where is the commandant?"

"Patience, patience," Lauridsen told Calicchio, "these things take time." In the short term, Dom thought, perhaps he needed some. Would give them some room. Hell, he could be a case. He knew that.

Then it was Thanksgiving, and nothing had been done. The winter of '84 was upon them. Old ships were going back into the North Atlantic. Calicchio went back on the attack. He called Lauridsen again. He called so many times and so many people that few any longer called back. These are important issues. These families deserve an answer. When are we coming out with the report?

Finally, Calicchio got a call, but not from Lauridsen. It was from a high Coast Guard official. They had Lusk call him. Calicchio's guardian angel, the guy who went to bat for him in Miami. "Can we talk sense?" Lusk asked. "No harm in talking," Calicchio said.

The general argument made to Calicchio by Lusk went like this. The real sticklers are your first two recommendations. You say we should get rid of the American Bureau of Shipping? And remove the Coast Guard entirely from inspections because they've been so bad? Turn it over to some new agency?

Dom, what's the point? Can't you reword them? Rephrase them, for goodness sakes. Soften it somehow. They are way too harsh. Over the top. And you know it will never get done. We want to do the right thing, but this is too . . . direct. Put something in a footnote. It looks bad for the Coast Guard, the way you have this. You know what the climate is in Washington. They want to outsource us completely! We'll take care of this stuff. Our own way. Create some really stiff regulations . . . some first-rate inspection teams. I've already started them.

"Sir, I'll think about it," Calicchio said. "But I've got to tell you now, my inclination is 'no.' Admiral, men died out there. We can't act like the Coast Guard had nothing to do with it. The way you change is to acknowledge that you have to. There is no shame in that. Let's do the right thing."

"Change it, Dom. You have no chance this way."

Calicchio thought about it. Could he get the point across another way? He would have to have Murphy and Lauridsen on board if he wanted to buck Washington now. Murphy was a good kid. Did the right thing. That Lauridsen had agreed to the report buoyed Calicchio, too. He had never thought he would get a majority on the board. It surprised him, sometimes, where you found good men. Where little acts, little decisions, made a difference. Pete Lauridsen could have sat it out, just puffing that pipe. This move wasn't good for his career. Wouldn't help him capture that flag. But he had seen what Calicchio had seen. Had known what they had to do.

What should he do? Lusk was a good guy. He knew that. There was no arguing with the direction of Calicchio's Coast Guard career. It was bouncing along the bottom, just as the *Marine Electric* had.

Lusk was a good man and had tried to resuscitate his career back in Miami. Maybe he was doing that again? Play ball. Be a team player. Get back in the game. We need men like you. Was that the message?

And there was a good chance this report *could* revive his career. Make him whole again with the brass. Restore him to pre-Miami status, the glory days when he was traveling to London, New York, Geneva. Lord of all Florida ports. The report could remake his career. All he had to do was say, guys, Pete, Ed, let's tone down the first two recommendations.

God, despite the problems he'd been having, despite Miami, he loved the Coast Guard. The one branch of the service, it was sometimes said, run largely for humanitarian, not militaristic, reasons. Those days, those days before Miami, they had been wonderful, beautiful times, and he wanted them back so.

Certainly, there was no hope in this quest of his. Almost certainly, those two lead points would be overruled.

On the other hand, if he was to get their attention, if any of the major problems were to be remedied, he had to keep the report extremely strong, in their face. Look what they had done to the milquetoastie *Poet* Marine Board? What had diplomacy won there?

No Marine Board report survived a commandant's review without changes. He knew there was a good chance they would take out the first two points. But if Calicchio took them out now, would the commandant then take out the next two tough points?

There is an old saying among negotiators. "If a man-eating tiger is advancing upon you and you throw him a T-bone steak, you are not negotiating. You are serving hors d'oeuvres." Calicchio recognized that instinctively. He would not throw those two major points away. They would just be back for more.

No one would blame him if he turned back. He would be rewarded. Get out of his cubbyhole in New Orleans. Back to the good times. Good times could roll again for him in the Coast Guard.

But what was his job?

Tradition. The Old Man's Code. More than twenty years at sea, doing things right. What was the Coast Guard's job? Calicchio's job? To aid those in peril on the sea.

The transcripts sat on Calicchio's desk. Paper clips, some of them already rusting in the New Orleans humidity, marked the key testimony. Much of it Calicchio did not need to reread. It stuck in his mind. Some of it was so tragic, so stirring, without anyone touching it. It read like verse.

Kelly, on the life raft. In his words:

> *When I turned around there was nobody there. I think we got separated by the seas.*
>
> *And it was about a half an hour, maybe a little bit less, that I swam away from the ship. . . .*
>
> *Finally, after some time in the water, I came across a life ring, and there were five other people hanging on. . . .*
>
> *It was the chief engineer [Richard Powers]; the third mate, Richard Roberts; one of the ordinary seamen, his first name is Harold—I don't know his last name; the day man, Joe, I don't know his last name; and it was the radio operator [Sparks Lane], and myself.*
>
> *We were on the life ring.*
>
> *Everybody was pretty well stunned.*
>
> *We sounded off so we could find out who was there. We sounded off by number and came out with six.*
>
> *And then it was just talking, giving each other encouragement, that we thought daylight was coming pretty quick.*
>
> *Several times the chief thought we saw a ship in the distance, or saw lights in the distance when we got to the top of a wave.*
>
> *The only lights I could see around me were the strobe lights of the life rings, the water lights, and I could hear people calling all the time, but I couldn't see anybody else. . . .*
>
> *And I don't know when I started to notice that people weren't on the life ring.*
>
> *I noticed that Harold wasn't there at one time.*
>
> *And then I turned around and the day man wasn't there.*
>
> *Right after that, I called out to Rich Roberts and I asked him how he was doing. He responded that he was okay, that he was cold, he was okay.*
>
> *I don't know how long it was on the life ring before I noticed that the only ones there were the chief engineer and the radio operator.*

He was stiffening up. He kept saying, "I'm cold. I'm cold. Help me."

At that point, I noticed that the chief—the chief—when we went into the water, had his spotlight and he had been shining it up into the air all this time.

I noticed that he wasn't shining it any more. I thought he might have lost it. So I whacked him on the back of his life jacket, and there was no response from the chief. And as I hit him, his flashlight floated away from him, and I was able to grab that, and use that as my signal.

I never looked at my watch in the water because I was afraid that I would lose my grip on the ring. So I wasn't concerned with the time element. I kept talking to Sparks. Sparks was the last one on the ring with me.

The helicopters arrived, and it seemed like I could see them passing over me two or three times before they spotted us.

When they lowered the basket, I turned to tell Sparks that the basket was here, and Sparks wasn't on the life ring anymore.

It was just myself.

The words of the transcripts, more than 2,000 pages, weighed on Calicchio. The words gave him chills. His eyes saw. His heart felt. His head could do only one thing.

How could you walk away, turn away from something like those words of Kelly? Of the others? Not remember, not care? Treat them like stray dogs? Kick them away?

What was going to happen here? How did you change the system? Not just put on a few more requirements. What? More lifeboats? Redo the EPIRB emergency beacons? Exposure suits were fine, but wasn't that missing the larger point here?

The ship was unsafe. It should never have gone to sea. The Coast Guard let it go. The ABS let it go. The *Marine Electric* never should have been in the water. The system did not work.

If Calicchio didn't do something, who would? Who would? And when? After the next thirty men died? The next 100? Another 500? Five years from now? Ten? Never?

It was almost two years now since the wreck. And nothing had happened. No report. If he did not take action . . . just a little act of heroism. The men had given their lives. He was giving nothing, nothing at all, really. And if he backed off on those first two points, what would they want him to take out next? He had seen forty years of appeasement and accommodation. How else did you tackle the problem except head-on? The more trouble he made now, the more they had to take this seriously. The report couldn't simply list a bunch of stuff to be done. He had to hit them where it hurt, wake them up and make them take action.

Then Calicchio turned his little boat into thundering waves of policy that had wrecked Coast Guard marine inspections over the decades. He steered toward those waves breaking over the bar. He steered straight for the commandant.

There is another saying of negotiators, used frequently by the communications mogul Michael Bloomberg in the 1990s:

"Always bring a gun to a knife fight."

And Calicchio now reached for the only "gun" he had. He knew the *Inquirer* was still out there, hungry for stories. The *Marine Electric* as an issue may have faded from the front pages, but no one could ignore Calicchio's gun if he had to use it. Calicchio made one last call to Lauridsen, in Washington, in December 1984.

No, Calicchio was not going to change the recommendations, and Lauridsen could tell Lusk and the commandant that. And further—Calicchio was speaking for himself now; didn't want to get the kid in trouble and Lauridsen in trouble—*further,* the Coast Guard brass had one month to get the report out the door, reviewed by the commandant or not, with the commandant's comments or not . . .

Respectfully, if the Marine Board report is not released in one month, with the commandant's decision, then I *will* release it publicly and I will say why I have to release it publicly without the commandant's comments.

Was he going to blow the whistle?

Implicit in his threat was a pledge. He was going to blow it so hard and so long that the men in the engine room of the *Marine Electric* would hear it.

Remove the offending two items about the ABS and the Coast Guard?

He was going to bring those items front and center. Far more front, far more in the center of the media crosshairs than if you guys would just do the right thing now and issue the full report.

If they withheld the report? He would get his part of the report to the *Philadelphia Inquirer.* The Washington papers, the New York papers, too, would pick up on it. And then the networks.

There were no pleas for consolation and reason after that.

Shortly, the report with the commandant's actions was ready to go.

The commandant issued his report in January 1985, nearly two years after the wreck of the *Marine Electric,* nearly six months after Calicchio and the board had finished their reports, and less than one month after Calicchio had phoned in his ultimatum.

The commandant summarily dismissed Calicchio's first two recommendations. But he upheld nearly every other recommendation, including crackdowns on the old ships and the potential criminal indictment of Marine Transport Lines.

Calicchio had done it.

He had lost the first two points, and in that Calicchio felt bitter disappointment. He had wanted so to reform the whole system, formally and frontally.

But his report was the toughest Marine Board of Investigation report in post–World War II America, and they could not ignore this one. Soon it would be policy, and finally, the old ships would be on their way out. Soon, one by one, they would be sailing to the scrap heap.

Little things. A man turned right. A man turned left. A man did nothing. It made a difference. A man did the right thing, sought change, and policy moved.

But the man often paid a price. In the Revenue Marine Service, a predecessor to the Coast Guard, Captain Alexander V. Fraser was a visionary who campaigned for steam-powered ships in the early nineteenth century. Those who favored sail dismissed him from the service in disgrace without a pension.

In the twentieth century, Captain Frank A. Erickson led the movement to bring helicopters to Search and Rescue during the 1940s and early 1950s. Entrenched advocates of seaplanes won out in the short term. Erickson, too, left the Coast Guard.

And now Calicchio would pay. He lost everything in his career. Status. Respect. Assignment. Promotion. Quietly, Calicchio began filling out his retirement papers.

But he had won.

And that, Old Man, felt sweet. Very sweet.

Chapter Thirty

HOME

*. . . we feel the undulating deck beneath our feet, We feel the long
pulsation—ebb and flow of endless motion; The tones of unseen
mystery—the vague and vast suggestions of the briny world—the
liquid-flowing syllables, The perfume, the faint creaking of the cordage,
the melancholy rhythm, The boundless vista, and the horizon far and
dim, are all here, And this is Ocean's poem.*

WALT WHITMAN

ABOUT 10 A.M. / TUESDAY, JUNE 29, 1983
BRIDGE OF THE *MOORMAC LYNX* / SAVANNAH, GEORGIA

On the bridge of the *Moormac Lynx,* as she left Savannah and headed
out to sea, Bob Cusick stood in his new clothes next to the master.
While he dearly hoped Calicchio would get to the bottom of the
lousy system that sent the *Marine Electric* to the bottom of the ocean,
he was not thinking Big Picture thoughts. His days as a reform
leader were already behind him, and his mind had turned to the
small things now in front of him.

The crease marks of the store wrapping still showed plainly on
his khakis and made him self-conscious, but foremost in his mind
now was the nagging little thought: "What the *hell* am I doing
here?" They had sailed down from Norfolk to Savannah earlier, but
he had only been along for the ride. Now, as the ship prepared to
leave, it was his watch.

The master was looking at him now, and for the last few still
moments had seemed about to speak. The bridge of a ship, like an
old-money gentleman's club, is no place for displays of emotion.

"How do you feel, Mate? Do you want to take her out?" the master asked at last.

For a beat, Cusick looked through the bridge window, at the future.

"Are you okay?" the master asked.

"Oh, I feel just fine, Captain," Bob Cusick said, though a part of him was not fine at all. He paused for another beat and then said it.

"I would very much like to take her out, sir. I would very much like to."

The captain seemed to smile.

"Well, she is all yours, then," he said quietly. "I'll be in my office if you need me."

With the utmost courtesy and a respect that was not stated but could not be missed—an implied salute, really—the captain turned away, leaving Cusick as the lone officer on the bridge.

Bob Cusick was not sure how it would feel when he took command. How it would be. A slight electrical charge ran through his body. Not a bad feeling. Anticipation. A little queeze there in his stomach, a pang.

He could feel the great ship shudder as he ordered a slight course correction. Shudder and shift. She was a young ship. The sea ahead was clear.

The ship turned. There were blue skies. Sun on the South Atlantic. A young, whole ship beneath him. He could feel the ship's movements in his legs. He set her on a rhumb line straight for the Cape of Good Hope in Africa, and she cut out of the harbor into the long, rolling rhythms of the open sea.

It felt great. Like before the war, when all his young friends were alive. It felt as if he was sixteen again, in the Sea Scouts.

It felt like the first time he had taken a ship to sea.

Bob Cusick was finally home.

Calicchio heard what Cusick had done and thought to himself: "The dumb sonovabitch. He had it made with damages. Why did he have to do this now?"

And a half-smile of admiration crept across his face.

The same half-smile covered Henry Howell's face. You won some, you lost some. Cusick had just kissed his court case for damages toodle-loo.

Well, Cusick wasn't the neck-brace wearin' type. Never would be. You had to smile at that.

Calicchio, Howell, the *Inquirer* team—all had helped keep Cusick clear of the bang and hang. The hearings, the testimony, the memorials—all had helped Cusick shed his guilt and the "why you's." Cusick had flourished in the crusader role for a brief moment, and the eventual knowledge of the system's reform would be no small comfort to him.

But in the end, Cusick knew, you had to be who you were. To find freedom, you had to do what you loved. To be free, he had to face his fear and listen to the song in his heart.

And in the beginning of his adult life and toward the end, it was the same for Bob Cusick.

It was the sea that freed him.

EPILOGUE

They are gone now—and it does not matter. The sea and the earth are unfaithful to their children: a truth, a faith, a generation of men goes—and is forgotten, and it does not matter! Except, perhaps, to the few of those who believed the truth, confessed the faith—or loved the men.

JOSEPH CONRAD

They were still out there in the dreary winter of 1984–1985, those old wartime ships. The *Penny,* the *Point Susan,* the *California,* and dozens like them wallowed in the North Atlantic, decrepit American merchant ships in various states of disrepair.

The *Penny* had a wobbly propeller. The *Point Susan* and the *California* were so worn out they could not steam under their own power and had to be towed.

But they would not be out there for long.

The hammer of the Marine Board of Investigation and the commandant's actions fell hard on the old ships and impacted the U.S. Merchant Marine and global maritime safety systems in a way that never has been widely acknowledged.

If you read formal contemporary histories of the Coast Guard today, they footnote the *Marine Electric* on one or two pages. The case caused the Coast Guard finally to require survival suits on North Atlantic winter runs, and created the Coast Guard rescue swimmer program. Coast Guard choppers would not have to rely on Jim McCann and the Navy. They would have their own McCanns. Men and women on cold winter runs would now have survival suits. The law said so.

But the paperbound historians were not privy to a more profound historical trend. This is because the trend did not set sail on a sea of paper and formal policies and proclamations but on the sea itself, where it counted most. The destination of the old ships out there in the winter of 1985 would mean that the sinking of the *Marine Electric* had produced some of the most important maritime safety reforms since the sinking of the *Titanic*.

The ships were heading home, to the home they should have reached at least twenty years earlier. The old warhorses were bound for Karachi, Pakistan, and other wrecking yards in the Far East, where the huge ships would be driven onto the beach. Hordes of workers then would descend on them with cutting torches, hammers, bars, and even fingernails, stripping them of everything salvageable.

Finally, the old ships were to be scrapped.

Commandant Gracey and Admiral Lusk may have rejected a formal policy ballyhooing Coast Guard failures, but nearly all the other tough recommendations from the Calicchio board stood firm.

Yes, Gracey said, the owners' agents should be investigated for criminal charges. Yes, the old hatch covers were the problem. Yes, there is an inspection problem that needs to be focused on.

Then Gracey and Lusk formally drilled down and drilled down hard this time on the inspection of old ships. It was similar to the action the Coast Guard took on the Great Lakes when the *Daniel Morrell* went down, but without the formal embarrassment of NTSB intervention.

Stated skeptically, the Coast Guard could not stand the pressure of Calicchio, the *Inquirer* stories, Jesse Calhoun's stealth crusade, and the gentle, compelling group of animated furies comprising the *Poet* mothers. The brass simply stalled on issuing the report so they could look better, try to get Calicchio to soften it. And when they could no longer stand the heat, they acted.

Stated complexly and with a grain of optimism, they realized the faults in the system and moved, finally, quietly to correct them.

The end came, no doubt, from a mingling of the pressure and the better instincts of the Coast Guard leaders. Lusk, Calicchio always knew, was a stand-up guy. Gracey, in official Coast Guard histories, is credited with navigating the agency through a sea of mines that included drug interdiction, pollution control, Reagan privatization, and boat people. The history makes no mention of marine inspection reform, but what happened to the old ships could only have happened because he placed his shoulder behind reform.

But from wherever it came, and whatever the motive, the crackdown came finally, and came down hard.

An "old ships squadron" of seasoned, serious inspectors was formed and activated even before the commandant's actions were issued. Senior inspectors like Lieutenant Commander Ogle pinpointed the old tubs, many of them mentioned in newspaper stories, and showed up at the ports where the old ships docked. No longer could a ship just switch seacoasts and start from zero with no Coast Guard records following the old girl about as she shopped for an easy out. Port swapping was over. They could run—when they worked well enough and could run—but they would just die tired—as tired as the tired iron in their hulls. Ogle and his colleagues would find them.

One by one, the old ships were cited, finally, for the true violations of safety codes contained in their old hulls and hatches. The inspectors and their bosses took to heart the admonitions of nearly three decades ago: that inspectors had to be *very* sure these old ships were seaworthy, or else don't send them to sea. So many violations were cited that the companies had no choice but to send them to the scrapyard. The inspectors, finally, were sending them to the dump. The accommodation of irresponsible, "one-more-trip" owners was over.

More than seventy very old vessels were scrapped or laid up in the two years after the wreck of the *Marine Electric,* many of them during the period when Dominic Calicchio and the Marine Board, Cusick and the *Inquirer,* made it obvious they were not going to back off.

The impact of inspections on the Merchant Marine fleet of the United States—on any postwar merchant fleet of any flag in peacetime—seems unparalleled. More than half of the large bulk carriers of the American merchant fleet were junked virtually overnight. Even more followed in subsequent years. The losses to owners were estimated at more than $1 billion.

And it was this tally that established the wreck of the *Marine Electric* as one of the most significant—if not the most significant—maritime disaster in the second half of the twentieth century. Reforms from the wreck of the *Exxon Valdez,* to be sure, saved sea otters, wilderness beachfront, and seagulls and set important oil transportation standards.

But the wreck of the *Marine Electric* woke up the marine inspection system and saved human lives. The *Titanic* tragedy had forced the codification of safety rules early in the century. The war years slackened the application of those rules as wholesale risk became necessary. The postwar maritime economy and the war-numbed seamen weakened enforcement further and accepted more risk.

And after dozens of structural failures in the old ships and more than 500 men lost at sea, the sinking of the *Marine Electric* and the deaths of its crewmen created enough public sentiment, finally, to produce change. Enough past-due bills from enough private consciences were called in. The rules at last were tightly enforced.

No catastrophic structural failures of an American ship have occurred since the wreck of the *Marine Electric* and the scrapping of America's aged wartime merchant fleet.

The plans to build toxic waste incinerators on T-2 tankers were scrapped, as was a plan to keep the old T-2s running for another forty years, favored at one time by the Maritime Administration and Marine Transport Lines. Abandoning those plans, adding Coast Guard rescue swimmers, requiring survival suits—all the result of the deaths of the *Marine Electric* men and the resulting campaigns—saved countless lives.

Perhaps the scrappings saved more than lives. The prospect of toxic wastes carried through major population areas on ships with brittle hulls was more than alarming. It was, as the *Inquirer* team thought at the time, madness.

The players in the drama of the *Marine Electric* sailed on, of course, and all of them, some for better, some for worse, found their ways to new ports.

If irony is a centerpiece of postmodern life, then the officials of

Marine Transport Lines met a finely honed postmodern justice. CEO James H. Rand and his team were removed by a rebellious board of directors in the mid-1980s because they were not producing adequate returns on the *new* ships the corporation had built.

The insurgent board members were prompted not by the loss of the *Marine Electric.* They were numbers guys. Thomas Rohrer had controlled settlement costs on the *Marine Electric,* so there was no problem there. The problem, one of the board members implied, was that Rand wasn't hungry enough. He wasn't pushing profits hard enough. Rand was trying to build too many new ships and not hitting the hurdle rates. The board wanted new energy in management, someone with fire in the belly who would push "production."

And one day, Rand and his team were simply out, set out in lifeboats in the huge waves of wealth easily found and easily lost in the financial weather fronts that nourished and then pounded the 1980s.

Farnham was installed as captain of the *Marine Princess* for a brief period, his former colleagues said, and in that sense the company took care of him. The Coast Guard did indeed move against his license, though. Investigators said he surrendered it and retired to Maine before his license could be reviewed. He never talked to the *Inquirer* about the sinking, but his testimony implied that Farnham felt he might have saved the ship, had he been there, because he knew her better than Corl, a man who sailed only as the relief. Farnham told the Marine Board how he could *feel* how the ship behaved, felt it in his legs as no other unseasoned master on the ship could.

Perhaps it was so. Both the Coast Guard and NTSB said, far down in their reports, that Corl might have fared better had he turned the ship stern to the waves, and then inspected what was wrong up front. Perhaps so. Safety standards do not prepare a ship for the best captain, merely a good one. And Corl was that.

Turning stern to the waves might have helped, but as Richard Cahill, a former master for twenty years, wrote, it was not Corl who sank the ship, "but the willingness of his superiors to avoid the hard and unpopular decisions required to maintain the vessel in a satisfactory state of repair. . . ."

Farnham to this day does not correspond or have any dealings with his fellow officers of that period, and he is viewed with scorn by the survivors, a man who knew things but did not step forward as Cusick did.

Downing, vice-president in charge of Marine Transport operations, had once been a seagoing officer, and sometimes let his feelings show. The MTL executive made few public statements that were not choreographed by spin artists. In one impromptu comment, however, he talked about the conditions he faced.

"Something like 80 percent of the U.S. domestic fleet are very old ships," he said in the 1980s. "That's something we're living with from an economic standpoint. We would love to renew all of our old ones with new vessels.

"You don't have the economic reasons. It's the state of the economy and the return in the domestic trade for the vessels.

"You're caught," he said sadly.

"I wish it weren't so. I am a seaman, too."

The *Marine Electric* civil litigation was settled, said one news article, for about $15 million—not even 10 percent of the cost of a new ship. Rohrer, who insisted the wreck was Cusick's fault, certainly did not win one, but he did not lose much, either. He did not lose much in dollars, at least. He did his job well as an attorney by limiting damages. Little is known of the settlements. Mary Babineau said only that she turned down the first offer of $500,000—Clayt's list said to—and then received a larger check.

"It was funny how they played it," she said of Marine Transport Lines. "If we claimed loss of earning power, then they'd say we could not claim loss of Clayt's personal company, because if he was earning money he would have been at sea and not company to us. They were very hard, very tough."

Some of the families with a young wage earner lost at sea were said to have received more than $1 million. If the news report of $15 million in total damages was correct, of course, then the average settlement was under $500,000 for the thirty-four—about the average settlement in the year 2000 for a single personal injury case involving an injured arm in New York State. Had the case gone to trial, it might have been a breakthrough in terms of record awards. So in *that* Rohrer succeeded, and when he retired from his firm, its newsletter noted that he most treasured his ability to protect his clients against "runaway juries."

Criminal proceedings moved slowly, and on that front MTL lawyers both won a small victory and lost big time, it seemed, in the long run.

After years of sitting on the case, the U.S. Attorney's Office in Norfolk, in 1986, assigned an earnest assistant U.S. Attorney named Robert Wiechering. He looked at the case and the recommendations to nail Farnham and Thelgie, and he made an important decision. In a very bad system, he would skip those little fish and fry the biggest ones he could find. He would prosecute the corporation itself.

Eventually, he would succeed. Marine Transport Lines—as a corporation—pleaded guilty to a felony. This was for failure to report the hole in the hull that Cusick patched with a tin coffee-can lid. Ironically, the hole was never shown to contribute to the sinking. It was just one clear violation that the feds had the shipowners on cold. An unreported hole in the hull, in fact, is about as flagrant a violation as you can get in the business.

Years later, Freedom of Information Act requests showed that the feds never turned the FBI loose on the case. The trend in white-collar crime at the time was more toward congressmen and Wall Street insiders—not the low-profile maritime sector. The earnest assistant U.S. Attorney did what he could with what he had. There was no public outcry for the heads of shipowners and no mandate to unleash dozens of feds on the owners. If the feds took the case further? Charged Thelgie or Farnham? Marine Transport Lines could mount a formidable defense over the years, and had one big closing line for any jury.

How can the government say we are guilty when the government in the form of the Coast Guard said these ships were sound?

So the criminal case stopped there.

It was no small achievement. Wiechering had secured what was believed to be the first-ever felony conviction of a major maritime corporation in modern times. The fine for the felony seemed ridiculously low at $10,000. The Coast Guard fined the company another $10,000. In total, the fines were no more than a rounding error for one ship's annual operations. About a half-day's expense for running a modern ship.

Yet Marine Transport Lines was thoroughly embarrassed by being the first modern American shipping company to bear the informal title "felon." And the lawyers' success in plea bargaining the fine to such a low amount backfired in many ways.

In the lore of mariners, the company was guilty, and even in its guilt had managed to cut corners. Had the company paid a million-dollar fine, say, it might have buried the matter and come to closure with the mariners. Bought some disposition.

It did not. Just a few years after the *Marine Electric* went down, John Babineau, Clayton Babineau's son, went to sea as an officer. He sailed for seven years and even signed on Marine Transport Lines ships.

"They had the worst reputation," he said. "Nothing to do with my dad's death. Just objective fact."

Even today—though MTL does not exist as a company, having gone private again and public again, and then merging into another shipping company—the Jesse Calhoun curse dogs the memory of the company among many mariners. *"MTL is a junk-ship operation, always has been, always will be."*

It is not a fair assessment. So many of the company's positive efforts, such as attempting to crack the Japanese auto-export business with U.S. ships, were overwhelmed by its bad image. The company did many fine things, some of them exemplary, at a time when most American ship lines were just running with the tide. James Rand had vision and good intentions. Some of the best of both at the time.

But even an industry jaded to losses at sea viewed the *Marine*

Electric case as clear-cut. Rand and his team were undone not by their grand vision, but by inattention to the most basic of details: Ships had to float.

Hughes, the MTL attorney on the ground in Norfolk, who thought the MTL case was just posturing, retired in 1989, six years after the *Marine Electric* board hearings.

Asked what he had done since then, he replied dryly, "Just about anything that has nothing to do with the law."

Clyde Lusk, the admiral who defended Calicchio's action on the passenger ship and implemented the old ships inspection task force, rose first to chief of staff to the commandant and then to vice commandant. He believes the Coast Guard has done the best it can in marine safety amid turbulent years when it assumed responsibility for more than twenty separate missions, ranging from small-boat safety to drug interdiction to pollution control.

Always, he said, there were pressures to keep the old ships at sea, to provide jobs and revenues. He and his colleagues, faced with those pressures, did the best they could. Always, he said, he saw the system as a series of protective nets, defensive obstacles to incoming missiles.

"Most of the time one net might fail and the others would hold up," he said. "In the *Marine Electric*, well, the missile just went through every one of the nets we had up. The owners, the officers, our guys, the ABS, all of them.

"There is a last net, and it is our most effective net, but you hate to see it come in to play because it's too late and men have already died," he said. "The last net is a Marine Board of Investigation and, in the case of the *Marine Electric*, that net worked."

Tough Marine Boards were something he always welcomed because it gave the Coast Guard and the system a prod to move on. The *Marine Electric* board and the deaths of the men gave the Coast Guard a mandate for change. The mandate pierced the political and economic powers that kept the old system in place. Calicchio's insistence on a strong report—even if, in Lusk's view, some of it was a bit heavy-handed—helped in the end.

"The old ships teams were something we were proud of after the *Marine Electric,*" he said. "Nobody was ashamed of that effort, I assure you, and we did something very good there."

After a long silence, Lusk, who believed in the system's ability to change, sounded eerily sad and remorseful. There was a reedy, husky quality to his voice.

"Too bad we weren't able to do it earlier, huh? Too bad for those men. Too bad we couldn't move the system faster."

Jesse Calhoun, the president of MEBA, bided his time and watched with amusement as the *Inquirer* ground out story after story about the old ships, bringing the heat to MTL and the Coast Guard, all courtesy of Jesse's guided secret tours.

Then, still officially friendly with MTL, Calhoun pulled a coup on the Masters, Mates & Pilots, his competition and the union representing the *Marine Electric* deck officers at the time of the sinking. In 1984, MTL rejected the Masters, Mates & Pilots and chose Jesse's union.

The shrewd union leader had had it both ways. He had, figuratively, walked down the table and kicked MTL in the teeth, just as he had wanted, using his skilled Washington lobbyists and the willing tool of the *Inquirer.*

And then he had called in past favors—calling the Navy, being flexible here, willing there—to gain the biggest deck officers' contract with the nation's largest bulk fleet operator.

The brave Navy diver, McCann, was given medals for his valor, but McCann was never certain whether he had saved anyone that day in 1983. He does not claim so. Kelly, though initial reports seemed to indicate he was helped by McCann, is not certain either way.

The Navy diver was still in service seventeen years later. He was a chief petty officer, devoted to training other rescue swimmers and running rescue operations. He retired in 2001. Whether or not he saved anyone that day in February 1983, the inspiration of his courage and daring have saved dozens of men and women since. The Coast Guard, asked by its search and rescue wing to establish rescue swimmers for such situations, finally did so. Those swimmers have plucked countless people from peril, when they were too cold or too tired to grab the baskets dangled by the rescue helicopters.

They owe much of that to McCann.

Calicchio got the little judge's office working pretty well in New Orleans. But he knew when he forced the report out the door that he would retire soon, and he did in 1985. Almost immediately, doctors discovered he had cancer. There were operations. Successful ones.

He moved back to Florida and began a successful consulting career as an expert witness in court cases. He specialized in passenger ships, and was hired by some of the very people who criticized his famous "Now row!" cruise ship episode. His big fear was that these big floating hotels did not have adequate firefighters, did not have adequate lifeboat plans, and that "the big one" someday would happen. He was called upon frequently by attorneys, but they had to be very, very careful. Their case had to match his findings, not the other way around.

He did not do flailing anchors.

He had convinced himself that he had largely failed in the *Marine Electric* case, had not changed the system much. He saved in his files as a most valued remembrance of the time a letter from Lisolette Fredette, the *Poet* mother who thanked him and told him he was a hero.

"We, the families of lost merchant seamen, would not consider the Coast Guard a particular friend of ours, however . . . I do find a long overdue place in my heart for you and say thank you, Captain Calicchio, for being so persistent and critical in your questioning. . . ."

It helped make up for the unanswered questions about the *Poet,* she said.

In a letter, Calicchio thanked her for the heartfelt words, then added almost mournfully:

"However, any investigative report regardless of its completeness and soundness, aside from good reading, has little or no value, unless immediate action is taken to implement reasonable and sound recommendations made by the board to prevent a repetition."

And in that, the unsaid part read, I have failed.

In recent years, Calicchio talked about his failures and accomplishments with a reporter from the old *Inquirer* team. The two had worked separately back in 1983, never in tandem. Only years after the case did they talk across the table. Calicchio the kind uncle still was there, as was the predatory prosecutor. When the reporter made a wrong assumption—that Dom was purposely put on the board by the brass, for example—Calicchio's brow furrowed, and the falcon asked the reporter quick and concise questions in a pitying, almost shaming manner.

But there was a third Dom, too, one who looked slightly in pain, suffering from a back spasm almost, every time the reporter mentioned the legacy of the *Marine Electric*. Calicchio would rise up from a slight slump at the table and grimace slightly.

"If nothing else, I suppose we put a scare into the inspection system, and the American Bureau of Shipping certainly cleaned up its act as a result," he said. "At least there was that, but overall it was very, very disappointing to see how it all turned out."

"I am glad I sailed," he said sadly, "when it was a good time to sail. I had the good years."

You know, the reporter said, your report basically scrapped more than seventy ships. You wiped them out, Dom.

Calicchio seemed surprised at that number. The fact was not widely known or publicized by a Coast Guard attempting to do much while being blamed for little. Besides, Calicchio had cut his strings to the Coast Guard, had never heard the count. Had never seen the *Inquirer* stories after January 1985. Had never looked back. Had assumed the task force of inspectors was more hot air. His face took on a look that was neither kind uncle nor predatory prosecutor. It relaxed, and tension seemed to drop off him like an eight-ton anchor.

"Well, if we did *that* . . ." Calicchio said after a long pause. His eyes teared slightly. "If we *did* that, then it wasn't a failure. We did get something done, and that makes me very, very . . . pleased."

Eugene F. Kelly, Jr., went back to sea. The union and his lawyer all told him to stay on the beach and claim injuries, that this was how you could run up the award. Maybe so, Kelly said, but what do I do in the meantime? I've got a family, a daughter less than a year old.

He was in line for the *Energy Independence*—the new ship planned to replace the *Marine Electric*—and he took the berth when she was launched. Eight months after the old ship went down, the new ship came into service. She was a beauty. A self-unloader. Brand-new and very efficient. The new berth went well.

It went well except for the times when the *Energy Independence* passed a lonely marker buoy thirty miles off the Virginia coast. Follow the line and you'll see that the buoy is moored to the *Marine Electric,* 130 feet down on the bottom. Dive expeditions lead dozens of amateur recreationists there each year, where they take lobsters and hang suspended in wonder at the remains of the encrusted old ship.

Kelly would go out to the flying bridge of the new ship, look at that buoy from the bridge, and quietly say a prayer for his old friends. Bits of it would come back. He could handle it, but it would all come back.

The young man who had wanted to handle tankers and at-sea refueling, who had wanted more adventure in his life at sea, listened now when his wife talked of life on shore. He had subbed at a vocational technical high school in Massachusetts when he was on the beach, and when a principalship became available, he applied and was hired.

The settlement in his court case was $75,000, and with part of the money he bought a thirty-four-foot charter boat and ran sportfishing charters out of Provincetown, Massachusetts, and other Cape Cod harbors in the summers. The Kellys had a son in 1986, and in the summer of 2000 Kelly's boy said, yes, he would like to work guiding sportfishermen with his dad. It is all the sea Kelly wants now, though he hopes his son may go to an academy—Massachusetts Maritime, maybe, or even Annapolis.

Maybe, Kelly said—he is not pushing it—his son will go to the Coast Guard Academy.

Kelly was smart about survivors' guilt. He went to a professional for help and was diagnosed with posttraumatic shock. It still comes over him some times. He is on the bridge, on the eight-to-twelve watch. What did he do? Anything wrong? Was there something he should have seen? Should have heard? Was there the clang of an anchor? God, he could always hear anything on the ship, a loose chain two decks down. Was there something that night he didn't catch? Seventeen years later, his mind drifts back and he is on the bridge, wondering. What did he miss? Always, he comes up with nothing, but the thoughts still come.

On a sunny day on the Cape Cod Canal, in front of the memorial to the *Marine Electric,* the former reporter said to Kelly, "Listen, if it means anything, I went over every inch of this I could find. Nobody gave credence to the banging anchor. No one, including the AB on the bridge, ever suggested in any way that you could have or should have done anything different at any time in any way."

Kelly paused. There was a nice rip to the water nearby, and bait fish were jumping. Kelly had taken big striped bass, right there. It was on this very spot twenty-seven years earlier that he had first walked through the gates of the marine academy. Behind him, one of the tall ships, bound for the Boston parade of tall ships in July 2000, was docked a block away. The memorial for his dead crewmen was twenty yards to his left. The air was filled with nostalgia, memories good and bad.

"I know that," he said with a comfortable smile. "Listen, I know that."

The thoughts still come, but he knows what they are. He lets them go, knowing they will come, then go, come, then go. Tricks of his mind and human conscience.

Every February 12, he and his daughter and son visit the memorial at Massachusetts Maritime.

"When I'm gone," he tells his kids, "you still come, okay? Do that for your old man. You keep coming."

. . .

Little went away for the Wickboldts. After their cadet died, with two sons claimed by the sea, they asked their other two to leave the sea. One was a top student at King's Point Maritime Academy. Another was an officer on a top-rated ship line, years of experience under his belt.

Both walked away from careers at sea.

The compound in New Hampshire where each son was to have a summer home is still there, and Catherina Wickboldt, the dead officers' mother, said they were just fixing up a place where George might have stayed, seventeen years after he died.

Richard Wickboldt, the boys' father, could not work for a year after George died. Catherina and Richard could not stay at home. A few weeks after their second son died, they packed the car and took off. They traveled through Florida, North Carolina, Texas, wandering through the country. Just wandering, Richard Wickboldt said. It was all that helped them bear it.

They were wandering but not running. Like Cusick, they tried to take the case to trial. Their attorney, with tears streaming down her face, finally told them there was not a good-enough case to support months, maybe years, of litigation.

"We won't go to trial," the attorney said.

"We don't want the money," Richard Wickboldt told her. "You can have all the money. We just want the trial and the facts."

But there would be no trial. Eventually, the Wickboldts were given $125,000 for George's death. They looked at the check and for months did not cash it. We will help the other kids, Catherina said to herself, finally, and signed the check that summed up the value of her young son's life in dollars and cents and pushed it across the counter to the bank teller.

"All these years later," she said. "We are still very, very angry. The ship should never have gone to sea. He should not have died. Very little happened to the company."

"It changes your life," Richard Wickboldt said. "It leaves a big hole. Only now, you see, all these years later, the grandchildren begin to fill that hole, and there is a lot I can do with my hands on the house, you see, in New Hampshire, lots I can do when I get these thoughts. . . ."

"But the hole is still there."

Heather Price, Mike Price's young daughter, is twenty-seven now, a remarkably poised young woman. The family attorney, Marsha Price said, did an excellent job in negotiating a settlement, and Marsha and Heather had what they needed for a good life, except of course, Mike. George Dolak, the night engineer who was Price's best friend, says Heather is the one precious part of Mike that lives on, a balanced young woman of great focus who reminds him of his old friend. Seventeen years later, it takes Dolak a long time to say that simple sentence, and it is more blurted out between strangled sobs and chokes than simply said.

But it is true that her father lives on in her. Heather Price still skis from the highest mountain, swims to the deepest water. Her senior year, she wrote of how her father had taught her never to hate, never to give up, to set goals and go for them. "One may think that because of my age at the time of my father's death, I would not remember all of this about him, but he made such a deep impression on me that I will never forget him or the love he showed me," she wrote.

There is a streak of stubbornness and a sense of duty in her that Marsha Price knows is from Mike. Heather understands what her father did and why. "If I had been on that ship, had a job to do, had said I would do it, there is no way I would have gotten off."

Heather talks about her life in a manner that is introspective and curious, detached and at the same time heartbreaking. It was six months before Heather accepted that her father was never coming back. Six months was the cycle, the longest he had been at sea. Slowly, she came to understand that her father was dead. And when she did, she did not want her mother to leave her, panicked if she could not see Marsha. She did not want another parent to leave and then just disappear. And she could not bear people crowding around her, as if to shelter her. She remembered that dreadful day, on some level, when her relatives and friends walked from the television room and gathered about her to comfort her. It is not comfort she gets when people crowd around her. It is memories of that day, and she cannot bear it.

Marsha Price found herself becoming more and more spiritual. She also went to a ten-meeting program for new widows, but came away from the first session tearful and angry as a hornet. "They are all eighty and ninety years old and had sixty years with their husbands!" she told a friend. "What have they got to be grieving about!"

But she went back and, by the end of the series, knew the truth of it. Love is love at any age. Grief is grief and loss is loss, no matter how old you are.

Her best therapy was simple and effective. She volunteered for twenty hours a week for six years at the local hospital working with seniors, often comforting patients who were dying. She helped them. They healed her. It was funny how it worked, but it did, she said. She would tell them her story, and they would tell her theirs. Sometimes, if she felt particularly close to the dying person, she would think about whispering to them as they neared the end, "If you see Mike, tell him to get in touch with me. Tell him I love him so. Tell him to send me a sign."

But she never did. She would hold the hand of the dying person and pray, for the person, and for an ever-so-small miracle that a part of her would be carried in the soul of the dying person, that the part somehow would reach Mike and let him know how she loved him. She would will a small part of her soul through the dying person's hand and pray.

Years passed before Marsha Price could walk beside the ocean she once loved. Time is a solvent, though. Time dissolves pain and heals grief and broken hearts. Now she lives on the ocean and walks on the beach routinely. Still, all these years later, she sometimes sees something washed up on the shore, a piece of steel, some wood, a part of a life preserver, and thinks, "That could be something from the *Marine Electric.*" Oddly, she thinks, all these years later when she has accepted it all, she will see a glint of goldlike metal at the edge of the surf and the thought will pop into her head, "That could be from Mike. His ring."

"When I walk by the sea, Mike is with me all the time, and I think of those things . . ." she said.

Marsha and Heather have yet to decide who will escort her down the aisle when Heather marries. Heather worries about that, about who could take her father's place. She does not worry about explaining her childhood to her fiancé, Jason, or whether Jason could ever understand her life. When he was nine, Jason's father went down on the *Captain Cosmo,* a fishing boat out of Gloucester. No boat or bodies ever were found. The bride and groom do not have to speak to have perfect understanding.

And Dewey, the survivor in the life raft? The young man who had just signed on the *Marine Electric?*

"Disappeared off the face of the earth," Kelly said. "I lost my guys," he told friends over and over after he tried to get Babineau and the others into his raft. Guys he had only known for a few days at most. Guys who slipped from his hand, one by one. Guys he never would have met if Cusick had not fired the Gashounder, opening the slot Dewey filled for 1.5 round trips.

Dewey himself seems lost. Those who saw him last, in 1993, say he is still shipping out, trying to stay scarce. The sea stories say he had bought a bar in Norfolk with the *Marine Electric* settlement money, but that the venture had gone badly. Services hired to locate him found nothing. Notices placed in mariner publications were not answered. Dewey is alive, at least, because no one has reported him otherwise to the Social Security Administration.

His former colleagues who last saw him say they heard reports he sometimes acts a "little kooky." Tells stories that are hard to believe. Mentions that he lost his guys, and people who do not know him wonder what that means and think him odd.

The U.S. Merchant Marine has sound hulls, but increasingly fewer of them.

There are some men to this day who curse the *Marine Electric* reforms as the destroyer of jobs and the American merchant fleet.

None of them was in the cold water off Virginia.

And most now think it was the other way around. That it was the extended, unnatural existence of the very old ships that prevented the formation of a workable maritime policy, the prolonged denial and delusion, the decades of embracing a pathological policy, that has placed the U.S. Merchant Marine where it is today.

Major ship lines have dwindled to a handful, many of them running fleets of modern ships under foreign flags with foreign crews. Increasingly, American officers sail under foreign flags. The military builds and buys its own special prepositioning and rapid-deployment fleets, which handled the sealift demands of Operation Desert Storm with aplomb. The few rust buckets broken out from the reserve fleet for that conflict were nearly useless, because many of them broke down at sea and wallowed helplessly.

There are some signs that overall policy is changing, that from the ashes of fifty-five years of protectionism and neglgence, a fleet that can compete on global terms may one day grow.

If ever it does, merchant shipping will have been the first sector of the American economy to experience the challenges of postwar globalization. And the last to respond to it. In that, there is a cautionary tale. Global economies, like the sea, batter and hole stationary objects turned sideward to the current. Only those that turn the bow into the sea manage the waves of either force and gain some control.

And Bob Cusick?

Bob Cusick sailed out of Savannah that sunny day in 1983 and stayed at sea for as long as he had a ship beneath him.

He sailed on first-rate ships owned by United States Lines, a premier American line, for nearly four years before the company began running into economic problems, scaled back, and sent many of its men to the beach.

It was a good time to retire, and Bob Cusick did.

He pressed the legal case, but his attorney had warned him what might happen. He was doing too damned well, was too healthy, had gone back to the sea. We can't mount a full-fledged case against

Marine Transport Lines. The resulting damages couldn't possibly pay for the costs, anyway. And these guys at MTL do not like you very much, for understandable reasons, and are not eager to settle, will screw you as best they can. They'll spend thousands to keep you from getting hundreds.

So Cusick eventually let it go. The song of a reformer was a good song, but not his song. The board report, the criminal charge, were enough. Proved the point. A letter came from the company offering $30,000. Bea called up lawyer Howell and said, "Henry, you know I'm no lady, but I can be one when I want to. I don't want to now. You tell them to shove that letter."

They came back with $50,000, and Cusick said, "Just forget the whole thing. I don't want their money." And there it stood until Bea said, "Think of it this way. If you don't take the money, they'll have it. Why let them have it? Take what they're offering," Bea said. "Money was never the thing. Let's end it."

And so Marine Transport Lines paid their former chief mate $50,000 in damages—about $35,000 after Howell took his fee.

Soon, Bob and Bea moved to Bea's small hometown in New Hampshire. He got a real estate license. With small-town entrée courtesy of Bea's roots, the man's quick wit and gentle humor soon made him known far and wide. "He flirted with every widow selling her house, is what he did . . ." Bea maintains. Robert Manning Cusick smiled at that as if he had seen God's Great Cosmic Joke and understood it well.

Cusick also kept his hand in at leading. He started a quiet and polite battle with the American Legion and Veterans of Foreign Wars. Neither would admit World War II mariners to their memberships. The Legion caved after a few years of fencing with Robert Manning Cusick and mariner groups. He became the historian of the local post. The VFW, who did not know in all of Christ's land who they were dealing with, declined the polite letters filled with facts contradicting their assertion that he never really saw combat. He told them in disarming and polite language about the V-1 and V-2 rockets that came over in Antwerp in '44, how the café ceiling fell on him and his crew one day. About the men and ships under him that went down. His polite, fact-filled letters never stopped, and he was admitted to the VFW.

Then in 1995, Cusick found he had advanced cancer. "Radiation or radical surgery?" the doctors asked. "Do what you have to do," Cusick said matter-of-factly. "Surgery. Don't waste time. Do your best."

The prognosis was not good. There was radical surgery. He recovered completely.

Then, in 1997, just before Thanksgiving, Bea and Bob were returning from a community service center where they had helped the Lion's Club prepare baskets of food for the needy. Bea recalled that he had said, in his typical manner, with the sparkle in his eyes, "We feel it is important to do our part, to share with the needy, to humbly prepare these packages and then give them to the deadbeats."

As he came into the house, his left foot dragged. Bea thought his speech was slurred. They called a neighbor, who asked Cusick: "Bob, have you been drinking?" A rescue squad volunteer down the street said he thought Bob might be having a stroke, so they called the ambulance.

The next morning, Bob Cusick could not move anything on the right side of his body. He was barely breathing. He had suffered a major stroke. "It could have something to do with the bad times in the water," the doctors said. "Certainly that didn't help."

He lay there helpless, paralyzed. They were not sure he would make it, and if he did, it was certain he never would be the same.

Six months later, after rehab and therapy, Bob Cusick spoke perfectly well and told jokes about his walker. Soon, he left his walker and cane in a corner. He had only a slight limp, a slight drag to his left foot. He was back joking with the locals and cheering up the new widows. They still use videos of his rehab in training classes. On those videos, he is a poster boy for stroke-recovery courses in New Hampshire, showing to those whom adversity has struck the final blow how one might rise again.

Then, in May 2000, as the New Hampshire spring moved temperatures over forty degrees, Cusick was stricken again.

Bea said he told her he had "The Dream." He had told her he had not had that Dream for, oh, ten years. Told her he thought he was done with it. But there it was again. He was back in the boat, he told her, kicking to keep warm. Muscles cramping. Thrashing around. Singing in his sleep. Oh, so cold.

"Get me covers," he said. "I'm freezing to death."

Which was strange, the cold, because Bea clocked his temperature at above 104 degrees and rising. She scrambled the local ambulance, and they took a barely conscious Bob Cusick to the hospital.

There the family and close friends gathered. Carol, his beloved daughter, was back from Australia, with her two dogs, one part dingo. The doctors were not sure what was wrong with him, only that he was not getting better and that his core body temperature this time was too high, so very, very high. Some sort of virus maybe, just consuming the guy, burning him up. Dangerous in an older fella, because Bob Cusick was now seventy-six. Worse in a guy who still had these hanging-on ailments from long ago, weak lungs and a funky heart, caused by the cold, now ravaged by heat.

There were a lot of tears as the hero of the *Marine Electric* began slipping away, slipping further and further. Bea had a thought to call one of the *Inquirer* reporters, tell him, "You'd better talk to him now, because he has lived up his nine lives now."

Cusick said little, and was conscious little. They all remembered his joke about what to do with him after he died.

"Bury me, don't cremate me," he had always said with a mischievous smile and a skeptical intelligence. "I don't know that it's true, but just in case there is a second coming . . . just in case all those things the Bible-thumpers say are right about Revelations, I want to come up out of my grave, you know . . . rise again. Doesn't cost you anything, really, so bury me in the ground."

Had he been joking? Or serious? Or both? Probably Cusick himself was not certain, but now they were to this point. Would be pretty soon.

At night, the nurses noticed, he seemed to be thrashing his arms and legs. Seemed to be mumbling. A course, hoarse sound. Almost humming. A mumbled song, perhaps, but they could not discern the words, if there were any.

Two weeks later, Robert Manning Cusick was back on his feet. Six weeks later, he was working outside, driving around, scouting real estate, and scouting, too, for wild blueberry bushes for the awful waffles of the fall.

It was not his time. Cusick knows this and only this for certain: Never did he see himself as a hero or as God's chosen instrument. He does not believe in a God who reaches down and singles someone out. He believes in a God who creates tides, waves, strong men, weak men, songs, gravity, greed, grain, and anchors and chains, and then washes them all together.

All of them, he knows, move in currents that send them this way and that with a purpose beyond his keening. A lifeboat drifts this way, a good man turns that way. A wave washes a line over here, a man reaches out over there. He hears a song. He is saved or lost. A good man acts, a weak man does not. Life and God wash together all the good and bad little things. Together, those little things can say when, where, and why. Save men. Drown men. Keep systems. Change systems. Say in their sum what will happen, to a man, to a society.

Your time is either up or it is not.

No power on this earth, Cusick knows, can change that either way.

Against all that, he knows, you can only listen to the song in your heart. You can only quiet your mind and listen softly for the song in your heart and pray hard that you hear the words clearly and do what is right.

NOTES AND ACKNOWLEDGMENTS

The book I have written is far different than the one I might have written in 1983. Then, it would have been a story of a system immune to change. Now it is a story of how change and reform did occur. Change came at a terrible cost in the lives of men and families. But it did come. It is my hope that the survivors and the families of those seamen who did not survive will take some comfort in this. And that they also will find comfort in the fact that the story was told.

Until the Sea Shall Free Them tells a story of the sea, but it is a nonfiction narrative told to the best of my knowledge with all sequences rooted firmly in fact.

The degree to which I succeeded in this intent is thanks largely to the cooperation of dozens of people and a rich source of written information from transcripts, studies, and some of the survivors themselves. In the course of writing this book, I consulted several thousand pages of documents, ranging from the Marine Board of Investigation public record to technical welding articles published in 1942. I also interviewed dozens of those who either were on or knew the *Marine Electric*, and families of men who died on the ship.

This information was added to the wealth of knowledge gathered by the original investigative team at the *Philadelphia Inquirer*, which I was privileged to help lead. This first leg of the research was based on dozens of interviews and many days and weeks spent in the "stacks" of Coast Guard archives and interviews with dozens of government, labor, and regulatory officials, as well as many days sitting in on the direct testimony of the board.

I could not locate all the families impacted by these tragedies. And in large part, senior officials of the company and the U.S. Coast

Guard chose not to sit for interviews. This was true back in 1983 and it was true in the months leading up to the publication of this book. Efforts were made to locate all parties impacted by the *Marine Electric* through calls, letters, notices in widely circulated maritime publications, and messages on web sites. I also used "locator services"—successfully in some cases, unsuccessfully in many others. Some government agencies—the U.S. Navy, for example, in helping locate Jim McCann—were superb. Others were less helpful.

As to the company officials and the Coast Guard officials, I have attempted to represent their case fairly, lacking direct interviews, based on statements of the time, and testimony. My regret in not having access to company officials was felt not in the lost chance to skewer them with prosecutorial questions, but in my inability to learn more about their points of view and how they coped with the tragedies, at sea and in the boardroom. In writing the book, it was my intent to represent these points of view fairly to the best of my ability with the information I had.

Any regrets I have regarding this book are far outnumbered by the debts of gratitude I owe. With the *Philadelphia Inquirer* and its remarkable editor, Gene Roberts, I almost certainly would never have written about maritime affairs, yet alone conceived of the story of the *Marine Electric*. Larry Williams, my working editor at the *Inquirer*, was equally essential to the original stories and has an extraordinarily gifted manner with difficult and stubborn reporters and writers. Tim Dwyer was the ultimate partner for a writer and reporter. It was a golden time and a golden team.

Thanks also go to the agent of all agents, Sterling Lord, who picked up my sample chapters and outline from a pile of manuscripts on his desk. And also special thanks must go to Shawn Coyne, then at Doubleday, who shared my vision, and to William Thomas and Deborah Cowell, who kept it alive and healthy and made it real. Bill Eddins, the best word editor I know, contributed significantly to this book. Mark Bowden provided both inspiration and unerring support.

It should go without saying but must be said that Bob Cusick spent many, many hours with me. His patience and honesty and willingness to share his innermost thoughts were essential to the book. Bea Cusick, his wife, and Carol, his daughter, were helpful in a similar manner. Their hospitality, humor, and patience made this book a far more enjoyable task.

A similar debt of gratitude must go to Dominic Calicchio, who agreed not only to do lengthy interviews on the topic, but also provided thousands of pages of documentation. Eugene Kelly was likewise extremely helpful in his willingness to relive the awful hours he spent in the water, as well as the years since.

Some of my most heartfelt thanks are reserved for the families of the men who were lost on the *Marine Electric* and in other shipwrecks. The Prices. The Wickboldts. The Babineaus. Lisolette Fredette, the mother of a missing *Poet* crewmember. Each of them agreed to relive painful events.

This book never could have been written without the support of my own family. Suzanne, my wife, helped edit the manuscript, and as importantly, put up with a writer's odd temperament on deadline. The personal integrity of Sarah and Caitlin, my daughters, was inspiration to pursue my own personal goal. Rae, my sister, and Helen, my mother, have insatiable curiosities and a love for learning that always have helped feed those qualities in me. L. Merle Frump, my late father, passed on his storytelling tradition to me without either of us ever quite realizing it while he was alive. It is my heartfelt wish that this book will honor all those who helped me research and write it.

One last note is necessary. The wreck of the *Marine Electric* helped tighten U.S. inspections of ships. It did not solve the global problem of loose ship standards. Big ships like the *Marine Electric* and their crews still go down. The tragedy related here is replicated somewhere in the world every month of the year. What John McPhee wrote some years back remains true. "Somewhere, anytime, someone is getting it."